BATTLEFIELDS

BATTLEFIELDS

The Chicago White Sox and the Great War

JIM LEEKE

BLOOMSBURY ACADEMIC
NEW YORK • LONDON • OXFORD • NEW DELHI • SYDNEY

BLOOMSBURY ACADEMIC

Bloomsbury Publishing Inc, 1359 Broadway, New York, NY 10018, USA
Bloomsbury Publishing Plc, 50 Bedford Square, London, WC1B 3DP, UK
Bloomsbury Publishing Ireland, 29 Earlsfort Terrace, Dublin 2, D02 AY28, Ireland

BLOOMSBURY, BLOOMSBURY ACADEMIC and the Diana logo are trademarks of
Bloomsbury Publishing Plc

First published in the United States of America 2026

Copyright © Jim Leeke, 2025

Cover images: © Chicago History Museum/Alamy Stock Photo, © istock/Phra yor Jitonnom

All rights reserved. No part of this publication may be: i) reproduced or transmitted in any form, electronic or mechanical, including photocopying, recording or by means of any information storage or retrieval system without prior permission in writing from the publishers; or ii) used or reproduced in any way for the training, development or operation of artificial intelligence (AI) technologies, including generative AI technologies. The rights holders expressly reserve this publication from the text and data mining exception as per Article 4(3) of the Digital Single Market Directive (EU) 2019/790.

Bloomsbury Publishing Inc does not have any control over, or responsibility for, any third-party websites referred to or in this book. All internet addresses given in this book were correct at the time of going to press. The author and publisher regret any inconvenience caused if addresses have changed or sites have ceased to exist, but can accept no responsibility for any such changes.

A catalog record for this book is available from the Library of Congress.

ISBN: HB: 979-8-8818-0228-8
ePDF: 979-8-8818-6619-8
eBook: 979-8-8818-0229-5

Typeset by Deanta Global Publishing Services, Chennai, India
Printed and bound in the United States of America

For product safety related questions contact productsafety@bloomsbury.com.

To find out more about our authors and books visit www.bloomsbury.com and sign up for our newsletters.

In fond remembrance of
Judith Irwin Berman

CONTENTS

Introduction 1

1 Commy 3
2 Sarge 15
3 Chick 33
4 Buck 43
5 Griff 55
6 Swede 67
7 Knuckles 77
8 Scotty 91
9 Doc 103
10 Kid 111
11 Phil 121
12 Shoeless 129
13 Red 143
14 Hap 153
15 Cocky 163
16 Cracker 175
17 Jenks 187
18 Kenesaw 197

Acknowledgments 213
Notes 214
Bibliography 250
Index 252

Introduction

Major League Baseball faced a roiled horizon in April 1917 as the United States declared war on Imperial Germany. The great uncertainty was whether anything resembling a normal season could possibly be played as America joined the fight "over there." Not even the government could answer.

Scrapping and squabbling among themselves, the sixteen clubs persevered until an armistice ended the conflict a year and a half later. None came through easily, smoothly, or unaltered. This book offers the wartime history of one, the Chicago White Sox. Many contemporaries claimed a greater number of stars on service flags honoring the departed. Most sent more combatants into the front lines of France. But the Pale Hose, in their struggles and victories, their ups and downs, best reflected the stresses and losses afflicting all.

Here, then, is a study of South Side fans, supporters, and writers, players who donned military uniforms and teammates who remained in flannels, and the half dozen who abandoned Chicago for the industrial leagues. We'll also examine the club owner's battle to keep his business afloat amid the first hints of the 1919 "Black Sox" scandal that followed.

The story isn't simple, pretty, or uplifting. It involves lives and careers in jeopardy, decisions made by people in tough circumstances, and a future that was unfathomable. Judge them as you will.

1

Commy

The winter of 1916–17 was frigid in Chicago but not nearly so cruel as in Europe, where the Great War raged into its third year. Byron Bancroft "Ban" Johnson returned to the city February 8 after visiting Capt. Tillinghast L'Hommedieu Huston at the Dover Hall Club near Brunswick, Georgia. The American League (AL) president was bursting to share an idea the co-owner of the New York Yankees had planted in his mind.

"Capt. Huston made a suggestion that may interest the baseball public," Johnson told reporters. "He would have all the major league players devote a portion of their time at the camps to drilling for military service." Huston believed such drills would set a good example for America's young men as the country skidded toward joining the war against Germany. A scribe asked Johnson if such a scheme would be popular among AL ballplayers. "Well, I don't know about that," he admitted. "It would give the players a chance to show their patriotism."[1] Any player in the circuit was free to volunteer for the armed forces without hinderance or complication.

"Not only would we release the players, but also would look to the welfare of their dependents," Johnson said. "Contracts will not stand in the way of American League players who wish to fight in the defense of their country. We would encourage the spirit to enlist."[2] The president added, however, that he didn't expect military drills to change any AL team's spring training plans.

"A war with Germany would, he believes, not cause a great deal of disturbance aside from the excitement attendant upon the mobilization of a big army of men," the *Chicago Examiner* reported. "Even in war time he thinks a nation must have some diversion, hence argues that the big leagues would have a place to fill. Even in England and Germany sports have survived the two and one-half years of hostilities."[3]

"Whether or not military service is made compulsory in baseball, it seems certain all the big league teams will go south to train, regardless of what may develop in the present crisis with Germany," twenty-five-year-old sportswriter John Alcock observed in the *Chicago Tribune* the next day. "That is the opinion of Ban Johnson who was back at his desk after an extended vacation in the south."[4]

Scribes like "Johnny" Alcock heeded the AL prexy because he was a heavyweight in both baseball and life. Historian Eugene C. Murdock later noted that Johnson was "for nearly a quarter of a century the guiding genius of our National Pastime."[5] Ban was also a military buff, the *Tribune* observing that he was "a keen student of military tactics, and has an extensive private library of writings on military subjects. He follows the present European war closely in both newspapers and magazines. From the first suggestion of participation in drill for players he has been enthusiastic for the [Huston] plan."[6]

In the fall of 1917, following the World Series, Johnson would try to volunteer for combat in France at age fifty-three. The US Army would tactfully turn aside his request.

Byron Bancroft "Ban" Johnson, American League president. Courtesy of Library of Congress.

The AL president had already participated in the war in a small way. Learning in 1915 that Canadian troops in France were writing home asking for baseball equipment, Johnson had promptly offered several crates of gear and asked league players to contribute autographed baseballs as well. Ty Cobb, for one, contributed fifteen balls and three bats. Canadian officials accepted the equipment with thanks, a Calgary newspaper noting that Johnson was "heralded all over the country as a great benefactor of the Canadian soldier."[7] An American paper added that Johnson "maintains his neutrality and if the Germans or Turks want to play ball in their trenches they can have balls and bats for the asking."[8]

Surely no sportswriter was surprised, however, that the idea of drilling AL players during the coming season had sprung not from Johnson, but from "Cap" Huston in New York. The former army engineer had made his fortune through construction projects in Cuba following the Spanish-American War, long before buying into the Yankees. Huston was also a mainstay of the Plattsburg Movement, a military preparedness program for American business and professional leaders.

Among its influential backers were former US president Theodore Roosevelt and Maj.-Gen. Leonard Wood, ex-army chief of staff who now commanded the eastern department. "Nearly every tent contains either a millionaire, a captain of industry or some man whose name is in the 'Who's Who,'" a wire report had said of the 1,200 participants at the first Plattsburg camp in upstate New York in summer 1915.[9]

Chicago White Sox owner Charles A. Comiskey now joined Johnson in helping to make Huston's drill plan a reality. Known as "Commy" to friends and sportswriters, Comiskey hadn't worn khaki at Plattsburg. But he did track useful ideas and focused on Huston's proposal like a first sacker eyeing a high fly ball. Along with a growing number of his countrymen, Comiskey believed the United States soon would be pulled into the European war.

The Allied powers of Great Britain, France, and Russia had been locked in combat with the Central Powers of Germany, Austria-Hungary, and the Ottoman Empire since August 1914. Fighting raged not only on the Continent but elsewhere across the world. The United States was still neutral but had drifted toward involvement since a German U-boat had torpedoed the British liner RMS *Lusitania* off Ireland in May 1915, killing 128 Americans and over a thousand others.

President Woodrow Wilson had won reelection in 1916 partly by campaigning that he'd kept America *out* of the war. Now provocations from Kaiser Wilhelm II's government and navy were pushing him closer to the Allies. Germany's policy of unrestricted submarine warfare, begun February 1, had brought the sinking of American and neutral shipping. Peace for America wasn't likely to last much longer. Comiskey knew it, as did Johnson.

The pair had known one another for a quarter century. Commy was an ex-ballplayer who'd helped Ban, a former sportswriter, launch the American League in 1900. They'd once shared an office in downtown Chicago, and although no longer close still kept in touch. Ban had given Commy a set of golf clubs for Christmas. His wife afterward had accompanied the Sox owner and Mrs. Comiskey on a trip south.

The Sox chief coincidentally had returned to the Windy City the day that Johnson came back home from meeting Cap Huston in Georgia. Commy joked that the weather in Florida had been so unusually chilly he'd come north to warm up.

Charles "Commy" Comiskey, White Sox owner. Oklahoma City Daily Oklahoman.

Chicago papers reported the next day that Commy and Chicago Cubs owner Charles Weeghman, his National League (NL) counterpart, both backed Huston's preparedness plan. Many serving army officers supported it too. "It will be a wonderful help if professional baseball can have 400 men in shape for service in case they are needed," an unnamed officer commented. "If the minor leagues should fall in line we could almost count upon another regiment."[10]

Comiskey and the other seven American League magnates wanted both Major League baseball and the country to be ready for war. They unanimously adopted Huston's plan during a February 16 meeting at the Wolcott Hotel in New York City, empowering Johnson to consult General Wood on details. The National League, in contrast, would never offer much in the way of military preparedness, although the Brooklyn Dodgers and Boston Braves would drill their players independently.

Huston contacted Maj. Halstead Dorey of General Wood's staff a week later, seeking help for drilling AL clubs. Dorey replied that recruiting sergeants might be available for a couple of hours daily, provided they were on leave. Cap telegraphed Dorey's reply to Johnson in Chicago.

"Clubs will be glad to compensate sergeants on furlough to do the drilling at spring training camps," Ban wired back. "It is a happy solution, but how soon can they be made available."[11] Timing wasn't immediately clear, but Chicago newspapers applauded the AL chief for backing the scheme. The White Sox owner leaped to offer support as well. Jointly, Comiskey, Johnson, and Huston comprised a strong, quotable triumvirate that attracted and held the attention of big city sportswriters.

Scribes often referred to Comiskey as "the Old Roman," a nickname coined by sportswriter Charles Dryden to reflect his personality, manner, and physique. The magnate wasn't as military minded as Johnson but had useful contacts in the army. During Brig. Gen. John J. Pershing's Punitive Expedition into Mexico a year earlier he had agreed to take his club south of the border for an exhibition game with an army team.

"Comiskey, who loves adventure, was keen for the jaunt," the *Chicago Daily News* now revealed.[12] The contest was scrubbed, however, after Pershing's troops withdrew back into Texas. The AL's pledge to drill its players during spring training again spurred Comiskey to act. Not content to wait for a sergeant to be assigned to his club, he meant to obtain the best damned drillmaster in the Windy City right away.

"If there is a man among the White Sox ranks whose past includes a term of service in the military, let him speak forth," the *Chicago Examiner* commanded. The boss would look elsewhere if the White Sox didn't have a veteran already under contract. "Commy believes it is a wise move, not only because it is in line with the preparedness campaign, but because it will serve as an ideal conditioner for the athletes who are soft-muscled after a Winter of ease and luxury."[13] The Old Roman turned to the AL honcho for assistance.

"That President Comiskey is in earnest regarding military training is shown by a request to President Johnson of the American league to secure a sergeant to accompany the Sox on their spring training trip," the *Tribune* said. Ban promptly passed Commy's request to Capt. Franklin R. Kenney at the army recruiting office at 526 South State Street, in "hopes to secure a man who will be able to make the Sox look a 'bit chesty' by the time the campaign opens."[14]

Comiskey also contacted Henry P. McCain, the army adjutant general at Washington, D.C. The AG sent word to subordinates in Chicago to give the magnate whatever he needed. "Gen. McCain is a pal of Comiskey; he'd give up the whole army for him," Kenney told the *Daily News*. "He was the guest of honor at Comiskey park last year."[15]

Kenney found the perfect candidate in Sgt. Walter Smiley, one of his recruiters. Smiley had enlisted in the army six years earlier under his family name, Smialowski, which he would change officially in 1918. Walter had been born in the Bridesburg section of Philadelphia, his father a naturalized citizen from Warsaw, his mother from Posen, Germany.

An army document listed him as a twenty-two-year-old glazer when he signed up in May 1911; different birthdates in other records indicate he may have been only seventeen when he first donned khaki at Fort Slocum, New York. Whatever his age, Smiley then began his army career 8,500 miles away in the Philippines.

Smiley was surprised but pleased by his sudden assignment to the White Sox. He was not an imposing man, standing slightly less than five-feet-eight and weighing 127 pounds. But he had "keen, piercing brown eyes that search you thru and thru, and he is, withal, a splendid type of the American soldier and, especially, the American sergeant, who has often been referred to as a backbone of the army," Malcolm MacLean wrote in the *Chicago Evening Post*.[16]

The soldier was also a fine ballplayer. Serving in Company A, Thirteenth US Infantry, he had led the 1914 Manila league with a .375 batting average. He'd later toured with an All Army team in China and Japan. Reassigned Stateside and promoted to corporal, he became a recruiter in Chicago while also attending business school. Smiley also held down second base for an Army All-Star team that played all comers in the Windy City.

"Mr. Weeghman, president of the Chicago Federal League club, has kindly loaned the use of his park for the army team and offered the services of manager Joe Tinker as coach at such times as that busy manager is available," *Baseball Magazine* said in 1915 (before the magnate had bought the Cubs).[17] The *Tribune* added that for the first time baseball was "recognized as a sport to promote efficiency amongst soldiers."[18] The secretary of war had even authorized funds to support the game.

With war approaching two years later, Johnson, Huston, and Comiskey hoped that the army might now do for the American League what baseball had done for the army. Smiley found himself in very fast company. Captain Kenney rightly expected the three-striper to fit right in with the White Sox.

"Most army sergeants are dyed-in-the-wool baseball fans and any of them would jump at the chance of being attached to a major league training camp," a newspaper said from Schofield Barracks, Hawaii, "for that matter we know of no officer of the army who wouldn't be willing to do the same duty."[19] Civilians who knew Sergeant Smiley thought well of him too.

"He knows the game and likes it," the *Examiner* said. "Therefore he is more than anxious to swap a little of his military knowledge for a few weeks of association with a major league crew."[20]

White Sox skipper Clarence "Pants" Rowland wasn't as enthusiastic as Smiley or Comiskey about drilling ballplayers. He probably had never considered it, and the proposal was sprung upon him without notice. "Manager Rowland yesterday did not seem hotly in favor of the plan, preferring to devote all time to putting his men in shape for the hard campaign that lies ahead in the flag hunt," the *Chicago Day Book* said as February waned.[21]

"The White Sox might engage in light military drill, but I have made no plans in that direction," the manager said. "My principal worry is to condition my men for the great race in the American league."[22]

But the prospect of war did worry others working for the White Sox, especially their longtime trainer, William Buckner. "Doc" likely was the first person of color ever to hold his position, although other African Americans followed him into the Major Leagues. "Buck has been with the club longer than any veteran on it and has stowed away much experience," *Daily News* sportswriter George S. Robbins wrote later.[23]

Buckner and his wife lived on the city's South Side, where when not tending to athletes, he operated the Colonial Barber Shop at Thirty-fifth and State streets, a few blocks from Comiskey Park at Thirty-fifth and Shields Avenue. Buckner's stepson served in the "Old Fighting Eighth," a Black Illinois National Guard regiment that had been in Texas during the border crisis months earlier.

"When the 8th regiment heard the sound of the tocsin calling it to arms, it took away about 800 of my cash customers," the trainer said. "If they take 'em away again, I'll be broke." Buckner added glumly, "We may be all be going to war before 1918."[24]

Sergeant Smiley hadn't yet reported to the White Sox when Johnny Alcock wrote in the *Tribune* the last day of February that military training for the team was assured, "provided other American league clubs go through with the project." Comiskey waited impatiently. "He is not certain that Ban has not provided for the instructors, and will not attempt to secure a drillmaster until Johnson reveals his plans in detail," Alcock added.[25]

The league president, however, was out of town. When Smiley finally received his orders March 1, the Sox became the first AL club officially to adopt the military program.

"It must be appreciated that this is only a beginning, a sort of experiment in training civilians in preparedness," Smiley wrote in the first of several articles he contributed to the *Chicago Herald*. "Consequently expectations must not be permitted to run too high, but I think that in the long run it will be a paying investment for country and men alike."[26]

Cap Huston, meanwhile, grew frustrated waiting for a noncom to be assigned to his club at Macon, Georgia. "Apparently the efforts of Mr. Johnson and myself have not shown good team work, although seeking the same results, viz., to obtain drill sergeants," he wired Major Dorey in New York. Huston asked the major to coordinate with Captain Kenney in Chicago. "I will depend upon you to have Sergeant [Smith] Gibson of the Macon recruiting station or other sergeant detailed to drill our club here. We are anxious to commence at once."[27]

Sergeant Gibson received orders March 4 to report to the Yankees' training camp. He and Smiley soon became the most famous sergeants in the US Army, mentioned on sports pages not only in Chicago and New York but across America. The army assigned drillmasters to four other AL teams. The last of the eight clubs, the St. Louis Browns and Detroit Tigers, were set to train in Texas; the war department ordered its San Antonio-based southern department to send noncoms to them as well.

The White Sox prepared to head southwest for the Lone Star State. Their spring trip differed from those of earlier seasons. The club was leaving Chicago later and training for a shorter time than usual. The Cubs began practice in Pasadena, California, more than a week before the Old Roman's boys even boarded a train for their training site at Mineral Wells, Texas.

"Comiskey has trailed through the south and the west with ball clubs more than any other living man, and he has concluded that there isn't much in it," *Tribune* sportswriter James "Jimmy" Crusinberry had written in January. "He knows the south is weary of big league baseball teams and will not pay to see them."[28]

Major League umpire and sportswriter William "Billy" Evans, like Crusinberry and others, considered Comiskey an exceptionally shrewd businessman who knew what he was doing. "He is rated as a millionaire, and he has made every cent of it out of baseball," the future Baseball Hall of Famer later wrote of Commy. "He has made it because he gave his attention to the game, because he always tried to figure what the public wanted, and then gave it to them. Mr. Comiskey is unique among magnates, because baseball is his business, not his hobby."[29]

Commy believed it was good business to shorten the 1917 spring trip, which would lead to higher profits once he opened his South Side park for the regular season. The magnate remembered his own big league days with the Browns, which he'd captained and managed back in the 1880s. The club had generally stayed in Mound City for spring training. Comiskey also recalled "an old German army officer" who'd hung around the park and convinced him that military calisthenics would help players stay in condition.[30]

Such conditioning could be crucial. The White Sox had finished second in 1916, only two games behind the Boston Red Sox, who'd gone on to win the World Series. Commy thought a brief spring camp might reduce wear and tear on his Sox and give them an edge during the coming 154-game season. "Any players who want more than a month for their training are fit subjects for the old men's home," he'd declared in January. "One month is amply sufficient for all practical training purposes."[31]

The greater variable this year, however, was America's possible entry into the war. The likelihood grew stronger the last day of February when news broke about the Zimmermann telegram, in which Germany had proposed a secret military alliance with Mexico should America join the fighting. The southern neighbor would receive financial aid from the Kaiser and reclaim much of the territory she'd lost to the United States during the war of 1846–8 should Germany triumph. The revelation exploded like a torpedo in the American consciousness.

"U. S. BARES WAR PLOT," the *Tribune* screamed March 1. "EXPOSES BERLIN INTRIGUE WITH MEXICO."[32] On the East Coast the *New York Evening World* blared: "PLOT STORY TRUE, SAYS WILSON; SENATORS DEMAND ALL FACTS."[33] And in the nation's capital the *Washington Herald* trumpeted: "UNCOVER PLOT AGAINST NATION / GERMAN-MEXICAN PACT FOR WAR AGAINST U. S. BARED BY GOVERNMENT."[34]

Despite the long history of friction between the two countries, Mexico swiftly disavowed any aggressive intent toward the United States. Nothing dampened the American anger toward Germany, however. The *Chicago Daily News*, at least, found one speck of humor amid the outrage.

"No wonder President Comiskey is strong for the military training," sportswriter David Rotroff cracked. "If the Germans helped Mexico take Texas from us, where would the Sox train?"[35] Commy readied his club for its southern trip, regardless of any prospect of Spanish-speaking German allies invading Texas.

2

Sarge

Temperatures hovered near twenty degrees at LaSalle Station the evening of Sunday, March 4, 1917. Three thousand White Sox fans shouldered their way inside to cheer the team's departure for Mineral Wells. "Throngs of South Side rooters assembled early, in order to have a first hand view of their pets as they embarked on the first lap of the American league pennant hunt, a journey local admirers strongly hope will result in a world's series for this municipality," an Iowa newspaper said.[1]

Charley Comiskey had heard complaints about travel accommodations in previous springs. This season he'd chartered a train from the Rock Island line for the thousand-mile trip to Texas. Reporters disagreed on the length of his "White Sox Special," which included several Pullman sleepers plus buffet, baggage, and observation cars, six to ten altogether. Among the sixty-four passengers were twenty-eight or -nine ballplayers, newspapers again unable to agree on the exact number.

Americans had suffered from serious food shortages and high prices since the previous summer, partly due to wheat exports to help feed Great Britain, France, and Italy. A shortage of railway cars recently had forced several key grain elevators outside Chicago to halt operations. "But a ball team, like those armies over in Europe, travels on its stomach, and the man who provides for the creature comforts of the athletes in the dining car should not be forgotten," George Robbins wrote in the *Daily News*.[2] The Comiskey train consequently was very well provisioned.

Scribes nearly salivated while writing about newly churned butter, crates of eggs, scores of hams, hundreds of chickens, and bushels of potatoes, onions, and other vegetables among the fresh consumables. "Even a bit of wet goods is provided for medicinal or emergency cases," Johnny Alcock added in the *Tribune*.[3] Players boarding the special were "grinning cheerfully at the prospect of free eats for at least a month."[4]

Sharp-eyed fans would have recognized pitcher Edgar "Eddie" Cicotte, catcher Ray "Cracker" Schalk, second baseman Eddie Collins, manager Rowland, coach William "Kid" Gleason, and owner Comiskey. Others of their favorites were missing. Many especially regretted the absence of future Hall of Fame pitcher Edward "Big Ed" Walsh, who was absent after thirteen seasons with the Sox.

"Up to the last moment it was thought Ed Walsh might show up, but the Big Moose never came," Alcock wrote. "Thus it is established finally that Ed Walsh is through as a big leaguer."[5] Trainer Buckner was sorry to see Walsh go. "I never put in more time on any player than on Ed Walsh," he'd said. "The Big Moose was always thankful for extra work on the massage table and I never worked harder to help a ball player."[6]

Outfielder Joe Jackson, pitcher Jim Scott, first baseman Arnold "Chick" Gandil, and nine other Sox weren't boarding the train either but would report to camp in the Lone Star State. Gandil had broken into the Majors with the Sox in 1910 and was returning to the club after stints in the Minors and with Washington, and Cleveland in the Majors.

"Gandil is of a peculiar temperament," Robbins had warned when the Sox acquired him a few days earlier, "but Comiskey believes that in Rowland and Gleason he has two men who will use Gandil's talents to advantage."[7] The returning first sacker wired assurances that he wasn't a holdout despite his absence in Chicago. "We're lucky in signing Gandil," Comiskey said. "He will complete a team of hard hitting players."[8]

Hopes on the South Side were high this season. Alcock called the assemblage that Gandil was rejoining "probably the greatest that has seen the Sox off in all the years that Commy has been carrying his team south or west on special trains."[9]

A number of non-players were also heading to Texas with the club. Comiskey's son, Louis, known to sportswriters as Commylou, was the club's vice-president and treasurer. Harry M. Grabiner was its secretary, equivalent to a modern general manager. The two executives stepped on board the "rattler" along with other team employees, family, friends, and scribes. Two passenger agents were going along too to help keep everyone happy.

Sgt. Walter Smiley, White Sox drill instructor, as an army baseball player. Lansing (MI) State Journal.

Sergeant Smiley, unmarried and unaccompanied, was the most conspicuous traveler on board. He appeared wearing a winter uniform and campaign hat, a full pack, and "a shooting iron, of the latest model."[10] Newspapers didn't say whether his weapon was a 1911 Colt .45-caliber pistol or a bolt-action 1903 Springfield rifle, both standard army issue. The sergeant lent "a military coloring to the scene," the *Daily News* said.[11] Had he worn civilian clothing he might have been mistaken for another player.

"Much interest is expressed here in the innovation of military drill for the White Sox," *Tribune* sportswriter Irving E. "Sy" Sanborn later wrote from Texas. "This state is militant in spirit, with its memories of the Alamo, and Sergt. Smiley will be as much of a hero as the ball players."[12]

The White Sox Special chuffed from the station at 6 p.m. and rolled through the night into warmer weather. It stopped briefly in the morning at the spacious new terminal in Kansas City. By Monday afternoon passengers saw sun but little snow outside their windows.

The special made another short stop at Wichita, where a prankster told Harry Grabiner that because Kansas was a dry state, authorities would have to disconnect the buffet car with its alcohol. The secretary glumly agreed. Afterward it was "a safe bet to say that he breathed easier when the train pulled out with the car still hitched on the train."[13] Sergeant Smiley made notes on drills and training throughout the day.

"Just what good the Sox are going to get out of this instruction rests with the players themselves," the *Tribune* said.[14] The sergeant made a point of wandering through the cars and speaking with nearly everyone. Encountering trainer Buckner, he promised to help the Sox care for their feet, the mark of a good noncom.

When Smiley entered the smoking car, one of Comiskey's musical pals struck up "We Can't Get 'Em Up in the Morning." The players welcomed him too. "It has been expected that the players would treat the military angle with a certain amount of levity," sportswriter G. W. Axelson wrote in the *Chicago Herald*, "but the opposite has been true, as there is hardly a mother's son in the crowd who does not fear the draft with a universal service bill in sight."[15]

The team rolled on toward Texas as the rest of the country focused on President Wilson's second inauguration in the nation's capital. The chief executive had taken the oath during a small ceremony Sunday, but his inaugural address and the celebrations were scheduled for today. *Chicago Day Book* reported that Wilson spoke of a new doctrine of internationalism, "but in the same breath warned that the United States may require 'a more immediate association' with the war than mere armed neutrality."[16]

The *Washington Star* ran a description of the military parade down Pennsylvania Avenue that would have caught Sergeant Smiley's attention:

> The demonstration today is featured by the presence of trained fighting men, not only men who have fought in the wars of the past, but who are ready for the wars that may come. All branches of the regular service, cavalry, engineer corps, marines, infantry and artillery are represented. There are the generals and the admirals of the future. Closely following them come a force of field-hardened citizen soldiers, such as the nation has never before had, fresh from duty on the Mexican border, whose bearing bespeaks efficiency and engenders a sense of security. The great zeal for preparedness that has been sweeping the country is expressed through the presence in the inaugural parade of cadets from military training schools in many states.[17]

The White Sox Special meanwhile chugged into a second night. Passengers glimpsed the lights of Enid, Oklahoma, "not through the rain and mist, but through a dust-filled whirl of Oklahoma wind."[18]

The train reached Fort Worth Tuesday morning and switched onto Texas and Pacific Railway tracks for the last stretch to Mineral Wells. Two freight trains had collided on the line earlier, smashing boxcars and rupturing tank cars, "which tied up the whole works for more than half a day while the right of way was being cleared of oil tanks, bean sacks, and other valuable debris," Sanborn wrote in the *Tribune*.[19] Kid Gleason considered the wreck a good omen. "That proves the Sox are lucky this year," the coach said. "We just missed that tank by a few hours."[20]

The spa town that Sanborn called "this medical burgh" lay 50 miles west of Fort Worth.[21] Mineral Wells advertised itself as an ideal place for visitors to rest, play, and rebuild their health in warm sunshine. It offered the mineral wells and baths that gave the place its name, hotels catering to all budgets, good railway access, and 175 miles of paved streets and roads.

"There is diversion for the athletically inclined—a beautiful new golf course—with interesting natural hazards—Tennis, Horseback Riding, Motoring, etc.," a newspaper ad promised.[22] In the springtime baseball fans also could watch Commy's club in action.

A brass band and several thousand people celebrated as the White Sox Special steamed into the station at 10:20 a.m., March 6, an hour ahead of schedule. Joe Jackson, Jim Scott, Jack Fournier, and Dave Danforth all were there to greet their teammates; several others were due in from Los Angeles that night. There'd been traces of snow in the coulees and fence corners earlier, Sanborn reported, but today the weather was fine.

"As suddenly as it can get cold, Texas warmed up today and under the influence of a blazing sun produced conditions so nearly ideal for training that Boss Rowland could not resist the call to arms and ordered the men into uniform as soon after lunch as possible."[23] The Sox changed into flannels and ran to the ballpark for pepper, hill climbing, and fungo, but no drilling yet under Sergeant Smiley.

"I prefer to meet the boys to-night and have a heart-to-heart talk with them about the seriousness of the undertaking," Smiley said the next day. "It is better to have all the men present when the drill starts. I am pleased to hear that American league officials have offered prizes for the best showing of clubs in military drill. Any incentive of the kind is commendable."[24]

Ban Johnson had announced a $500 prize in gold for the club that performed best during a drill competition planned for the summer, plus $100 for that team's sergeant. Commy and president A. R. Tearney of the Illinois-Indiana-Iowa (Three-I) League soon chipped in another $100 apiece for the drillmaster's prize. A $300 bonus was a dazzling goal for any poorly paid noncom like Smiley. The Sox began the drills that might help him earn it Thursday, March 8.

"They're gonna introduce setting up exercises and some other few army stunts to the Sox, according to dope," a Texas columnist wrote. "But if it comes to company drill and somebody yells, 'Strike one!' the drill master is likely to see the discipline shot to smithereens."[25] Rowland split his players into two groups for the hour-long sessions, one in the morning, the other in the afternoon. "This will compel Sergeant Smiley to make two trips to the ball park and spend two hours each day," a wire report said, "but he is keen for the job and so are the boys."[26]

Smiley began each session with ten minutes of "setting up" exercises, a limbering routine designed to develop military bearing and carriage. Next came fifteen minutes of squad drill, ten minutes of instruction on the army rifle (if there was an actual Springfield in camp, Smiley had brought it with him), ten minutes of the Butts manual of arms, and fifteen minutes of company drill. Lacking proper weapons, Smiley had the Sox drill using baseball bats, with the barrel in their palms and the handle over their shoulders.

"The bats are several pounds lighter than army rifles, but they are about the same length," the *St. Louis Star* said. "The fact that they are somewhat similar in shape will enable the players to make the shift from bats to rifles without difficulty."[27] Second sacker Eddie Collins thought it was just as well the Sox hadn't begun with nine pound Springfields, since combined with regular diamond work it "might have turned out a little too strenuous while the boys were still soft. The bats made a good substitute."[28] The other AL clubs began by drilling with bats as well.

"Tramp, tramp, tramp, the boys are marching," Robbins wrote after the "imposing spectacle" of the first morning's drill.[29] The Sox took the work seriously. Robbins noted that Oscar "Happy" Felsch, Joe "Blitzen" Benz, and every player of German heritage was a loyal American, reassuring to know as anti-German sentiment flared across the country. Press photographers asked Smiley to form up his men for pictures.

"With a few words of preliminary explanation the sergeant commanded in rapid succession 'left, face; left forward, march—column right, march—company halt—about face,' and there they were facing the sun in two ranks so straight that the sergeant exclaimed 'fine,'" Sanborn reported.[30] "It was a fine drill, just what we needed," outfielder "Shoeless Joe" Jackson said. "We'll be real soldiers in a few days."[31] Owner Comiskey agreed, later writing, "When they win the world's championship this fall, just remember that it was military drill that started them on their winning fight."[32]

Sanborn dubbed Smiley's recruits "the White Sox company, B. B. N. G. (base ball National Guard)."[33] *Tribune* colleague and columnist Ring Lardner Sr. suggested a special manual of arms for use at Comiskey Park during the season. It began:

1. On opening day, instead of singing "The Gang's All Here," White Sox rooters shall, just prior to the game, arise en masse and say to the head umpire: *Sir, all present or accounted for.*
2. Instead of "batter up," the umpire shall summon the hitter with the single word, *Front.*[34]

"Evidently Ban Johnson and President Comiskey don't intend the American League shall be found wanting in case of a declaration of war," the *Daily News* said, above photos of the Sox drilling in flannels and heavy cardigan sweaters.[35] Eddie Collins later recalled the Pale Hose as a mouthy bunch at first, continually telling one another to watch their feet or keep in line.

"It took the sergeant a couple of days to suppress this wordy mutiny, but once it had been accomplished the drill went like clockwork," he wrote. But Smiley was no martinet, and Collins added that "no man could have worked more smoothly than he did, or with more diplomacy."[36]

The condition and quality of his ballplayers pleased the young sergeant. While on a recruiting trip to Wisconsin the previous spring, Smiley had been appalled by the number of recruits he'd had to turn away, either because they fell short of physical standards or couldn't read or write English. A Racine newspaper reported his astonishment at "how many men are walking the streets with diseases of one kind or another which would keep them out of the army, and who do not know there is anything the matter with them."[37]

The brash and healthy Sox lightened the sergeant's heart. Collins, Schalk, and Scott took a special interest in the drills, Sanborn dubbing them Smiley's corporals. "We are now entirely surrounded by corporals," scribe Axelson cracked in the *Herald*.[38] The baseball ranks were flexible, however, and Rowland was later identified as the first sergeant, with others rising and falling from private and corporal.

Naming Columbia University-educated Collins a corporal made good sense. The Sox captain's $15,000 salary was at least double any teammate's, which gave him added stature. "Sergt. Smiley pronounced Eddie one of the brightest men he had ever seen in the army," the *Daily News* said.[39] Many fellow Ivy Leaguers were involved in the Plattsburg Movement, and the star second baseman likewise embraced the notion of military instruction for civilians.

"Corporal Collins is declared to have the best drilled squad among the White Sox, closely trailed by the one led by Ray Schalk," Robbins told readers.[40] A wire story later described Collins drilling Sox players in his hotel room from 9:30 to 10:30 every night. "The maid could never understand why the bedslats were in such confusion every morning, and she had to rearrange things daily," it said. "The reason was that Eddie's squad used the slats for rifles in their drill."[41]

Smiley's men grew fond of him, and upon his retirement long afterward, the army would note his "host of friends including officials and former stars of the Chicago White Sox."[42] When he gave his recruits a Sunday off to reward their hard work, Collins and Schalk called a team meeting and got unanimous approval to drill anyway.

"Sergeant, the boys are disobeying your command and breaking the Sabbath," a guest complained. "Tickled almost to death to hear it," Smiley replied. "They may break the rules that way all they choose."[43] A passing Sox player delivered a smart salute, which the drillmaster returned.

Numerous sports pages published colorful stories about Smiley and the Sox. Many were inaccurate, especially those about pitcher and Sox corporal Jim "Death Valley" Scott, the longest-serving player on Commy's club following the departure of Big Ed Walsh.

Papers said Scott had grown up on a military post out west, was the son of a colonel, and even that he'd served a hitch in uniform himself. None of it was true. Even his nickname was a myth, coined by a scribe when the hurler reported to the Sox after playing winter ball in California's Imperial Valley. Scott had never visited nearby Death Valley in his life.

Other details were accurate, though. Scott *had* pitched in London before King George V during the White Sox-Giants world tour of 1913–14. He *had* been born in Deadwood, South Dakota, although raised in Lander, Wyoming, where his father was a government weather observer and telegrapher. Scott *had* occasionally played ball against troops from an area army post, and he certainly looked the part of a proper White Sox soldier.

"In that weather bronzed face and stalwart frame is a graphic story of many seasons spent in the wholesome air of forests, plains and mountains," *Baseball Magazine* had once gushed.[44] But Scott had additional reasons for aiding Sergeant Smiley.

The big righthander became a star in 1915, winning twenty-four games and losing only eleven. But in 1916 he'd been banished by the club at the height of the pennant race for breaking rules and not staying in shape. Afterward he'd briefly played industrial ball in Beloit, Wisconsin, attempting to get back into condition. "Jim was away up on the pinnacle, and began to think he was not like other players. He didn't have to train to keep his place as a regular on the club," *Day Book* sportswriter Mark Shields wrote.[45]

Scott now sought redemption in the eyes of the fans and his teammates. "The suspension he was handed hurt his pride and also lowered his prestige around the circuit," Shields said. "Jim is out to win back all of this."[46]

Pundits had reported during the winter that Scott was on the trading block and suggested his career was over. The Sox absolutely denied it. "Scott is not on the market, and never has been," Commy said before spring training. "As a matter of fact, we expect Jim to be one of the mainstays of our pitching staff this season." Skipper Rowland acknowledged that his pitcher's lapse had harmed the club but said everyone slipped sometime. "I am willing to wager there will be few better pitchers than Jim in the American league this year," he said.[47]

Sergeant Smiley wasn't concerned with such issues. With Scott, Collins, and Schalk under his command, the Sox at Mineral Wells picked up military drills quicker than any recruits he'd ever handled. The discipline shown in drills carried over onto the diamond and prompted Smiley to write in the *Herald* that "no better behaved set of men have ever been on the field than the White Sox."[48] What surprised many observers, though, was that the players kept at it.

"No one in particular figured that it would stick," Eddie Collins later wrote. "This attitude was undoubtedly due to the fact that we are a nonmilitary nation, free and easy going on our ways, and always prone to drop anything which does not suit our fancies." But, the second sacker said, the players changed their minds:

> The greater number of the boys had never had the advantage of a single military drill in their lives, but it soon became apparent that the discipline of the ball field was a great help. . . . As a matter of fact we were more fit for ball playing after a week of drill than we would have been without it.[49]

The Sox were missing one player in Texas who'd have been ideal for leading a squad in the B. B. N. G. He was Alfred H. von Kolnitz, known as "Fritz" to his friends and "Baron" to the sportswriters. He had attended a military academy in Charleston, South Carolina, before studying at the College of Charleston and earning a law degree from the University of South Carolina.

Von Kolnitz had left baseball to enter business after playing two seasons as a utility man in Cincinnati (1914–15). He'd soon changed his mind, however, and returned to the Reds in June 1916. Commy acquired him the next day, writers figuring that Fritz would become pals with fellow South Carolinian Joe Jackson.

"In his brief appearances with the Sox he more than made good," the *Daily News* remembered of the Baron. "He was stationed at third base and his fielding and timely batting made him look like a find. He was handicapped by a bad leg, however, and when the bum prop went back on him he lost a chance to break in as a regular."[50]

Von Kolnitz had appeared in only twenty-four games with the Sox in 1916, guarding the hot corner or pinch hitting, but the club hoped to see him again this season, perhaps as a regular. He dashed those hopes in a letter to Rowland at Mineral Wells, saying he was retiring again to become assistant general manager for a potash company his father owned near Philadelphia.

"I'm a manager myself," he informed Rowland. "It's a case of business before pleasure. I wish the Sox the best of luck."[51]

The journeyman's departure was good news for one new Sox. Charles Risberg was a rookie infielder from the Vernon Tigers in the Pacific Coast League (PCL). The Cubs and other teams had coveted "Swede's" services. He was so good that when Commy had tried to grab him in 1916, Vernon's owner said he was available for "$20,000 and Eddie Collins."[52]

Before spring training some observers thought Risberg might challenge sophomore Zebulon "Zeb" Terry for the starting shortstop's slot. More likely, though, he would have contended with von Kolnitz to fill in as needed on the infield. "Risberg looks like a welcome addition to the White Sox force," the *Daily News* said after Fritz bowed out. "Even if the coast leaguer does not fight his way into a regular berth, it seems certain he will be retained for utility purposes."[53]

Commy said little about the challenges facing his infield, or whether he was disappointed over losing the experienced South Carolinian, or pleased at having the tough Californian step in. No matter his feelings at Mineral Wells, the owner would warmly embrace von Kolnitz later—once the Baron had enlisted in the army, to learn its ways without the aid of Sergeant Smiley. For now, the Sox soldiered on in Texas without him.

Captain Kenny wrote from Chicago after two weeks' drill to say the next step should be hand grenade practice. Rowland agreed, the sooner the better.

"In order to make it realistic some of the players want to dig a trench and hurl the grenades at silhouette targets," a wire report said.[54] Fortunately for everyone, the Sox practiced with baseballs rather than real grenades. The players were good at it. "If they ever are called to the colors the enemy would better keep their trenches far removed from the ball tossers," Robbins wrote. "Such eminent flingers as Happy Felsch, Joe Jackson and Buck Weaver would play havoc with the enemy."[55]

A couple of fans watching the Sox march in formation wondered if they were drilling for war or to prevent going to war. Kid Gleason overheard them. "The men are drilling to be prepared," the coach said, a comment Cap Huston and Teddy Roosevelt both would have applauded. "That's what you fellows ought to be doing. If a sharpshooter swooped down on the park you would be the first to take cover."[56]

Neither the Sox nor their sergeant realized how far Smiley's influence would spread. The club released catching prospect Wilbur "Dolly" Gray in March to the Fort Worth Panthers of the Texas League. Several weeks later, the president of that Class B circuit urged his clubs to begin military training. The Panthers were already drilling under their skipper and new catcher, who'd taught during the winter at a Missouri military academy. "Gray is the drill master of the team, the peppery receiver having been put through his paces under Sergeant Smiley during his stay with the Chicago White Sox at Mineral Wells," a local paper reported.[57]

Other Minor League circuits and individual clubs followed the example set by the American League and began drilling too. The Pale Hose, meanwhile, tired of marching with bats on their shoulders and asked Rowland for rifles. The skipper kicked the request upstairs. Comiskey said he'd buy Springfields from the government but none would arrive before the club left Mineral Wells.

The Sox wound up their intersquad games March 16 and got ready to hit the road for outside competition. Manager Rowland assigned the second team to Kid Gleason. White Sox historian Warren Brown later described Gleason as "a belligerent little man whose playing career had dated back to the horse-and-buggy days."[58] The *Chicago Herald* called the former second baseman "one of the scrappiest players that ever pushed a runner off a base."[59] *Chicago Evening American* sportswriter Harry Neily labeled him "the grandest old character in baseball . . . the understudy to the manager."[60]

Using the parlance of the day, writers called Gleason's second squad the Yannigans or the Goofs. Along with numerous youngsters he also had Jim Scott and a few regulars. When faced with a possible rail strike some Sox players regretted not bringing automobiles to Texas. Sergeant Smiley told them not to fret. "Why," he said, "by the end of the month you will be in shape to march from city to city between games."[61]

Rowland took his regulars to Fort Worth for a game versus the Texas League club there. Sergeant Smiley led his customary drill before batting practice rather than immediately before the game. "The players are not far enough advanced in their military team work to be confident of their appearance before a critical 'audience,' and preferred to take their evolutions while the stands were nearly empty," Sy Sanborn explained in the *Tribune*. The Pale Hose then ran and slid so hard during a 10–4 victory that their uniforms were filthy. "They may have to change their name from White to Black Sox," Sanborn quipped.⁶²

The Sox were more confident in their military abilities during games versus a Texas League club the following week in Houston. "Sergeant Smiley had his squad out for action with baseball bats instead of guns," a *Houston Post* columnist wrote. "The men went through the different formations without a hitch and used their bats in the manual of arms just as well as they use them in a game."⁶³ The scribe later called the visitors "the best drilled baseball team in either big league."⁶⁴

Houston fans were especially happy to see the return of catcher Joe Jenkins, a hitting star for their Buffaloes the previous season. "Even with such stars as Schalk, Eddie Collins and Jackson in the lineup, Jenkins was the most applauded player," Robbins wrote. "They are strong for the native son star in the Lone Star state."⁶⁵

Jenkins had reached the big time once before, with the St. Louis Browns in 1914, but soon slipped back to the Minors. He blamed only himself. "When I was with Manager [Branch] Rickey I had the chance of my life, but I mixed with the wrong crowd," he told Robbins. "My mind was not on baseball because my associates made me think of other things. They were out for a good time. That's why I was sent back to the bushes. It was good experience and now that I am up again I'm going to give myself a fair chance."⁶⁶

Commy was pleased with his Sox as they prepared to head north for the season, "more enthusiastic over his chances than he has been for years," according to Alcock. Gandil would fill the hole at first base. Risberg might become a dependable regular. Catchers Schalk, Byrd Lynn, and Jenkins all were ready to go, and the outfield looked good too.

"On the whole, I am entirely satisfied with our chances," the owner told Alcock. "If our pitching comes close to what it should be we ought to win."⁶⁷

The B. B. N. G. did the club proud as the regulars and Yannigans headed north separately toward Chicago. Smiley remained with the first team, and traveling secretary Joe O'Neill took charge of drilling the Goofs. A sandstorm prevented the regulars' April 3 exhibition game at Wichita, Kansas, but the sergeant drilled the men anyway. "A regular army captain detailed to recruiting service here complimented the men and Smiley on the wonderful results of less than a month of training," the *Tribune* said.[68]

Eddie Collins drilled his squad the next day in the hotel corridors at St. Joseph, Missouri. Both Sox teams were still traveling April 6 when the United States declared war on Germany. Black headlines everywhere announced the calamity. "HOUSE FOR WAR / VOTE IS 373 TO 50 / FULL POWERS ARE GRANTED TO PRESIDENT," the *Tribune* declared.[69] "U. S. AT WAR, WILSON FIAT" the *Daily News* trumpeted.[70] The Sox regulars heard the news at Ottumwa, Iowa, where they were scheduled to play an exhibition versus a local all-star team.

Several hundred Iowans applauded the players as they drilled in the street outside the Ballingal Hotel. "It was an inspiring site to see Eddie Collins, world's greatest second baseman, tutoring his mates in advanced evolutions learned from Sergeant Smiley, U. S. A., and from a book of military tactics which Eddie had been studying," Robbins wrote in *The Sporting News*.[71] Collins's reward for his patriotic display was a wild pitch to the head during Chicago's 15-0 rout of the locals.

The Sox second team was in Kansas when the news broke, preparing to play the Wichita Witches of the Western League. Like the regulars, the Yannigans drilled and played their game. "Corporal Charles Leksell, a Chicago boy, here on recruiting detail, drilled the Yannigans before the game," the *Tribune* said. "He was surprised at the snap of movements and said he thought they drilled better than the Sox regulars or Detroit."[72] Robbins believed such drills by the Pale Hose and other AL teams had rescued the 1917 big league season before it even began.

"The shutting down of the major league parks following the declaration of war probably would have occurred," Robbins wrote, "had not Johnson had the foresight to accept Captain Huston's proposal and declare for military drill even before the Congress of the United States had gone on record for universal training."[73] The scribe didn't doubt that Commy would have shuttered his South Side yard if his players hadn't begun drilling.

Mark Shields of the *Day Book* thought the drills also would benefit the Sox on the field once the season began. "This drill has proven more of a recreation than a hardship to the players and has taken their minds off baseball when necessary," he wrote. "Rowland gives the soldierly stuff great credit for the condition in which his team is as the season draws near."[74]

Walter Smiley, at his retirement as a master sergeant, 1939. United States Army Recruiting News.

Sergeant Smiley was the only real soldier among the lot. He believed that the effects of the Huston-Johnson-Comiskey drill plan went far deeper.

"The baseball drilling has done wonders in helping arouse young America," Smiley said in Iowa. "The drill of these major league ball clubs has been flashed on the [movie] screen in every city, town, village and hamlet in the United States. Baseball drill has been an educator and has helped the universal training idea immensely. This country at last has awakened from its sleep. Few citizens want war unless it is forced on us, but we owe [it] to ourselves and posterity to be prepared."[75]

"With talk of war and preparation wherever we go it is really wonderful how ball players fall in line with the spirit of the times," Smiley later added in *The Sporting News*. "Baseball players as a rule have a lot of other things to think about besides trenches and marches, but since the situation has taken on a serious aspect there has almost been as much conversation about war as the national game."[76]

3

Chick

The day after the nation entered the European conflict, Ban Johnson still expected the 1917 baseball season to proceed as planned. The AL president said his circuit would close its gates if war demanded, but he didn't foresee any actual disruption to the schedule.

"Every club will have a drill sergeant from the regular army with it all season and military training will be practically compulsory," Ban explained. "Thus the players will advance in army drill just as well as if they were in active service, and they will be ready for the call whenever it comes." National League president Gov. John K. Tener agreed. "Unless great loss of life is suffered through impending hostilities," he wrote, "I confidently believe base ball and other sports will have as many participants and patrons in the summer as heretofore."[1]

The presidents' view wasn't universally accepted. Charles W. Murphy, ex-president of the Chicago Cubs, dismissed their "czar-like attitude" and took a wait-and-see attitude. "In my judgment we do not know enough now to base any calculations on," Murphy wrote. "I think the clubs that play winning ball will draw the crowds, but whether the turn-outs will be as large as if the nation were not at war, I very much doubt."[2]

The White Sox were still on the road, the first team visiting Minnesota for an April 8 exhibition game versus the American Association St. Paul Saints. "Sergt. Smiley put the regulars through a more ambitious drill than usual just before the battle and their work drew volleys of patriotic enthusiasm from the crowd," Sy Sanborn wrote.[3]

The big leaguers beat the Class AA club, 7–4, then traveled 250 miles back to Iowa for a final tune-up versus the Class A Western League Des Moines Boosters. A local newspaper made no mention of Smiley's troops after an 8–1 Chicago victory, but did note the first drill by sixty businessmen from a preparedness group at a Des Moines coliseum.

Commy's team began the regular season Wednesday afternoon, April 11, versus the Browns at Sportsman's Park in St. Louis. Sergeant Smiley and his local counterpart, Sgt. Winfred B. Wisener, had their troops out for a ten-minute drill an hour before game time. The two teams marched around the park behind a band in squads of four. Several hundred fans were disappointed at missing the performance, a local newspaper later asking why the clubs had sent the boys out so early.

"Some of the best drill Sergeants in the service were detailed to train the athletes," the *St. Louis Star* said. "Now that the players are ready to go through exhibition drills they should be required to drill at the most favorable time."[4]

The Pale Hose trotted out for the opener wearing special blue uniforms with a faint white stripe and a silk American flag patch hand-embroidered on the right sleeve, an alternative to road grays and home whites. One of Comiskey's old skippers, Fielder Jones (1904–8), managed the Browns, who quickly roughed up Sox starter Claude "Lefty" Williams for a 1–0 lead.

"Holy smoke, how the Browns did pepper him in the first inning," Sanborn wrote in the *Tribune*. "Only brilliant throws to the plate by Jackson and [Harry] Leibold kept the locals from winning the game right there."[5] Manager Rowland yanked Williams and sent Jim Scott out for the second inning.

Scotty gave up only one run over six frames before handing the ball to Dave Danforth, a late Sox rally giving Chicago a 7–2 victory. "Jim Scott has come back—in this way: He has gone back to his old style of delivery," the *Daily News* said. "Jim swings around and covers up before delivering the ball. He has started out well."[6]

Sanborn added that the Sox also had "trimmed the Browns in the military preliminaries. Both teams drilled under orders from their respective sergeants, but the locals used simple formations and didn't attempt anything in the manual of arms."[7] The *Star* pointed out in their defense that the Browns had begun drilling two weeks after the Sox.

Rain postponed the second Sox-Browns game, but Sergeant Smiley managed to get the reunited regulars and Yannigans out for ninety minutes of drills beforehand. "The second squad had missed a couple of evolutions while on the trip, and Sergeant Smiley took the Goofs in charge as soon as they appeared on the field," an Iowa paper said. "A couple of more drills and they will be able to step with the rest."[8]

St. Louis rebounded the following day to beat starter Urban "Red" Faber, 4–3, with Danforth again in relief. Eddie Cicotte ended the series in spectacular fashion April 14. He set the tone for the rest of the season by tossing an 11–0 no-hitter, the first of six to be thrown in the majors that season.

The righthander arrived in Chicago from the Red Sox in 1912, and fans still argued over how to say his name. It has come down to us as "SEE-cott," but the hurler himself said otherwise —"you pronounce it 'Sy-cot,' with the accent on the first syllable. It's different in French—but I am an American."[9] Cicotte was now nearly thirty-three years old, the second oldest pitcher in the circuit behind forty-one-year-old Eddie Plank of the Browns.

Eddie allowed only five men to reach base this afternoon while striking out five. The *St. Louis Globe-Democrat* praised his "unimpeachable" performance.[10] "Eddie Cicotte, the little old man of the White Sox, is not yet ready for the scrap heap," the *Chicago Examiner* added. "He showed it here to-day when he hurled the best ball of his historic career."[11]

About three-quarters of Cicotte's deliveries were knuckleballs. He hadn't invented the unpredictable pitch but had mastered it, earning the nickname "Knuckles." A variety of other pitches helped Cicotte baffle hitters, including a new one dubbed the shine ball. The offering so bewildered batters that

Washington Senators manager Clark Griffith would later grab a couple of game-used balls and send them to President Johnson for analysis.

Ban would find nothing wrong and return them to the White Sox. "Whether he was sailing or sinking the ball, shining it or darkening it, the 5-foot-9, 175-pound Cicotte had more pitches than a traveling salesman," writes Jim Sandoval, his biographer for the Society for American Baseball Research (SABR).[12]

The Sox ran their record to 5–1 with a three-game sweep in Detroit before finally heading to Chicago for the April 19 home opener, again versus St. Louis. "President Comiskey had prepared for the occasion by decorating his improved stadium with more American flags than we supposed there were in the world," Sanborn wrote.[13] Portraits of presidents Washington, Lincoln, Grant, and Wilson, plus Admiral George Dewey, hero of America's most recent war, adorned the Comiskey Park scoreboard. Lettering on the outfield wall spelled out the address of the army recruiting office on South State Street.

"The god of war is a rooter at the White Sox park this afternoon," the *Daily News* said.[14] Sergeant Smiley had his troops ready. "Twenty-five khaki outfits were delivered to Secretary Harry Grabiner yesterday, with the same number of Springfields, for the athletes," the *Tribune* had said beforehand.[15]

Maj. Gen. Thomas Barry, commander of the army's central department, was ready to toss out the first ball. Barry, his staff, and Captain Kenney were Commy's guests in a special box. Over 25,000 civilians filled the park, the bunting partly compensating for the gloomy weather. Most fans were already in their seats when Sergeant Smiley marched his men out between the pavilion and grandstand, all wearing regulation khaki and shouldering rifles.

"For an instant there was a pause of surprise, then as the rooters recognized their idols they realized the transformation that had taken place since they last saw them," Sanborn wrote. "There was a roar that fairly drowned the band, which was trying to furnish a quickstep for the Sox to march by."[16]

Smiley halted his little command before the grandstand. General Barry inspected the Sox and complimented the noncom on the progress they'd made in six weeks. Then the city's board of trade presented the Sox with a regimental flag, a practice dating back to the Civil War and beyond. A spokesman addressed the sergeant, manager, and team.

"I am deputized . . . to present you with this flag—the flag of our country," he said. "In giving it into your care we charge you to cherish, honor and protect it and if called upon to battle in its defense, we expect you, when the battle is over, to return it bright in all its pristine loveliness and glory, unstained by defeat, or to remain buried on the battlefield with it."[17]

Everyone in the park rose and civilians removed their hats as bands began to play. The tune wasn't "The Star-Spangled Banner" or "God Bless America" but "God Save the King," a salute to the country's new ally, George V of Great Britain. The Sox then changed into home flannels and trotted out to face the Browns. The game, alas, was a letdown. The field was muddy, the contest interrupted by showers, the ball filthy as soon as it went into play.

"The skies were dark, and it was impossible for the gardeners to see the pill in the air until it had risen above the shadow of the grandstand roof," *Chicago Day Book* said. "Further, there was a high wind from the south which caused the ball to twist like an unmanageable aeroplane."[18] Even sure-handed Eddie Collins booted a fly ball as Fielder Jones's men took what Sanborn called a "sloppy 6 to 2 victory."[19]

Eddie Plank, a future Hall of Famer, pitched a complete game victory. Jim Scott took the loss, although relievers Ewell Russell (called "Reb" or "Tex") and Danforth allowed most of the damage. Perhaps the earlier surge of emotion had overwhelmed the Chicagoans.

The White Sox and the other AL clubs continued their drills before games on orders from President Johnson, usually in flannels and shouldering bats rather than rifles. "Ban Johnson wants both clubs to drill ten minutes every day before the assembled fans as incentives to patriotism," an eastern paper said.[20]

Besides drill exhibitions, the White Sox on the road began performing in what newspapers called a choir. The players marched around a field under Sergeant Smiley, then lined up before the grandstand to sing two verses of "The Star Spangled Banner." The singing was Rowland's idea. He'd gathered his men to ask who among them knew all the words to the patriotic tune (which wasn't yet the national anthem). Only Scott, Buck Weaver, and Joe Benz did.

"Rowland then told us to sing the two verses as well as we could and that those who didn't know the words could make a bluff until they learned them by singing 'Hum-hum-hum,'" an unnamed player recalled. "After our first appearance Gandil came in the clubhouse after the game and approached Rowland. 'I can't help it, boss,' he said. 'I'm a bum hum-hum-hummer.'"[21]

Sergeant Smiley accompanied the club and especially looked forward to a road series the first week of June in his old hometown, Philadelphia, versus Connie Mack's Athletics. "I want to visit with the home folks and then it's all off," Smiley said. "I don't care how soon Uncle Sam calls me to the battle front in France."[22] Commy was assured, however, of retaining his services for as long as he needed the sergeant.

The Sox played streaky baseball early in the season. After dropping the home opener, they reeled off four straight wins. Then came three more losses, a win, another loss, another win, four losses, three wins, and a pair of losses. May 12, they began a stretch of sixteen wins over eighteen games, with one loss and a tie. The 1–1 tie came May 26, at home versus Washington. Neither run was earned and the umps called the game for darkness after six innings, Scott pitching for the Sox. The streak ended June 5 after a three-game sweep in Philadelphia.

"There were more thrills in the final game of the White Sox-Mack series than one would expect in a whole season of watching games in which the Athletics were playing," Jimmy Crusinberry deadpanned in the *Tribune*. Scott pitched five innings of relief behind winner Benz. The Sox under Sergeant Smiley also impressed onlookers before the game, Crusinberry added, with "some marine maneuvers, running over the diamond and dropping to their stomachs like sharpshooters."[23] The 6–3 victory completed the second eight-win stretch for the Sox (punctuated by the tie).

Eddie Cicotte notched five of the sixteen wins during the run, including a 4–0, three-hit complete game June 2 in Philadelphia. Crusinberry said he'd done the job "so precisely that it was not even interesting."[24] The victory extended Cicotte's record to 9–2. When the winning streak ended, Chicago was a hair behind champion Boston, at 30–13 (.698) and 29–12 (.707), respectively, in the standings.

Cicotte was vital to Chicago's success. Despite the club's good record, the other Sox starters struggled much of the season. Reb Russell was occasionally brilliant but often hurt, as was Red Faber. Scott generally fell short of expectations, Lefty Williams was hard-working but luckless, and Meldon "Mellie" Wolfgang was ill and reduced to throwing batting practice. Danforth, at least, was effective off the bench. "Cicotte was my one dependable pitcher from start to finish," Rowland said later.[25]

Complicating the Sox pitching woes was the decent but unspectacular play of Joe Jackson, Hap Felsch, and Harry "Nemo" Leibold in the outer gardens. Slugger Jackson's .301 season batting average would be noteworthy but 40 points lower than in 1916. "The Sox outfield, I will frankly say, is not a feature of the team's work," Scott said later.[26] Focus therefore shifted to the infield, where many fans and scribes thought Chick Gandil was a fine addition.

Baseball writer and editor F. C. Lane recalled telling Charley Comiskey what a great club he'd had during the near-miss season of 1916. Commy had disagreed. "No, it isn't a great club," he'd said. "I haven't any dependable first baseman and I am weak at third. No club is a great club which is weak at first and third."[27] Gandil now capably filled the gap at first base.

"I am glad that fate has brought me back to the Chicago club," Chick had said in March after agreeing to his contract. "And I am going to try to help land a flag for the Sox."[28] It appeared he was doing just that.

Swede Risberg had arrived at the same time as Chick. He'd come from the PCL, "where they think he is the greatest infielder the coast ever produced," Sanborn wrote.[29] With Gandil playing first, Rowland could use Swede at short (after shipping Zeb Terry to the Minors) and use Buck Weaver at the hot corner, where, according to Lane, he became "lo, the greatest third sacker in the American League."[30] Jim Scott thought their new shortstop "made" the team.

"Without Swede the Sox presented a club formidable in every respect but one—they lacked the punch," Scott said later. "Risberg got off to a poor start but he handled himself in such a way that there was no mistaking the future star."[31]

Arnold "Chick" Gandil, White Sox infielder. Courtesy of Library of Congress.

But it was Gandil who became the key in the improved Sox infield. Born in Minnesota and reared in Berkeley, California, the first sacker was tough, troublesome, and superb. He'd posted the top fielding percentage in the American League for his position in 1916 and would repeat this season. With Chick, Eddie, Swede, and Buck, plus able Fred McMullin filling in as needed, Commy finally had the solid infield he'd lacked. Gandil never seemed to enjoy his success, however. He was broke, for one thing, and filed for bankruptcy during the summer, listing his clothing as his only assets.

"He didn't smile much, was quick to draw a line in the dirt over what he perceived to be assaults on his manhood, and was in the forefront of every battle, *mano a mano*, in which the Sox were involved," Sox historians Warren Wilbert and William Hageman write of Chick.[32] Rowland summed him up this way: "Chick is a fighting ball player. He has no friends among the opposing players during a game, and his presence on first base will liven up our infield and keep the other boys battling all the time."[33]

Gandil hated not only the men in the opposite dugout. He also despised teammate Eddie Collins and never spoke to him after joining the club. The poisonous feeling arose from a game in Philadelphia in 1912, when the Sox captain was a member of the Athletics' famous $100,000 infield and Gandil a Washington Senator.

Collins had leapt high for an errant peg at second base. Coming down, he'd shattered runner Gandil's nose, from which a surgeon later removed a small bone chip. The Nats thought Collins had intentionally struck him with his knee, a D.C. sportswriter calling it assault. The A's star reportedly had looked down at the prone and bloody runner and said, "Well, I got you, didn't I?"[34]

The account doesn't coincide with Collins's reputation, however. He never spoke about the event in 1917, and Chicago papers kept mum about any grudge between the pair. The first and second basemen were badly mismatched, no matter their history. "The educated and by now quite wealthy and refined Collins was the polar opposite of tough and tumble Gandil," writes Rick Huhn,

Collins's biographer. "Eddie would fight given significant cause; Gandil would fight just to fight."³⁵

"They could call him 'Fighting Chick' Gandil and never misname the big first baseman of the White Sox," a Texas newspaper said, attributing the infielder's pugnacity to determination to prove his worth despite demotions or trades by Chicago, Washington, and Cleveland. "Or they could term him the savior of the White Sox and do his pals no injustice. Or they could call him any one of half a dozen other names that stand for aggressiveness, fight, that indicate the possessing of the punch, of the ability to hit in the pinches."³⁶ Windy City sportswriters acknowledged Gandil's aggression too.

"Some of the White Sox have taken the military drill too much to heart," an *Examiner* columnist wrote. "Chick Gandil, for instance, can't wait until he lands in France."³⁷ Robbins also pointed to the Sox first baseman in the *Daily News*.

"The White Sox have progressed in fighting spirit in the last year," he'd write late in the season. "In 1916 Manager Rowland had to do most of the battling himself. The coming of Kid Gleason, the advent of Swede Risberg and the signing of Chick Gandil transformed the White Sox into one of the fighting machines of the American league."³⁸ Robbins considered Gandil "a surprise player of the year."³⁹

4

Buck

The day the White Sox finished sweeping the Mackmen in Philly, June 5, was Registration Day in America. Every male citizen who'd passed his twenty-first birthday but not yet celebrated his thirty-first had to appear before a government registrar. He was to provide his name, address, date of birth, citizenship, employment, dependents, race, marital status, and other details. His draft board would record a sequential serial number in red ink on the registration card. The man himself would receive a small blue card to prove he'd registered.

Conscription was a complex procedure surely born of governmental committees. It would include a July 20 draft drawing at the Senate Office Building in Washington, D.C. The *New York Tribune* tried to explain what it called the greatest lottery in history. "Of the 4,557 registration districts throughout the country the largest district has something over 10,200 numbers," the paper said, "while the smallest has only about 185, and the average is around 3,000."[1]

Blindfolded men would draw 10,500 capsules from a glass bowl, each containing a serial number. The hours-long process was to determine each man's place in the draft, with the results to be printed in local newspapers and posted in long lists at local draft offices.

"In districts where there are fewer than 10,500 men registered, any 'draft numbers' corresponding to a 'red ink number' higher than the number of registrants will be disregarded and the draft number next on the list will be called," the *Tribune* added.² During the first round the government expected to call 900,000 to 1.5 million men out of nearly 10 million anticipated to register. Exemptions might reduce this number to 625,000 actually sworn for duty.

Every Major League team observed Registration Day along with the rest of the country. The Athletics opened Shibe Park for service members and veterans, who had only to come in uniform to be admitted free to the game with the White Sox. In Chicago, three companies of sailors and marines from the Great Lakes Naval Training Station north of the city marched on the diamond at Weeghman Park before a Cubs-Phillies game.

Cap Huston missed a Tigers-Yankees doubleheader in New York because he was again an army captain. Nearly fifty years old, the Yanks' co-owner had hurriedly left a game the previous day to report to his regiment of railway engineers in Michigan; by autumn he would command troops in France.

Rowland and other skippers with road games made sure their draft-age players were registered before boarding their trains. Rowland and secretary Harry Grabiner had escorted twenty-two Sox to the Chicago city clerk's office at 9:00 a.m. May 24, a day when over 300 other young Chicagoans also registered.

Emotions were running high in the Windy City following America's declaration of war. Captain Kenney had tried to raise what the *Herald* called a "flying squad of 'American beauties'" to lobby against wartime marriages of convenience.³ The superintendent of the Cook County social service bureau, believing prospective grooms hoped only to avoid military service, had screamed "Shame! Shame!" at couples waiting for marriage licenses, believing the prospective grooms hoped only to avoid military service. "What a mockery this all is!" she'd exclaimed. "Can it be that my own sex can so disgrace itself by supporting and encouraging men who shirk their duty?"⁴ The *Daily News* had accompanied its article with a poem:

I am a slacker. My colors are yellow and black.

I have no manhood, no name, no pride, no ambition, no self-respect, no sense of duty.

I hide behind women's skirts. I grovel in the dust of shame. I am a worm.[5]

Five clerks stood waiting to help the White Sox register. Joe Jackson signed his draft card within ten minutes, about the limit of his literacy. The team was amazed to learn that Hap Felsch was a married man, a fact he'd never revealed. Outfielder John "Shano" Collins registered too, only to receive a telegram from his hometown seven weeks later saying it wasn't necessary. "Instead of being born in 1886, Shano first saw the light of day in 1885," the *Tribune* explained. "This makes him nearly a year over the draft age limit."[6]

"War apparently has no terrors for them," the *Daily News* said of the Sox. "There was a little 'kidding' back and forth, but for the most part the players took the matter seriously."[7] But as *Baseball Magazine* had noted in a profile of the army's All-Star team two years earlier, "the lot of the soldier has never been made as attractive to the average, healthful young man as it should have been."[8]

Secretary Grabiner told the Sox to send their completed cards to their local boards by registered mail, to avoid any questions about their status. Such precaution was important because anyone certified for military service had to return to his local jurisdiction to leave for training with other draftees from his hometown. That wasn't likely to occur anytime soon, however, since the government was still frantically building cantonments around the country to handle millions of raw troops needed for the new National Army consisting largely of conscripted men.

Rowland, Gleason, and pitchers Cicotte and Benz were above draft age and didn't register. The government would raise the age limit later, which would require the two hurlers and Shano Collins to register in September 1918.

The men who did register in 1917 endured several unsettled weeks of waiting before learning their places in the draft. The process was laden with uncertainty and anxiety. The draft lists took time to reach local draft boards following the big lottery in July. Sox players were uncertain for a few days whether they could even leave Chicago for road games, lest they miss an order to report for physical examinations for the army. The *Tribune* shared what little it knew about their status the day after the drawing.

"Weaver's number, 938, was the 782d one drawn, and it is likely that all up to that number will be in on the first call," the paper said. "Other Sox players who knew their numbers and who are drawn early enough for a possible call were Ray Schalk and Chick Gandil. Ray had number 3,405, and it was the 1,138th number drawn. Gandil had number 1,716, and it was the 1,584th number drawn. [First Baseman Ted] Jourdan's number is 1,510, and it was pulled out after about 2,050 numbers had been drawn." Swede Risberg didn't know his status, but he was single and fit and "has a feeling that his number was drawn among the early ones."9

Risberg later learned he had a high draft number. The *Tribune* figured Weaver, Schalk, and Gandil needn't worry yet either, because they were married and wouldn't be among the first called. But vague suppositions weren't enough, and many of Commy's men telephoned or wired their hometowns to learn where they stood on the lists. Millions of other American young men shared the same boat.

Charley Comiskey did his bit for the war in his usual businesslike manner. Back in March he'd pledged 10 percent of his club's daily gate gross receipts to the Red Cross, should America enter the conflict. Cubs owner Weeghman had done the same.

Comiskey was "one of the first to recognize the drill as a means of softening the opposition to the professional sport in war time, and he has now come through as the first of the major magnates to offer a percentage of his profits to the Red Cross, if war should be declared," sportswriter Daniel Rice had written in the *Brooklyn Eagle*. "Other magnates have talked about it. Comiskey has acted, and more power to him."[10]

The Sox owner exceeded expectations. His team rode the train to Madison, Wisconsin, during a chilly free day in April for an exhibition with a team from the university. The players carried their regimental flag during a drill under Sergeant Smiley. "I couldn't tell from the uniforms whether the boys were the regulars or a bunch of soldiers from Uncle Sam's army," a fan said.[11] The game netted $500 for the Red Cross.

The club then visited Wisconsin national guardsmen at nearby Camp Randall to play a casual exhibition (the score not recorded) for some 3,000 fans. By June 1, the Sox owner had handed the Red Cross two checks totaling over $5,000, which was generous but much less than Commy had anticipated.

"Cold weather and continued rain have played havoc with the White Sox schedule during their home stays," Johnny Alcock wrote in the *Tribune*. "Besides many postponements, the games played have attracted only a percentage of the crowds that would have turned out with anything like real baseball weather." Alcock pointed to a rained-out Memorial Day doubleheader that might have drawn 30,000 fans. "The Red Cross fund lost 10 per cent of whatever would have been Comiskey's share from such a gate."[12]

Commy constantly looked to boost attendance and Red Cross contributions in the park that bore his name. The *Daily News* suggested holding a France Day should Marshal Joseph Joffre, former commander of the French armed forces, visit Chicago during an American tour. "Bully," the Old Roman replied. "It's the best suggestion I've heard for a long time. Yes, sir, we're right in line for a 'France day,' which will also be a Red Cross day. Every day is Red Cross day at my park."[13] The event never came about, but Commy's total Red Cross contribution would top $17,000 by the end of the season, the equivalent of over $400,000 today.

The White Sox weren't alone in their altruism. Every Major League team supported war charities and local troops, as did many Minor circuits. Clark

Griffith was particularly brilliant. He had been a player-manager for Commy's first two AL clubs (1901–2) and now managed and partly owned the Washington Senators. During the spring Griff had hit upon the idea of supplying baseball equipment for bored, sports-crazy troops at home and overseas.

America had several nicknames for its boys in uniform. Soldiers were doughboys or Sammies; sailors were bluejackets or jackies; and marines were devil dogs, from what the enemy called them (*Teufel Hunden*). Griffith supported them all. When he wrote to big city sportswriters to publicize his notion, fans from President Wilson to John Doe began chipping in coins and bills, starting at a quarter.

The Clark C. Griffith Ball and Bat Fund became immensely successful. It assembled $30 packages that included a catcher's mask, chest protector, and mitt; first baseman's mitt; three bats; three bases with pins; a dozen baseballs; a rulebook; and twelve scorecards. Griffith eventually raised nearly $150,000, thanks in no small way to Charley Comiskey and fellow owners. A postwar list of recipient units would run thirty-two pages.

The White Sox climbed into first place in the American League with a June 9 win over Griffith's club in Washington. After a single game in Cleveland, they headed east again for two games with the Yankees. In New York they learned of Sergeant Smiley's promotion. The noncom would snip the chevrons from his sleeves and pin the single silver bars of a first lieutenant to shoulder straps.

"His commission has not arrived, but is expected shortly," the *Tribune* said. "With the promotion there is danger of the Sox losing their drillmaster."[14] The Yankees received similar news about their drillmaster, Sergeant Gibson.

The Chicago club chugged into Boston in mid-June for a series with the second-place and suddenly struggling Red Sox. Trainer Bill Buckner bought a bull terrier for luck and named it Pennant. Later, the dog became a regular at Comiskey Park. The *Chicago Defender* even credited Pennant with a fifteen-inning victory over Cleveland, saying a loud bark startled an Indian outfielder into dropping the fly ball that put the winning run into scoring position. But the mascot only helped the White Sox break even in Beantown.

Lefty Williams beat Ernie "Long" Shore 8–0 in the first game, Friday, June 15. Eddie Cicotte faced hurler Herman "Babe" Ruth the next day. The Saturday game was damp, dark, and chaotic. Gamblers in the crowd of 9,400 grew increasingly loud and unhappy as Boston trailed amid a light rain.

"The legion of gamblers in the bleachers was well aware that if the game was called before becoming official, all bets would be canceled; shouts of 'Call the game!' began ringing out from the stands," Sox historian Don Zminda writes.[15] "The truth is that during the last two weeks, the gamblers here have been stung, stung for a greater amount than in years," Jimmy Crusinberry reported in the *Tribune*. "When they saw they were likely to get another trimming and that it might be averted by breaking up the ball game, they incited the fans to riot."[16]

Several hundred Bostonians stormed the field. Police tried to reassert order but got little or no help from Red Sox owner Harry Frazee. The fracas landed on the front page of the *Boston Globe*.

"There was a delay of 45 minutes before play was resumed. It never should have continued as the grounds were in an unfit condition," a Boston sportswriter wrote. "During the intermission there were a lot of interesting goings on under the stand, the Chicago players, it is alleged, figuring in several mixups [sic]." Catcher Ray Schalk, "in language not of the parlor, is said to have questioned the courage of a patrolman from the Boylston-st station."[17] The *Tribune* added that during the ruckus a fan "is supposed [to] have bumped McMullin's fist with his eye. Also he is supposed to have had his fingers on the railing just when Weaver let his bat fall."[18]

George "Buck" Weaver, White Sox infielder. Courtesy of Library of Congress.

Little fazed Buck Weaver, a twenty-six-year-old third baseman in his sixth season with the big club. "Weaver was knocked off the back of an automobile returning from the ball park to the hotel," the *Tribune* had reported after an out-of-town exhibition game a season earlier. "His injuries were slight, and he walked to the station. It is hard to hurt Buck."[19] Chicago novelist Nelson Algren later described him as a territorial animal who "guarded the spiked sand around third like his life."[20]

Boston cops slapped Buck and Fred with arrest warrants for assault. The case wouldn't be heard until late September when the Sox made their last trip to Boston, then be tossed out quicker than a catcher trying to steal second base. "Both athletes appeared in court and the judge then dismissed the case and talked baseball to them until time for the next case," the *Tribune* said.[21]

The pair also refused to settle a damage suit that dragged deep into the 1918 season and likewise went nowhere. Meanwhile, even devout Boston fans thought things had gotten out of hand at Fenway Park.

"Those first-base bleacherites need a strong restraining hand," a *Globe* columnist wrote following the Saturday invasion, "and the quicker it is applied the better."[22] Once play had resumed Cicotte cruised to a 7–2 win, both he and Ruth throwing complete games.

The Red Sox didn't play Sunday ball at Fenway. The White Sox dropped a doubleheader to even the series Monday. Commy's club then left town exactly as it had entered, three games ahead of Boston atop the American League standings.

Chicago dropped out of first place with a July 6 loss in Detroit, four percentage points behind the Red Sox. That same day, newspapers also reported Jim Scott's intention to enlist and attend an army reserve officers' training camp at Leon Springs, Texas.

Pitcher Scott was only the second active Major Leaguer to sign up. Catcher Hank Gowdy of the Boston Braves had joined the Ohio National Guard a month earlier. Remembered as the batting hero of the champion 1914 "Miracle Braves," Gowdy had entered the army to applause from the nation's sportswriters. Scott didn't say whether he'd consulted Sergeant Smiley before making his decision, but it wouldn't have been surprising.

The B. B. N. G. corporal was always enthusiastic about military drills, whether with bats or rifles. Scott even had taken command at Philadelphia on what the *Chicago Examiner* said was one of several occasions. "In the absence of Sergt, Smiley, Jim Scott acted as commander of the White Sox forces and put them through the stunts like a regular army captain," the *Tribune* added.[23]

Sy Sanborn thought the hurler was facing reality when he "surrendered to Father Time before the season was over and volunteered his services to Uncle Sam."[24] Commy, Ban, and Captain Kenney all supported Death Valley Jim's application, making it a near certainty that the army would accept him. "When the first call for the second officers' camp was issued Scott made application and anxiously awaited the call that he hopes will give him shoulder straps and service in France," the *Examiner* said later.[25]

The White Sox ended their road trip with the loss in Detroit and headed home to Comiskey Park. "Since leaving home the Sox have won five games and lost four and yet they were shoved into second place," the *Tribune* said. "They will be at home now for a long spell, meeting all of the eastern clubs, and when that period is over the boys expect to be back on the top."[26]

The first series was with Connie Mack's Athletics, last in the American League, as they would be at season's end. Paradoxically, Philly was the team skipper Rowland feared most. His South Side club played hard against tough opponents like Boston. "But there was a disposition to take the Athletics as a more or less safe proposition," Pants said later. "And Connie's team being good sluggers and whaling away at anything, caused us more damage than I care to admit."[27]

The Sox dropped the Saturday game, 4–2. The following day brought a change in routine. The two clubs caught an early train up to Fort Sheridan, an old army post beside Lake Michigan, where they played an unusual Sunday morning exhibition for 6,000 officer candidates and their friends, sweethearts, and families. Soldiers met the teams at the station and drove them in trucks to the fort, where engineers had laid out a diamond on the parade ground.

"The embryo soldiers did the fair thing, half of them sitting on one side and the other half taking opposite benches," the *Philadelphia Inquirer* said, "each side pulling lustily for the Sox or Mackmen, according to their location."[28] The colonel in command sat beside Rowland during the game "and learned some new things about strategy," according to the *Tribune*.[29]

Players and spectators took the game lightly. Weaver offered an entertaining fake rhubarb that made even the umpire smile. The *Examiner* ran a photo of cheering doughboys above a story that said the Sox "allowed themselves to be driven to cover by the pesky Athletics, who did things that they usually are not guilty of on a big league diamond. The score was 5 to 1."[30]

The teams left Fort Sheridan after seven innings to head back to the South Side for an afternoon game that counted. Eddie Cicotte almost inevitably was the starter, versus Alexander "Rube" Schauer for the Mackmen. The contest nearly mirrored the morning's. Philadelphia led 4–1 after their half of the sixth, baffling even the visiting sportswriters. Eddie Cicotte uncharacteristically surrendered ten hits and looked in danger of being yanked.

"For some unaccountable reason the Mackmen hit Cicotte harder than any other American League team this season, although the 'Shine Ball Kid' appeared to have his usual stuff," the *Inquirer* said. The headline called the AL race "as tight as a miser's purse strings."[31]

"Eddie stuck to the job as if convinced it wasn't possible for the Philadelphia outfit to beat him, and he was right. The blowup finally came, and Eddie's record stands unharmed, regardless of the swats," Crusinberry wrote.[32] "The Rowlanders uncorked a vial of pennant-winning dash that carried them through to an 8–4 victory," the *Inquirer* added. "At the same time Cleveland trounced the Boston Red Sox again, so White and Red Hose exchange places in their pet scrap for the flag."[33]

The victory boosted Cicotte's record to 13–6. With the season half over, the hurler led the White Sox, and the White Sox led the American League.

5

Griff

The White Sox were locked in a tight pennant race but were still leading the Red Sox and Tigers entering August. The weather had been lousy much of the season and the prohibition on playing professional baseball on the Sabbath in some cities complicated making up the rainouts. After a Friday road win and a Saturday doubleheader sweep versus the Mackmen, the Pale Hose looked forward to a free Sunday, August 5. They didn't get it.

"Instead of that they have learned they will be expected to make a hurried getaway out of Philadelphia next Saturday, ride all night and part of Sunday, play a game in Detroit, then board an early train out of Detroit, ride all night and part of Monday back to Philadelphia, then tackle the Athletics, who will have been resting over the Sabbath," Sy Sanborn said in the *Tribune*. He withheld the names of the Sox who grumbled about their owner's plan for getting back on schedule. Sanborn added, however, "All the players know Comiskey's reputation for being willing to spend money to win a pennant, but they cannot see how that reputation fits the present case."[1]

Manager Rowland sent pitcher Red Faber ahead to Detroit and took only fifteen men with him for the game. The Tigers faced a similar pinch. They had to leave a series in New York, travel home to Navin Field for the makeup game, then immediately head back east to continue playing the Yankees. Neither team was happy. They got even grumpier when a deluge stopped the Sunday contest with the scored tied 2–2 at the bottom of the third inning.

"The teams waited half an hour and then a dozen turf manicurists, armed with brooms, came upon the field and started sweeping off the water," the *Tribune* said. "They brought forth wheelbarrows filled with rich earth and spread it around the sacks. While they were thus engaged the heavens opened afresh and the umpires, after several minutes of hesitation, called play off."[2]

President Johnson was in the stands and agreed with the decision by head arbiter Francis "Silk" O'Loughlin. The Tigers handed out nearly 15,000 rainchecks.

"As far as the game had gone it was an argument worthy of teams ranking well up in the American league pennant race," the *Detroit Free Press* said.[3] The exhausted Sox completed their unprofitable thousand mile round trip by dropping the last two games of the A's series in Philadelphia, which they followed with another loss at Washington. The equally drained Tigers lost their next two games with the Yanks in New York.

Meanwhile, another imperative matter had occupied several Sox. Weaver, Felsch, and Gandil had undergone draft physicals August 7 in Philly, before the club left for Washington. Buck and Chick were registered in Chicago and Hap in Milwaukee, but taking their exams elsewhere was "perfectly regular and will be effective in the case of many baseball players, as well as traveling men."[4]

Pitcher Dave Danforth had taken his exam a day earlier a hundred miles south in Baltimore. The four Sox players all passed and asked for draft exemptions on the grounds they were married. Unhitched bullpen catcher Joe Jenkins also wanted to be examined, but didn't have permission from his board in California, so he took and passed his physical later in Chicago.

Jim Scott appeared for an exam too, with a regular army surgeon prior to his enlistment. He passed and received word to report for training August 27. He would head not to dusty Leon Springs, Texas, or Fort Sheridan outside Chicago, but to the San Francisco Presidio, where the war department sent prospective officers from Wyoming and seven other states comprising the army's western department.

His teammates' requests for exemption looked shabby compared with the hurler's determination to don khaki. But a player's career was short, and losing any portion of it materially affected him and his family. Debates over pro athletes volunteering for service continued throughout the war. Nothing happened quickly for Scott or others like him, however, and various delays left him not knowing when the army expected him.

Scotty pitched five games in August as starter and reliever. His last appearance came August 17 in Chicago when he threw two- and one-third innings in a 9–7 loss to the Athletics. "Jim Scott, once a main reliance of the staff, was of little use," Rowland said months later.[5] *Baseball Magazine* said "the club can survive without him."[6]

The pitcher's record for the season ended at six wins versus seven losses, but his earned run average (ERA) of 1.87 would have been good enough for fifth in the AL had he thrown more innings. Despite his unimpressive stats, some commentators thought Scott had erased the stain of his 1916 suspension. "His 'come-back' from that episode this year has been notable in baseball circles," the *Chicago Eagle* said.[7]

Charley Comiskey looked forward to the drill competition that would award the $500 prize to the top AL squad and $100 to its drillmaster. "The White Sox say they are going to reward Serg. Smiley by earning the hundred bucks for him," the *Tribune* said.[8] Commy meanwhile continued to host thousands of Sammies and jackies in his ballpark, particularly men from the Illinois National Guard.

"While the enlisting squads were out hustling for men the rest of the [Seventh] regiment continued the inexorable drill in Humboldt and Douglas parks," the *Tribune* said August 23. "President Comiskey of the White Sox invited the entire regiment yesterday to see the ball game today. P. S.—The entire regiment accepted."⁹

Thursday the twenty-third was also Military Day, when the White Sox and Senators were to demonstrate their drill proficiency at Comiskey Park. At Ban Johnson's request General Barry had appointed Maj. Raymond Sheldon, a regular army officer, to judge all the AL squads that week. Each team drilled in a fifteen-minute program prepared by its drillmaster.

Sheldon had already reviewed the Athletics and Indians at Cleveland and the Yankees and Tigers at Detroit. In Cleveland he'd learned of his promotion to lieutenant colonel. After Chicago he would continue to St. Louis for the Red Sox and Browns. Expectations were high on the South Side for the B. B. N. G.

"Unless they fall down through nervousness today the White Sox are thought to have a swell chance to win the military prize, as they have worked persistently under Sergt. Smiley ever since March to perfect themselves," the *Tribune* said.¹⁰ Morning downpours held attendance to about 8,500 before giving way to sunshine. The weather didn't matter to the 7,500 soldiers, sailors, marines and six military bands also on hand.

"There was khaki to the right, and khaki to the left. . . . Flags fluttered in the breeze, bands played, and for the first time this year a pennant battle was overshadowed at Comiskey Park," the *Herald* said.¹¹ "Parades, martial music, flag raisings, and the other military features completely swamped the national pastime," Sy Sanborn added in the *Tribune*.¹²

Watching from the stands were President Johnson, the governor of Illinois, the mayor of Chicago, Generals Barry and McCain, and 300 other officers. The White Sox marched out for the drill competition wearing khaki and carrying Springfield rifles, while the Senators wore travel flannels and had bats over their shoulders. Many fans mistook Commy's boys for regular soldiers.

"When it was discovered they were ball players all hands joined in a cheer," Sanborn wrote. "The Rowlands made a much more impressive showing than the Senators on account of their better equipment."¹³ Some observers argued that khaki gave the Sox an unfair advantage, but the *Examiner* disagreed. "The fact that some of the teams appeared in army uniform and used real rifles made no difference to the regular army officer," it said of Sheldon. "He judged them on what they knew of military formations."[14]

The Senators went through their paces under drillmaster Sgt. John Dean, followed by the Sox under Sergeant Smiley. Sheldon watched both with an experienced eye, judging them for punctuality, number of men in the squads, appearance, military courtesy, variety of movements, discipline, and military drill.

"Both the Chicago and Washington teams made a good impression in the drill, and their maneuvers were roundly applauded by the huge crowd," sportswriter Denman Thompson wrote in the *Washington Star*.[15] The *Daily News* thought the Pale Hose looked fine but noted "several members of the Sox squad who couldn't keep step and they had a ragged line for the same reason. In the eyes of a trained soldier like Lieut.-Col. Sheldon military drill counts for a lot."[16] Overall, though, the officer was impressed.

"Without question all teams have had good instruction and great interest in their work," Sheldon said later. "The drills in company close and extended order, the manual of arms, bayonet exercises, advance by rushes, the facings, etc., showed plainly that much time had been devoted to these movements, and I was surprised to see how well the teams were drilled." Sheldon gave Smiley and the other sergeants "great credit for the results they have achieved in such a short time."[17]

Once the judging was complete the Sox and Senators marched together behind an artillery band and a squad of marines to the right field flagpole. They raised Old Glory, then marched to the left field pole to raise the city championship pennant the Sox had won from the Cubs the previous fall. Sheldon joined Ban Johnson in his box as Eddie Cicotte took the mound for Commy's nine. The hurler notched his nineteenth win, 6–0, keeping his club a game and a half ahead of the Red Sox. The event was such a smashing success that the Sox owner wanted to make Military Day an annual affair.

"I could not stand there and watch those soldiers and sailors marching without choking up, and many people who were at the park on Thursday and today told me the same thing," Commy said. "I believe it is a great help to make us all better citizens to see our soldier boys oftener."[18]

Military Day 1917 also gave a boost to Washington's manager. Before the game an officer handed Clark Griffith a check for over $700 for his Ball and Bat Fund, which the *Chicago Herald* had collected at the Sox-Athletics game the previous Sunday.

Not to be outdone, Commy decided to offer another extravaganza Saturday. The Sox returned to the South Side for Clark Griffith Day after a Friday exhibition in Peoria. Griff planned to deliver several of his baseball sets to local troops and give fans an opportunity to donate toward buying gear for troops elsewhere. "All of the baseball material was purchased from local sporting houses yesterday and packed ready for delivery," the *Examiner* said on the big day.[19]

The Senators were making their last appearance at Comiskey Park this season. The game promised to be a beauty, Red Faber pitching for the Sox versus Washington's great ace, Walter "Big Train" Johnson. Commy again flooded the stands with local troops. "The military, while not in as great force as on Thursday, was made a more elaborate feature of the day," Sanborn reported. "For an hour and a half before game time the field was a moving picture of khaki."[20]

Among the Sammies attending were the Second, Seventh, and Eighth regiments of the Illinois National Guard. The Eighth was the African American unit in which Sox trainer Doc Buckner's stepson had served since 1914. Buckner's wife, Maggie, was keenly interested in the Eighth and served as president of the Kit and Comfort Club, a women's group that supported the regiment. One company of the Eighth (soon to be redesignated the 370th

Infantry) was already in Houston, Texas, where Illinois guardsmen trained for France.

Two days earlier, Military Day in Chicago, Houston had been rocked by violence as Buffalo soldiers of the Twenty-Fourth US Infantry rebelled against racial abuse from civilians. Rioting during what became known as the Camp Logan Mutiny left nineteen people dead. Army courts would convict 110 soldiers of crimes and hang nineteen (the convictions were overturned 106 years later). Chicago's Black troops hadn't been involved in the fighting.

"The members of company G, Eighth Illinois national guard, Chicago's Negro regiment, who conducted themselves like true soldiers last night, obeying orders of their commanders explicitly, were kept closely within their camp—not under guard, but under orders," the *Tribune* said later.[21] The paper also editorialized, "If the southern communities cannot respect the color they might respect the uniform that covers it, and if there is danger that they will do neither then our colored soldiers ought not to be sent south."[22]

Memories of Houston were fresh Saturday afternoon as nearly 20,000 fans watched 6,000 to 7,000 thousand soldiers, sailors, and Boy Scouts march into Comiskey Park. The fans alone were the biggest crowd Washington had played for all season.

"As regiment after regiment poured through the gates, parading the field, the fans stood up and cheered. Each military organization was led by its band and was given a rousing reception," the *Daily News* said.[23] Sy Sanborn particularly noted the Eighth Illinois in the *Tribune*, writing, "The colored soldiers were given a remarkably warm welcome by the spectators and the other soldiers in recognition of the loyalty of their comrades during the Houston riots."[24]

The seven African American companies would be ordered to Houston too, in mid-October, the last Illinois troops to head south. Bloody memories aside, the afternoon was a huge success for the manager of the sixth-place Senators and his baseball fund.

George "Buck" Weaver, White Sox infielder. Courtesy of Library of Congress.

"If they don't think much of Clark Griffith back home, he, at least, is held in high regard in these parts," the *Washington Times* said.[25] Following drills and the flag raising, a band led the Washington skipper as he circled the field in a car. Griffith stepped out at home plate, where both teams were lined up, and distributed seventeen baseball sets. He suggested to appreciative Sammies that they wait to open the packages until they got overseas.

"With these balls and bats go the best wishes of thousands of red-blooded Americans who contributed money so that you boys may indulge in the grand old game during your spare hours back of the trenches in France," Griffith said. "It has been said that baseball civilized the Filipinos. When you get to Berlin turn these balls and bats over to the Huns. Maybe baseball will help to civilize them."²⁶ Sanborn added that a detachment from each unit "passed before Griffith at the home plate and carried away the souvenirs of a great day for them, for Chicago, and the American league."²⁷

Although his team's record was 54–61, Griffith had reason for optimism about the game about to start. The Big Train was surging at 16–13, while Faber was struggling through a mediocre season at 11–11. But the contest didn't break the Senators' way.

"Amid a military setting never before equaled on a ball field Walter Johnson today attempted to hang up a new league record for the season by annexing his tenth straight victory at the expense of the White Sox, but was compelled to bow before the superior prowess of Urban Faber, supported by a team that outplayed the Griffmen," Thompson wrote in the *Star*. "The score was Chicago 4, Washington 1."²⁸

The Senators' overall performance this season at Comiskey Park was disastrous. "Yes, the fans here were sorry to see the Griffmen depart," the *Washington Times* said. "Out of the eleven games played, the Washingtonians won just one."²⁹

Two days and a handful of hours later, the evening of August 27, the army announced the winner of the American League drill competition. To much surprise the prize went to the St. Louis Browns and Sergeant Wisener. The Sox under Sergeant Smiley finished fourth and the Yankees under Sergeant Gibson seventh, no doubt disappointing Commy and Cap Huston, who'd done so much to establish the program. The *Tribune* credited the St. Louis skipper and Wisner for the winners' martial bearing.

"Fielder Jones of the Browns, it seems, stole a march on his rivals," the paper said. "For two weeks preceding the test he personally supervised a two hour drill of his men each morning."³⁰ The *St. Louis Globe-Democrat* frankly admitted, "The majority of baseball fans did not think that the Browns would win anything."³¹ The *Chicago Examiner* likened the club to Ulysses Grant, who "as a salesman for tanned hides in civil life fell far short of championship caliber, but, given a uniform and a complete equipment of shoulder straps, he became the champion hide tanner of our Civil War."[32]

The *Daily News* had been right about the drill sloppiness of the Pale Hose, judge Sheldon noting "three movements improperly executed with some confusion."[33] But no Sox player had dropped his rifle like an unnamed Indian had done, twice. Scoring was tight, with the Browns earning 90.5 of a hundred points, the fourth place Sox fewer than five points behind at 85.8. Sheldon appreciated the entire experience.

"The drill, as a rule, was excellent and the players received most hearty applause from those in the stands, who took intense interest in all they saw," the lieutenant colonel wrote. "I was very much impressed with the patriotic outbursts, the excitement, the spontaneous enthusiasm of the people at the game. It was something I shall always remember. The American League has performed a wonderful service for the United States of America."[34]

The Sporting News added that Ban Johnson was "highly pleased at the good report made by the Army officer and the evidence of the benefits of the drill is so apparent that it probably will be continued as a regular feature in the American League each season."[35] Til Huston, however, thought the AL hadn't done enough.

"The original intention was that after the ball players had become proficient in military drill they would in time drill a company of say 150 fans not subject to draft, giving them an annual pass as a compliment, thus to aid in creating a home guard," he wrote from France. "The magnates fell down on this feature. It should still be put into effect." And Huston was outraged by the Browns. "It was suggested that they give the prize to the Red Cross. They refused and each individual pocketed the lucre."[36]

With the drill competition over, the army quietly reassigned its eight sergeants to new duties. Officers thought the experiment had been worthwhile. "The American league's introduction of military features at all its parks, beginning with the drilling of the ball players in their training camps and leading up to big spectacles by national guard units," Sanborn wrote, "was admitted by army officials to be of much benefit in spreading the spirit of patriotism which the nation lacked at the outset."[37]

Sergeant Smiley left the Sox club the day results were announced. Commy praised him to the army as "very efficient in every way. I am further pleased to state that he proved himself to be a gentleman of exemplary habits in every way."[38] Army needs had shifted, and Smiley never became a first lieutenant, instead resuming recruiting duties in Chicago.

Smiley again sought a commission in 1918, only to see the war end before he received it. He stayed in the army during peacetime and earned a reserve commission in the 1920s while retaining his regular noncom rank. Smiley retired as a master sergeant in 1939. Later, he briefly returned to active duty during World War II as a captain at Fort Sheridan.

6

Swede

The victories over Washington after the drill competition and on Clark Griffith Day marked the start of a pennant-winning run for Chicago. The White Sox won eighteen of nineteen games August 23 through September 15, in two nine-victory streaks separated by a loss. The second streak began with four wins over Detroit in front of big home crowds as the Sox swept doubleheaders September 2 and 3, the latter being Labor Day.

"From one of the most desperately fought, hair curling finishes ever seen the White Sox emerged with a double victory over Detroit in yesterday's nerve raking [sic] test and increased their advantage over the Red Sox to four and a half games," Sy Sanborn wrote after the initial double bill. "The first game was annexed by the comfortable score of 7 to 2, but the second was bitterly fought for ten innings before the Rowlands copped, 6 to 5."[1]

Eddie Cicotte notched his twenty-second win with a complete game in the opener. Lefty Williams won his sixteenth in relief during the second game. Michigan papers took a gloomy outlook on the losses. "Detroit was expected to offer strenuous opposition to the onrush of the Windy City boys and because they fell in the first two games, it is not expected that they will be much bother from now on," the *Detroit Times* said.[2]

"Some of the 'wise guys' among the fans had it all doped out that Detroit didn't want to win the second game when [George] Cunningham was put in to pitch," the *Detroit Free Press* added. The grumbling died, however, as

Cunningham threw a complete game before losing 6–5 on a sacrifice fly in the tenth. The *Freep* also noted the many Sammies and jackies among the crowd of 35,000. "As the pass list here is very heavy and Comiskey has a free gate to soldiers and sailors in uniform, the paid count probably was about 28,000."[3]

The Tigers fell twice again Labor Day, 7–5 and 14–8, as the teams "vied with one another in smashing the ball over Comiskey park this afternoon with a rooting, yelling, highly entertained crowd of 25,000 watching the performance," George Robbins wrote in the *Daily News*.[4] Dave Danforth won the first game in relief of Red Faber. The second game then got so out of hand that the managers used Cicotte and Cunningham as relievers, although both had pitched complete games Sunday. Eddie ultimately notched his twenty-third victory.

"It's doubtful if ever such a day of wild pitching was staged in a major league before yesterday. . . . Buck Weaver was warming up out in the pen at the conclusion of the second game ready to spell Cicotte, if necessary. He was about all the pitchers Rowland had left," the *Tribune* said.[5]

Sanborn called the holiday games "the wildest, wooliest and most exciting pair seen at the south side park in a long time. . . . No adequate word picture of the details is possible without more space than the inside of a city directory."[6] Detroit writers considered the four games a debacle as the doubleheader losses propelled the White Sox six and a half games ahead of Boston in the pennant race.

"No language that a respectable family newspaper would print would do justice to this carnival. It was a grand medley of bad pitching, loose fielding and hard hitting," the *Free Press* snorted after the final contest. "Chicago played horribly at times but the Tigers were infinitely worse and deserved the beating that was handed them."[7] The *Detroit Times* consoled readers with the notion that the Tigers merely had aimed for uniformity over the holiday, noting, "Every team in the American league either won or lost both games."[8]

Charles "Swede" Risberg, White Sox infielder. Courtesy of Library of Congress.

Concerns over the Chicago-Detroit series would arise three years later during the early days of the Black Sox affair. The *Chicago Tribune* would mention that attorneys for the accused Sox players "expect to drag into the case instances of alleged crooked playing and the 'throwing' of games dating as far back as 1917."[9] In January 1927, Swede Risberg, banned from baseball for his part in the scandal, said in sworn testimony to new baseball commissioner Judge Kenesaw Mountain Landis that the Sox had paid Detroit players $1,100 to "slough" the four games. Landis asked how.

"I figured the pitchers didn't put much on the ball," Swede said. "Ground balls were booted." Risberg also told the commissioner about a chance meeting with manager Rowland on a Chicago street in September 1920. "For heaven's sake, don't let that 1917 business get out!" the ex-skipper supposedly said.[10]

Rowland bitterly denied it all. So did Sox players. Only Chick Gandil, another of the "eight men out," publicly supported Risberg's account. But big dollars clearly *had* changed hands.

"When confronted with the undeniable evidence that they did pay the money, the Chicago players said the money was paid to the Tigers as a token of thanks for their beating the Boston Red Sox three times later that month, September 19–20," baseball historian Steve Steinberg writes.[11] "Ultimately, Commissioner Landis found the White Sox guilty of poor judgment, but not a fix, accepting the players' explanation of the cash gifts."[12]

What really happened between the clubs? White Sox historians Wilbert and Hageman call the charges leveled by Risberg and Gandil "unfounded and peevish."[13] But historian Don Zminda takes a far dimmer view. "If any dates could be said to have marked the start of the 'Black Sox' era," he writes, "September 2–3, 1917, would be the logical choice."[14]

The Sox next traveled to St. Louis for two games with the last-place Browns. They won both. Newspapers afterward quoted Browns owner Phil Ball saying his club was "laying down" on manager Fielder Jones. When his players objected the magnate told them he'd been misquoted.

"When asked by a reporter if you were doing that, I told him that I did not know: that all my friends told me you were and that you might be, for all I knew, but that I wasn't competent to judge of that," Ball said.[15] The clarification flopped so badly that Browns pitcher John "Doc" Lavan and infielder Derrill "Del" Pratt each sued Ball $50,000 for slander.

Ban Johnson downplayed the whole matter. He said Ball hadn't meant to imply dishonesty or crookedness, only indifference or lack of ambition, and that the owner hadn't specifically named either player in any case.

"Had such a thing been meant by Mr. Ball I would have suspended those players promptly, taken the case to the national commission, and if after a fair trial they had been found guilty they would have been expelled from baseball," the AL prexy said.[16] The Browns later traded Lavan and Pratt, and Ball quietly settled the lawsuits.

The Sox, meanwhile, returned to the South Side and took two single games from visiting Cleveland. Local troops preparing to leave Chicago packed Comiskey Park both days. A prosperous boosters group called the Woodland Bards helped give them a sendoff.

The Bards were "died-in-the-wool Sox fans with a cultural, that is to say poetic bent," according to historians Wilbert and Hageman, and even had a clubhouse under the stands.[17] Before the first Indians game the Bards presented Illinois guard units with new baseball uniforms to complement all the gear they'd received on Clark Griffith Day.

Commy said he would also ship flannels to the artillerymen of the First and Second regiments, now in Texas. "The good old sport has made the boys of this regiment so happy to-day," the colonel of the Second, now the 122nd Field Artillery, would say when the suits arrived.[18] But for now, Sanborn captured the scene at the first game, Saturday, September 8.

"For nearly two hours previous to the game," Sanborn wrote, "the men who are going to blaze the trail to Berlin paraded around the playing field punctuated with bands of music, and found their allotted sections in the big stands, while more than 15,000 people who had arrived early for the big demonstration, cheered at every possible opportunity."[19] Surprisingly, Cicotte then started the game for the Sox.

"Eddie was supposed to be enjoying a well-earned vacation," the *Examiner* said, "but the little hurler decided that he had enjoyed enough rest and was ready to resume his work."[20] The ace won a complete game, 2–0, for his twenty-fourth victory.

Danforth won in relief of Russell and Faber the next day despite a chilly drizzle that kept attendance down. The game ended bizarrely in the tenth with the score tied 3–3. At the top of the inning, with the bases loaded and two men out, catcher Ray Schalk tried to nip Jack Graney off third base. Schalk overthrew, and the Indians might have scored two runs if Graney hadn't become entangled with the runner coming down from second base. He was called out for interference, killing the rally.

The Indians complained for ten minutes and continued beefing in the bottom half of the frame with "some of the worst kicking and burlesquing seen in the American league for years," according to Sanborn.[21] Umpire Clarence "Brick" Owens reached his limit after one batter and declared a 9–0 forfeit, putting Chicago seven games up over the Red Sox. Even a top Ohio newspaper pinned the loss on "the dilatory tactics of the Cleveland players."[22]

Jim Scott wasn't around to see it, though. He was suddenly off to the army. Through some mix-up, the order had gone first to his winter home in Wyoming instead of his summer residence in Chicago.

"On receiving it he wired to learn his status and received a reply at 7 o'clock Friday night, instructing him to leave at once for San Francisco. He was aboard the train at 10 o'clock the same night," a Bay Area paper said.[23] Shano Collins became the senior Sox player following the righthander's departure. The *Tribune* reported that Scott "will not rejoin the Rowlands until the war is over."[24]

Philadelphia Evening Ledger sports editor Robert "Tiny Bob" Maxwell was a Chicago native and a former football All-American who knew the city's sports teams well. He reported that Scott was reluctant to leave his team, fearing he'd leave it in bad shape, and that he'd offered to give up his chance to become an officer and enlist as a private instead after the World Series.

"Comiskey would not listen to it," Maxwell wrote. "Instead, he shook his hand and congratulated him, saying that he would not be forgotten when the spoils were divided."[25] The *Tribune* added that Death Valley Jim was assured of receiving a full series share, since "the pitcher's teammates made that arrangement before wishing him Godspeed from the Windy City on his trip to join Uncle Sam's forces."[26] The owner promised to pay his salary during the final few weeks of the season.

"I had to lay off Scott last Summer for not being in condition," Commy commented. "I hated to do it because I always admired him, but it became necessary. When he expressed a desire to go to an officers' training camp I encouraged him, although I hated to lose him on my ball club. It gives me great pleasure to learn that he has put himself in position to be useful to our country."[27]

The White Sox finished the season playing fifteen of sixteen games on the road. The exception wasn't a makeup game but an unusual single tilt at home versus Phil Ball's club Sunday, September 16.

"Those St. Louis Browns refused to 'lay down' to the White Sox in the final game of the season at Comiskey park," Jimmy Crusinberry wrote, "but the Sox went out and won the battle anyway."[28] Eddie Cicotte won his twenty-sixth game in the tenth inning, in relief of starter Lefty Williams. The club then hit the trail again.

"The pace-making White Sox were joy riding eastward to-day to clinch an American league flag," George Robbins wired Monday from a train at Geneva, New York. The idle Sox figured to own the flag by week's end. "It's all peaches and cream," bullpen catcher Joe Jenkins said.[29]

The Chicago and Boston clubs had tangled bitterly all season, sometimes literally duking it out. Ty Cobb of the Tigers knew a thing or two about scrapping for a flag. "The way to beat the Red Sox," he said, "is to fight 'em."[30] The battle would renew and end in Beantown, but first the Sox played a three-game series with Connie Mack's last-place Athletics in Philadelphia, beginning Tuesday, September 18.

Red Faber won the first game, 6–1. Then the club's ace lost a 2–1 heartbreaker Wednesday.

"Eddie Cicotte was after his twenty-seventh victory and felt the defeat keenly," the *Tribune* said. "He wants to win thirty games, but will hardly have a chance now unless lucky."[31] The Sox took the third game Thursday, 5–3 in extra innings, and headed north to Boston. The pennant race ended there Friday, September 21.

The Sox clinched with a 2–1, ten-inning win, Faber and Hubert "Dutch" Leonard of the Red Sox each going the distance. Commy followed the game via telephone in Chicago, a local sports editor relaying ticker reports. The suspense was almost too much for the Old Roman until the final score arrived.

"His hand shook so that safety required he hang up the telephone receiver," Johnny Alcock wrote. "But he turned to his son, Commy Lou, and said: 'Better tell your mother.' Big Lou had Mrs. Comiskey on the phone in a minute or so, and the whole family was rejoicing long before Chicago fandom knew the glad news."[32] The Sox owner congratulated his manager in a telegram that evening: "Fondest hopes of all Chicago," his wire said, "and the wonderful legion of White Sox fans as well as myself have been realized after eleven long years of patient waiting. . . . Give the team and party as fine a dinner as you can, with my compliments."[33]

Congratulations flowed the other way too. Commy heard from Connie Mack, Big Ed Walsh, Til Huston in France, and many others. A wire also arrived from federal Judge Landis, a big fan of Chicago sports and not yet baseball's commissioner. "My congratulations to you, Rowland, and the team," the jurist said from his second home in Michigan. "Not in my memory has any one achieved a more deserved victory."[34] Commy was especially glad to hear from Jim Scott at the Presidio.

"Our entire camp joins me in congratulating you and all the boys on your well earned success and in the confidence that nothing can stop you in the final series and that your ultimate joys will be mine," Scotty wired. "I am proud to have been one of you."[35]

Following Boston, the Sox wound up their regular season with series in Washington and New York. They ended 1917 with an even hundred victories, more than they've won during any season since.

7

Knuckles

Eddie Cicotte had propelled the White Sox into the World Series. Had it existed in 1917, he surely would have won the league's Cy Young Award. His twenty-eight wins (versus a dozen losses) were best in the AL, ahead of Babe Ruth's twenty-four and Walter Johnson's twenty-three.

Cicotte also led in ERA (1.53) and innings pitched (346.2). By modern reckoning, he topped the circuit in walks and hits per innings pitched (WHIP) at 0.912, and in wins above replacement (WAR) for both pitchers (11.8) and all players (11.9). Many fans and writers credited his phenomenal stats to his famous shine ball, which Cicotte later claimed didn't exist. He'd say instead that he and Hap Felsch had concocted the ruse back in Mineral Wells.

"Why not rub the ball on the uniform and make the batsman believe I was doing something with the leather," Eddie recalled thinking. "It was a capital idea. . . . The shine ball is a myth. When we heard [managers] Griffith, Jones and others wasting time discussing the subject we were amused."[1] Many sportswriters accepted this story.

"It doesn't stand to reason that rubbing a wee shiny spot on the ball would place Cicotte where he is today," Malcolm MacLean wrote in the *Chicago Evening Post*.[2] "The rules object to discoloring a ball, but there is nothing against cleaning one, as Ban Johnson found when asked to investigate Cicotte's delivery," the *New York Times* noted before the 1917 World Series.[3]

But AL umpire and future Hall of Famer Billy Evans had seen the pitch up close and concluded it was real. Cicotte rubbed one side of a dirty ball against a wet spot on his jersey, the arbiter said, making one side smooth and clean while the other remained rough and grimy. This gave the ball uneven friction in the air.

The shine ball was "a great fooler, but there's nothing illegal about it," Evans asserted.[4] Damon Runyon believed much the same. Cicotte had a "trick of rubbing the ball on his shirt front before delivering, first, however, applying it to a spot on his knee," Runyon wrote in the *New York American*. "Ball players have claimed that this rubbing produces a small shiny place on the ball and makes it take odd quirks and turns."[5]

SABR's Jim Sandoval offers another, slightly different take. He writes that Cicotte "rubbed one side of the ball against the pocket of his right trouser leg, which had been filled with talcum powder."[6]

No matter how he achieved it, the difference in surface textures gave Cicotte a good grip, and the alternating bright and dark spots on the rotating ball created an optical illusion that flummoxed batters. "I have no doubt that imagination greatly increases the effectiveness of the shine ball," Evans wrote.[7]

Doc Buckner grinned at such theorizing and confusion. He believed the key to the hurler's dominance lay elsewhere.

"First it was the mud ball, then the licorice ball, then the oil ball. Now it's the paraffin ball that is giving Cicotte his shine ball," the Sox trainer told George Robbins. "Eddie is in the best condition of his career. He's the smartest pitcher in the business and his great condition has enabled him to employ psychology in his pitching. . . . Half of Cicotte's success lies in making his opponents believe he has an uncanny delivery."[8]

Decades later, although still not fully explaining the pitch, Cicotte agreed that his delivery gave him near perfect control over the shine ball. Ban Johnson, he went on, repeatedly asked him not to throw it. The hurler responded: "What do you want me to do, pitch lefthanded?"[9]

Edgar "Knuckles" Ciciotte, White Sox pitcher. Chicago Examiner..

Sy Sanborn thought the Sox would mainly rely on Cicotte as well as Red Faber during the World Series, the right-handers giving Chicago a "decided advantage" over New York. "The Giants have no pair of hurlers who pitch from the north side of their anatomies with whom to match those two if Faber is given sufficient work before the combat to assure control of his stuff," Sanborn wrote.[10] He was spot on.

Cicotte and Faber would pitch fifty of fifty-two innings for the Sox during the series. The showdown began October 6 in Chicago. Each team hosted an initial two-game series, followed by alternating single games. A coin toss had determined the Sox were at home first; another would determine the site of a seventh game if needed. The South Siders were tickled to see one of their rooters in particular at Game One.

"Sergeant Smiley, who acted as drillmaster for the Sox this year . . . came out on the field in uniform, and was surrounded by a bunch of the Sox," Runyon wrote. He added that the soldier was "warmly greeted by the ball players."[11] The Sox also welcomed their North Side counterparts.

"Almost every member of the Cubs was out at the game helping Clark Griffith pass the hat to collect money to buy baseball stuff for the soldiers in the new national army," the *Tribune* said. "Among the outsiders who assisted were Johnny Evers of the Phillies, Duffy Lewis of the Red Sox, and George McBride of the Washingtons."[12]

Rowland dispatched Cicotte to the mound to start the club's first World Series game since 1906. The team sported new uniforms with a star-spangled Sox logo. (They'd also have a road version, totaling five sets of flannels for the season.) Comiskey Park was packed. Fifteen hundred officer candidates from Fort Sheridan jammed the right field stands. Hordes of civilians filled the rest of the park. Those who couldn't find or afford tickets crowded into Chicago halls and pavilions to follow the game on scoreboards.

Several hundred uniformed Sammies got a closer look from the towers of their nearby Seventh Regiment armory. Thanks to news agencies and the signal corps, thousands more troops followed play on scoreboards erected at American army headquarters in France, where it was nighttime.

Cicotte was brilliant in Game One. His wife and two daughters watched him nip Giant southpaw Harry "Slim" Sallee, 2–1, each man throwing a complete game. But most of the ink went to Hap Felsch, whose fourth-inning homer gave the Sox the winning run.

Commy's boys continued winning the next day in Game Two. Red Faber beat four Giants hurlers, 7–2, with hundreds of Sammies and jackies attending. Faber also entertained fans on the basepaths when he tried to swipe third base with two men out in the fifth inning. Red found the bag already occupied by Weaver, whom he'd mistakenly thought had scored.

"Where the hell are you going?" Buck asked in astonishment. "I'm going to pitch," Faber replied.[13]

"'A thousand, thousand years' from now it will be dug up by the historians as the feature of the 1917 world's series," Sanborn wrote of the blunder.[14] "I was a surprised boy to find Weaver there," Red admitted. "I won the game and I want the fans to understand I'm a pitcher, not a base runner."[15]

Commy called his winning Sox "the greatest ball club I ever saw."[16] The team boarded a train of ten Pullman cars and headed east in high spirits for the next pair of games in New York. The owner rode another, sixteen-car rattler as a guest of the Woodland Bards. Cold and torrential rain then delayed play for twenty-four hours to October 10.

The man of the day at Game Three wore the uniform of neither the Giants nor the Sox. Ex-Boston Brave catcher Hank Gowdy, baseball's favorite Sammy, came up from nearby Camp Mills, where he was preparing to ship out for France with the army's famous Forty-Second "Rainbow" Division.

"Gowdy, now a sergeant in an Army camp on Long Island, got a brief furlough and was drafted to assist in collecting quarters for Griffith's Bat and Ball Fund," *The Sporting News* said. "When he appeared in the stands in uniform he was given a tremendous ovation—a fitting tribute to a real hero—to the first major league ball player to enlist in Uncle Sam's service."[17]

The Woodland Bards presented Gowdy with a timepiece at home plate before the game, his seventh since entering the army. "Hank is now said to wear wrist watches all over his person," sportswriter Irwin Cobb wrote.[18]

Fans entering the Polo Grounds received envelopes for the Griffith equipment fund. During the game, Gowdy and fellow big leaguers Walter Johnson, Walter "Rabbit" Maranville, Johnny Evers, and others took over from local Boy Scouts to circulate through the stands and collect donations.

"Coins and bills poured into the huge paper baseballs the players used for collection boxes and enough money was obtained to outfit several regiments in France with baseball paraphernalia," the *New York Sun* said. "Griffith ardently is hoping that the next boatload of bats, balls, gloves and masks does not meet with the fate of the first consignment, which unfortunately was part of the cargo of one of the ships sunk by a U-boat."[19]

The two earlier tilts in Chicago had been sellouts, but Game Three in New York saw "scads of vacant seats," according to Jimmy Crusinberry.[20] Sox fans probably wished the stormy weather had continued. Two runs in the fourth inning "dimmed the luster of Cicotte's so-called shine ball," Charley Dryden wrote in the *Chicago Examiner*, the Sox losing the 2–0 squeaker to John "Rube" Benton.[21] Manager John McGraw's Giants also won Game Four the next day. Faber, with Danforth in relief, bowed to Ferdinand "Ferdie" Schupp, 5–0, centerfielder Benny Kauff belting two home runs as "the whole Sox machine sort of crumpled," Dryden wrote.[22] The clubs left Gotham for the Windy City with the series tied.

"The Sox haven't given their supporters a run for their money for the last twenty-two innings, which is the largest collection of goose eggs gathered by a world's series loser since the Giants took three shut-out victories in a row from the Athletics in 1905," the *Chicago Examiner* said.[23] "All the Chicago fans in New York tonight sneaked down to the railway station by back streets and got out of town as quietly as possible, because all of New York's fans were laughing at them," Crusinberry added.[24]

The journey home brightened no one's mood. The Sox awoke on their train at Cleveland to see lake effect snow blanketing the tracks outside the windows. "We have had shine balls, high balls, spit balls and yesterday the world's series ran into snow balls," scribe Hugh Fullerton wrote.[25] "Guess we'll have to transfer the world's series to Florida," manager Rowland cracked.[26]

The snowfall became nearly a blizzard farther west along Lake Erie but soon melted. The Sox were an hour late reaching the Windy City, where 500 undaunted fans greeted them at LaSalle Station. The wintry conditions didn't improve much for Game Five the next day, October 13.

"That concrete park of Comiskey's was like an icebox for frigidness," Cobb reported. The crowd, "considerably abashed in the face of those last two drubbings which its favorites had suffered in New York, reflected in its general behavior the prevalent chilliness."[27]

The contest began badly for the Pale Hose. Starter Tex Russell couldn't get anyone out and allowed two runs. Rowland quickly yanked him for Eddie Cicotte, who threw six innings, surrendering another two runs, one earned. Lefty Williams threw in the seventh, giving up one more run. The Sox trailed Giants starter Slim Sallee, 5–2, entering the home half of the inning. The game suddenly turned and South Sider fans began screaming themselves silly.

"Apparently beaten—hopelessly, disgracefully licked by themselves instead of by the Giants—the White Sox staged a tremendous comeback late yesterday afternoon in Comiskey park and won the fifth game of the world's series by a score of 8 to 5 after almost all the fans who bet on them had torn up their tickets," Sanborn wrote.[28] "The Sox did the baseball impossible," Damon Runyon added. "They came on and on, and always on, even when their most devoted followers were submerged in gloom, with not even a periscope of hope showing."[29]

The Sox scored three times in the seventh, tying the score 5–5 on two singles, a double, a walk, and an error. Rowland sent Faber to the mound for the eighth. "Joe Jenkins, captain of the bull pen, had one of the busiest days of his career in the pen," the *Tribune* said. "He warmed up four different fellows for service and had a fifth on the fire when the game was over."[30]

Faber faced only three Giants to retire the side. At the bottom of the inning, the Sox rapped out another three runs on four singles and a sacrifice bunt. When Faber returned to the hill in the ninth Crusinberry figured Chicagoans could hear people cheering all the way over in Cascade, Iowa, the hurler's hometown.

"Red did come forth and he saved the game," he wrote, "largely because the Giants continued to blow all to pieces, while Red pitched in his steadiest and truest form, and when his mates garnered three runs in the eighth, it was all over except the shouting in Cascade."[31] Faber's victory was his second of the series.

"Saturday's free-for-all was a gift to the Sox as magnificent as anything Andrew Carnegie might have given," sportswriter Louis Lee Arms lamented in the *New York Tribune*.[32] After the game, both teams boarded rattlers back to New York for Game Six.

"Going east the Sox players had their chests out so far they wouldn't talk to newspaper men. Coming back newspaper men wouldn't talk to the players. We ought to have a social time this trip," Crusinberry commented.[33]

"Judging from scenes at the Grand Central station when the White Sox special arrived tonight there will be eltopay [sic] at the Polo grounds tomorrow," Crusinberry added the next day from Gotham. "There was such a maddened throng to meet Rowland's invaders that ropes had to be stretched in order to leave an open passageway for the Chicago athletes to pass out of the station."[34]

Commy and his party left Chicago on the Twentieth Century Limited half a day behind his club. He arrived Monday morning, October 15, for the game that afternoon. The home team had won every contest so far, a bad omen for the Chicagoans. Game Seven, if needed, would be Wednesday.

The clubs wouldn't enjoy a free day Tuesday, however, but were slated instead to play a game for Sammies. The National Commission had agreed beforehand to stage an exhibition at the army cantonment nearest the city hosting the final series game, which in this instance was Camp Mills. But meanwhile 34,000 people inundated the Polo Grounds for Game Six, the largest crowd thus far.

"It was a delightful day for the game, warm and bright with sunshine," the *Times* said. "The crowd jammed the grand stand and filled up the bleachers. Overcoats were in the way and there wasn't even a breeze to chill the afternoon as the sun dipped over Coogan's Bluff."[35] Faber started for the Sox versus Benton for the Giants. The game was scoreless until the visitors batted in the fourth inning, when the NL champions flew apart like a dollar watch.

Eddie Collins led off with a grounder to Henry "Heinie" Zimmerman, the only native New Yorker on the Giants' roster. The third sacker had played well all season but was having a poor series. Zim's bad peg to first base let Collins reach second. After twice failing to bunt, Joe Jackson lofted an easy fly to right, which Dave Robertson dropped, putting runners at the corners.

Hap Felsch, next up, bounced a ball back to the mound. Rather than throw to first and surrender a run, Benton whirled and froze Collins along the third base line. The Sox captain figured he was caught, so waved Jackson and Felsch to keep running. Benton turned Collins back toward third and tossed the ball to Zimmerman. Eddie broke for the plate.

"The Great Zim is graced with a single track mind, and now and then a few cinders clog his mental calculations," Louis Lee Arms wrote.[36] Zimmerman set off after Collins. "Well, it has been a tough era for Teutonic thought, one way and another," Runyon wrote. "Von Kluck thought he was going to eat dinner in Paris. The Kaiser thought he could lick the world. Heinie Zim thought he could outrun Eddie Collins. It has certainly been tough!"[37]

Collins was the faster man, and slid home with the first run as Zimmerman leaped over him. "Heinie chased him almost into the Chicago bench, for he was going so fast he couldn't even stop after he passed the plate," the *Chicago Herald* said.[38]

"That play killed the Giants deader than Dickens's door nail, as Gandil immediately sent a long single to right, scoring Jackson and Felsch. After that it was only a question whether Faber would be able to hold the Giants down," sportswriter Fred Lieb wrote in the *New York Sun*. "What Zimmerman tried to do is not particularly clear, unless he hoped to get Collins immediately so he could whip the ball to third and get Felsch going into that bag."[39]

Giants fans couldn't believe it. Zim's blunder overshadowed even Faber's goof in Game Two. "The great crowd shook with laughter and filled the air with cries of derision at one of the stupidest plays that has ever been seen in a world's series," the *Times* said.[40]

Many scribes agreed with this assessment. Runyon, Sam Crane, and a few others, however, pointed instead toward Giant catcher William Rariden. Photos showed "Whoa Bill" standing well up the line as Collins slid home, looking toward the mound or first base. Benton and first sacker Walter Holke weren't anywhere in the frame, prompting more criticism. Someone asked the backstop about the play.

"'Throw the ball,' I yelled to Heinie," Rariden explained. "'GET OUT OF THE WAY. I GOT HIM,' was Zim's reply. Then I stepped out of the line."[41] Collins challenged the implication. "Zim wasn't to blame," he said decades later. The Sox captain believed the key to his scoring had been to slip past the catcher, not outrun the third baseman. "Who the hell was I gonna throw the ball to," Zim demanded in the same article, "the umpire?"[42]

The Giants scored twice the next inning and the Sox once more in the ninth, handing the South Siders a 4–2 win and the championship. Ex-heavyweight boxing champ James J. Corbett singled out one hurler for praise in the *Examiner*.

"The hero of the series is Urban (Red) Faber," he wrote, "the sorrel-topped right-hander who figured in four out of six battles—and won three. . . . Before the big fight began he wasn't figured among the valuable assets of the Chicagoans. But it was 'Red' who hurled the Sox to the pinnacle of the baseball world."[43]

Judge Landis had been presiding at a trial in Chicago during the game. "He couldn't see the game, as it was played in Gotham," the *Tribune* said, "but he did the next best thing." An aide in chambers followed the play-by-play by telephone and passed the scores along to the bench, which the judge relayed in "Landisgrams" to reporters. His last scrawled message to the press table said "WHITE SOX, 4" in large letters scrawled across the page and "Giants, 2" in small print in one corner. "Well, we did a good day's work today, anyway," Landis said at adjournment. "We disposed of the Giants."[44]

"Three of the games were exhibitions of high-class, skillful baseball," the *Times* said afterward, "while the other three games were far below the standard of play expected of clubs of World's Series calibre."[45] Commy celebrated for an hour, then caught a train home to Chicago.

"The White Sox once more are champions of the world and I feel as if nothing in baseball matters from now on," the magnate told Crusinberry. "I wanted to win one more time before I got too old and the boys this year have gone out and turned the trick. . . . It always has been my wish to play New York for the championship of the world, and now that we have played it and won I feel as if my life in baseball is completed."[46]

Rowland hosted a party that night at Shanley's Restaurant, an immense eatery on Times Square. The players gleefully took over the stage following the formal speeches. Ex-Cub second sacker Johnny Evers was called up to say a few words. Afterward he and Collins were hailed as the Keystone Kings of all time.

"Because of this party there wasn't a great deal of pep on tap at the soldier ball game" played the next day, a wire report said.[47] After the players' midnight revelry, "it was tough to get them out early for the trip to Long Island, and some of them went away without breakfast," Crusinberry added. "A few of them didn't want any breakfast anyway."[48]

The champs and Giants played for 8–10,000 Sammies at the St. Paul School field in Garden City. "There were no stands, but standing six deep around the field were khaki fighters, generals, colonels, nearly four regiments of officers and men," the *New York Evening World* said.[49] An Illinois regiment cheered from one side, countered by a New York regiment from the other. The game began with numerous substitutions among the regulars and soon devolved into a burlesque that the troops enjoyed.

"Several two sackers [doubles] were made, but the Sox made more than the Giants, and the war scribe who was detailed to keep score finished his job with the result 6 to 3 in favor of Chicago," Crusinberry wrote. "Not many others had the same score, but all were agreed the Sox had won."[50] The Sammies marched back to camp as the Sox quickly changed back into street clothes to catch a slow train back into Manhattan. They then rushed across town to Grand Central Terminal, and caught the last train for Chicago at 5:30.

Hordes of fans plus naval and civilian bands began gathering two hours early to welcome the Sox home. The train huffed into LaSalle Station late Wednesday afternoon.

The arrival was "the signal for an outburst from fandom the like of which never before occurred in this or any other great city. A modest estimate places the 'reception committee' at 50,000," the *Examiner* said, perhaps inflating an impressive figure. "There were judges, lawyers, bankers, hodcarriers—in fact, it was a reception committee (each member self-elected) made up from all walks of life. Chicago has pulled lots of big stunts, but the homecoming given her world's champions outshines everything done before in the world of sports."[51]

"Never before in the history of baseball has such a welcome and reception been tendered to a baseball squad returning home after a big series," the *Daily News* said. The paper added, "Tears seemed to appear in the eyes of Rowland as he saw the remarkable greeting prepared for him by the fans."

The Sox waded through the wild crowd, eager to pick up their winners' checks the next day and head to their hometowns for the winter. Several had left the club already in New York. Secretary Grabiner said no victory parade was scheduled.

"The ovation they had received at the station amply rewarded the returning heroes for their efforts at trimming the New York Giants for the baseball championship," the *Daily News* said.[52] As the Sox left Chicago with World Series money filling their pockets and bank accounts, the chorus of a popular wartime ditty they'd sung on the train may have echoed in their heads:

Where do we go from here, boys,
Where do we go from here?
Slip a pill to Kaiser Bill
And make him shed a tear;
And when we see the enemy
We'll shoot them in the rear.
Oh joy, Oh boy,
Where do we go from here?[53]

8

Scotty

Jim Scott knew where he would go from here, or as much as any soldier knew during wartime. Confusion over his orders almost had proved disastrous. After various delays he'd been told to report to the army September 10. He didn't make it.

Scott reached San Francisco late the tenth after three days on a train from Chicago. He reported to the Presidio early the next morning, "hopeful the short delay will be overlooked," according to the *San Francisco Chronicle*.[1] Another tardy officer candidate might have landed in the guardhouse, but commanders decided Scott's "desperate" efforts to reach California entitled him to some consideration.[2]

"From what I hear of Candidate Scott, I am inclined to believe he will make a first-class officer," a colonel said. "Few men have come to us with the recommendations that Scott brings."[3] Even fewer arrived from a Major League diamond. Death Valley Jim was enrolled without reprimand.

The government wanted several types of men for officers. Scott fit best into category (h): "Citizens with valuable military experience and adaptability for commissioned grade, or citizens who have demonstrated marked ability and capacity for leadership, and are clearly adapted for military service in commissioned grade."[4]

The war department accepted candidates from twenty years, nine months to age fifty but preferred men thirty-one or older. The Sox hurler was single and twenty-nine. Scott's military experience, though, went beyond growing up in the West or drilling with the B. B. N. G. at Mineral Wells.

He'd accompanied the PCL Venice Tigers on an exhibition tour to Hawaii after the 1914 regular season with the White Sox. Future teammate Swede Risberg went too. When the Venice squad faced a strong Twenty-Fifth Infantry team at Schofield Barracks, Oahu, Scott struck out thirteen and won easily, 3–0.

"My boy, you would make a fine soldier, and I hope that you will some day be with us," the white colonel commanding the African American regiment told him.[5] The hurler replied that he'd like an opportunity to wear the khaki sometime. Now he was doing just that, a Sammy stationed at the Presidio overlooking the Golden Gate. He met a captain there who'd played against him at Schofield nearly three years earlier. "Well, Cap," Scott said, shaking his hand, "here I am."[6]

The camp assigned the new officer candidate to the Fifth Company. Scott wrote that he was "leaving the excitement and turmoil of a pennant winning fight far behind me and taking up the duties and tasks of a man struggling for a commission in Uncle Sam's new army. . . . Uncle Sam is a hard taskmaster these days."[7] Few instructors knew who Scott was. One asked his name after watching him perform drills flawlessly.

"Scott, sir."

"Did I understand you yesterday that you had had no previous military training?"

"Yes, sir."

"Well, where did you learn to handle a rifle as you do?"

"With the Chicago White Sox. We were drilled all season."[8]

Officer candidates earned a hundred dollars a month, a pittance compared with the $4,000 Scotty had earned per season in Chicago (although Commy continued paying him through the World Series). Training was hard and varied, ranging from marching in formation to learning to read maps and understand terrain to mundane physical tasks. Many newspapers ran a photo of Scott digging a trench.

"The students yesterday became convinced, they said, that there is a vast discrepancy between the 'soil' of the written instructions for 'digging in' and the adamant exterior of the Presidio hillsides," the *San Francisco Examiner* said after one such exercise.[9] Scott and fellow candidates also practiced tossing hand grenades.

The army taught Sammies to throw using the lobbing overhand motion from British cricket. But baseball was a great help in judging distances and throwing accurately. Scott got so proficient at lobbing grenades that he wound up teaching other men in his squad. Again, an officer who didn't recognize him marveled at his ability to hurl wooden dummy grenades so precisely.

"Ever throw one of 'em before?" the officer asked.

"No, sir."

"Ever play cricket?"

"No, sir."

"How do you happen to know how to toss the blamed thing so far?"[10]

The PCL San Francisco Seals, at least, knew who Scott was. They'd noted his arrival and hoped he might pitch for them during off-duty hours. Commy wired his willingness but said any agreement would violate the rules of the National Commission then overseeing Major League baseball. Scott did throw batting practice one weekend.

Seal pitchers were "greatly interested in his work and stood behind him watching his every move," the *San Francisco Call* observed. "A very wise idea on the part of the boys."[11] The Merced Bears, a semipro club in the San Joaquin Valley, also tried to convince Scott to pitch a game for them, "but Jim had been digging trenches at the Presidio and had blisters on his pitching hand."[12]

When the 1917 World Series began in October, the Presidio and many other installations erected scoreboards for Sammies to follow the games. Scott took more interest in the play-by-play than most others.

"But, as luck would have it, the commanding officer took it into his head to send the Fifth Company to Fort Barry [on the Marin headlands] for rifle practice this week of all weeks," the *Chronicle* said. "So it happens that Scott, who might have landed a pass from the Presidio to watch the scoreboard, is tied up good and properly on the other side of the bay." As the pitchers warmed up for Game One in Chicago, "one James Scott, with many fellows, was trying to see how many bullseyes he could score over on the rifle range."[13]

Scotty got to play a little ball in mid-November. The occasion was a benefit game at Recreation Park between PCL players and Major Leaguers spending the winter on the west coast. Ten thousand fans watched the big fellows beat the coasters, 3–2.

"Jim showed conclusively that his right wing has not been impaired by the military uses it has been subjected to while undergoing training in the officers' reserve camp at the Presidio," the *San Francisco Examiner* said. "'Death Valley Jim' went through the motions of shouldering a musket, coming to attention with the regulation salute and other drills for three innings, with but one Texas Leaguer credited to the attack."[14]

It was an open secret during his training that Scott was engaged to Harriet Belle Cook of Chicago. "Hattie" and her three sisters were well-known vaudevillians who toured as the Cook Sisters. One sibling, Margaret, was married to Sox third baseman, Buck Weaver.

Scott had met his fiancé in 1915 when he and Weaver joined their tour after the baseball season, trying to "make their clubhouse strain jibe with trained tones of the Cook sisters."[15] A manicurist had filed a $25,000 suit against Scott a few months earlier for breach of promise to marry *her*. The suit quietly dropped from the newspapers following a lot of messy publicity. Now Weaver and his wife traveled to San Francisco for Scott's nuptials.

Buck found his pal extremely fit and enjoying life at the Presidio. But the engaged couple delayed their wedding when Scott was assigned to a chow hall detail, leading to jokes about too many Cooks in the Presidio kitchen. Scott married Hattie November 17 in San Francisco, making Weaver both his teammate and his brother-in-law. "And mebbe, in the days to come," the *Examiner* said, "the former Miss Cook will endeavor to cook some nice biscuits for Jim, or he will remember when he reached 'somewhere in France' that he married Miss Cook a week later than the original date because he had to cook for his brother officers."[16]

Scott received his commission November 26. The army needed far too many officers for all to begin as second lieutenants. Candidates at the Presidio learned if they were to become second lieutenants, first lieutenants, or captains only when the commanding officer announced their names during the ceremony. "When he came to Scott he called 'Captain James Scott,'" the *Bulletin* reported. "Instantly a shout went up from the other men and several grabbed him and hoisted him on their shoulders. He passed second in the list of candidates."[17]

"Jim Scott, White Sox pitcher, knew more army ways, work and regulations than any member of the graduating class," said a newspaper in Washington state.[18] A pastor working with the Young Men's Christian Association (YMCA) admired the captain and other officers he'd met at the Presidio.

"They came from all walks of life—farmers, doctors, lawyers, teachers, one state normal principal, two preachers, and Jim Scott, a former pitcher for the White Sox," the reverend said. "Jim got a commission—as did the preachers and the normal professor, and a good percentage of the others—and I think he will make just as good an officer for the United States as he did a pitcher for the White Sox."[19]

Among the men commissioned with Scott were an international rugby player and former collegiate rowing, track and field, tennis, football, and baseball stars. The army assigned them to the various branches, Scotty going to the infantry. "Scott's commission can be attributed to the fact that he had several months of drilling last season under Sergeant Smiley," the *Chicago Daily News* said.[20] Some pundits thought the commission redeemed Scott for his 1916 suspension by the Sox.

"It would have been easy to drift away and become a common floater among men," Jimmy Crusinberry wrote.

But something stirred him. There have been great fighters among the Scotts. Perhaps a bit o' the auld spirit of his ancestors rankled in his breast. Anyway, Jim Scott picked out the toughest way of all to conquer himself and regain his place among men. He joined the army. . . . Uncle Sam isn't worrying about Capt. James Scott. He has won his first and biggest fight already and is well fitted to take his place in the world war for democracy.[21]

Bob Maxwell in Philadelphia found a moral lesson in "an athlete who was hopelessly in bad with his club and the home public and who was thought unable even to conquer himself." Scott, he wrote, "has arisen rapidly in the service until now he has become a captain, full of pride in his work and a man of recognized value to his country in the great work facing it."[22] Commy was as pleased as anyone by the pitcher's turnaround. "Scott deserved such a promotion," the White Sox owner said, "and he is certain to make a good officer, as his past experience will come in good stead now."[23]

A widely published newspaper photo showed Scott in uniform, complete with pack, canteen, and rifle, "receiving the felicitations of his wife on his success in winning a captain's commission."[24] Hattie's congratulations, in public at least, consisted of a prim handshake. The newlyweds then traveled north for Scott to assume new duties at Camp Lewis, American Lake, Washington. Had they remained in California a few days longer the captain would have encountered another Sox teammate.

"'Swede' Risberg, having helped the White Sox win a championship, promises to do much the same for the quartermaster's detachment baseball club at the Presidio," the *Chronicle* said in early December.[25] The *Bulletin* added that the Bay Area native was an "adviser extraordinary" to the army ballplayers.[26] Swede had several former minor leaguers on his club, whose games would be reported in local sports pages during the winter.

Scott meanwhile arrived at Camp Lewis (called Joint Base Lewis-McChord today). "Jim says he likes the army life," a wire service reported, "as far as it has gone, but realizes that getting a commission is mere child's play in comparison to what is bound to follow on the other side of the pond."[27]

"Here Is Man Who Will Make Germans 'Duck,'" a headline in nearby Tacoma declared as Scott prepared to report for duty December 15.[28] His pay now was 200 dollars a month, less board and uniforms, still far less than he'd earned as a hurler. Hattie didn't return to Chicago but stayed in Tacoma, a challenge during explosive wartime growth. The army appointed her husband an instructor in Company F at the Officers' Training Camp.

James "Death Valley Jim" Scott, White Sox pitcher, Captain, USA. *Tacoma (WA) Sunday News-Ledger.*

"'Capt. Jim' says the assignment is for three months, after which he hopes to be sent to France," the *Chicago Examiner* reported.[29] The Ninety-First "Wild West" Division also was training for Europe at the cantonment. Among his other duties Scott helped supervise camp baseball leagues, working with Capt. Leonard A. Wattelet of the 364th Infantry and other officers. Wattelet was an ideal partner, a former minor league player, manager, and executive. Scott was as excited by the army games he helped arrange as any he'd ever pitched in Chicago.

"Why shouldn't I be?" he asked. "We're in the biggest game of our lives right now, and when we strike France we shall feel as if we had never played in anything but bush team [sic] before."[30] Scott added in a letter to the *Examiner*, "I will feel greatly honored if I can represent the White Sox club and Mr. Comiskey with our boys at the front; that is what we of the 91st division are waiting for."[31]

The captain was starting to understand what New York sportswriter Grantland Rice was also learning as a second lieutenant in South Carolina. An ex-Minor League manager serving there as a captain and company commander told "Granny" exactly what officers were up against:

> Baseball is a great game, but it is strictly minor league compared to the game of war. Its emotions, its problems, its development are insignificantly small compared to the red game now ruling the world. One company commander in one year will have more hard work and a far greater variety of problems to face than John J. McGraw or Hughey Jennings or Connie Mack has known in any ten years of his existence.[32]

The Ninety First Division completed training in late June 1918. Early the next month, it began moving eastward to join Atlantic convoys for England, Scotland, and France. The entire Wild West Division was on the Continent by late July and after more training it entered combat in France. Captain Wattelet died in action in Belgium the last day of October.

Captain Scott, however, remained Stateside. No matter his hopes and expectations, the army valued him most as a trainer, a famous athlete the Sammies would listen to and heed. Scott was also useful as an unofficial recruiter while playing baseball versus civilian squads and service nines. The war department regarded many big leaguers in the armed forces the same way, and Scott would meet several old opponents on diamonds up and down the Pacific coast. Meanwhile, the captain received further training himself.

In late May 1918, Jim and Hattie headed east from Camp Lewis. They stopped briefly in Chicago and took in a Cubs game because his old team was on the road. Scott continued alone to Camp Perry on Lake Erie east of Toledo, Ohio, where he attended a school of instruction and learned more about handling weapons. He visited the White Sox in Cleveland while on a pass and threw batting practice before a Memorial Day twin bill.

"Scotty was given a royal welcome by his old pals of the diamond. He looked in the pink of condition," George Robbins wrote in the *Daily News*. "Army life apparently agrees with him."[33] The *Tribune* added, "After completing the course at Camp Perry, Scott will return to Presidio [sic] as instructor in small arms practice."[34] In fact the captain returned to Camp Lewis in July wearing a sharpshooter's medal he'd earned beside the great lake. Scott stopped in Chicago again on his way back.

"We have more baseball diamonds at Camp Lewis than at any other camp in the United States or in the world," he told the *Daily News*. "We have a little organized baseball game of our own—a national commission that handles all the disputes and two major leagues. . . . The rivalry is spirited and the interest of the soldiers and their friends is intense. They are playing for the championship of the camp and may carry their baseball argument to France if necessary."[35]

Robbins lauded Scott and the other ex-pros playing for him at Camp Lewis. "The morale of the whole army has been boosted by the spirit shown by these graduates of the big leagues," he wrote in *The Sporting News*.[36]

In August, the army temporarily relieved Scott of his instructor duties to lead his crack Camp Lewis ballclub down to the Bay Area. The competition was topnotch, the rosters of military nines there likewise filled with former big leaguers. This was a reasonable if unheroic use of athletes, which the government would again employ during the Second World War. Fans in San Francisco and Oakland greeted Scott warmly.

"Some real baseball will be dished up and handed to the fans during the next few weeks when Captain 'Death Valley' Jim Scott and his string of Camp Lewis ball players drift into town for the purpose of taking the army, navy and marine teams stationed hereabouts on for a series of games," the *San Francisco Examiner* said. The paper called his club "just about the best baseball outfit yet produced in the Northwest."[37]

Scott pitched a few innings but mostly managed. His club lost twice to a strong army Letterman General Hospital team, once on a no-hitter thrown by former St. Louis Brown Walter "Lefty" Leverenz. Camp Lewis then did the same thing to a Mare Island navy team led by Red Sox outfielder Chief George Lewis. "Duffy" delighted the captain by unaccountably taking the mound in relief. "Come on, boys, here's where we score a million," Scott shouted.[38]

The highlight of the trip was a three-game series with an All Army squad at Camp Fremont down the San Francisco peninsula in Menlo Park. Camp Lewis lost the first game, 10-9, as 17,000 doughboys and civilians cheered the home nine. Walter "Dutch" Ruether, who'd hurled for the Cincinnati Reds until drafted, won the second matchup for Camp Lewis, 12-9 (newspapers didn't record attendance).

Captain Scott had "rounded up a great ball club for that army training place," the *Oakland Tribune* said before the rubber match, "and is now here trying to take the service men's championship back to Camp Lewis with him."[39] Twelve thousand spectators saw Death Valley Jim's men win, 5-3, to capture what a San Jose paper called "the inter-cantonment baseball championship."[40]

Scott went north the following month for three charity games in Canada with a civilian all-star team at Vancouver, British Columbia, and a single game at nearby Blaine, Washington. Camp Lewis easily swept all four. "Vancouver people can be depended upon to shell out for patriotism anyway, and didn't have to endure the experience of seeing the local team walloped by a coterie of visitors just as an excuse for digging up," a local paper said. "They attended for the love of the game, and moreover thoroughly enjoyed themselves."[41]

Scott concluded his army sporting career that fall. He never set foot in France or fired a shot except during training or while instructing others. He was still a captain when the war ended November 11, 1918. The army later sent him to Seattle to create a program of talks and business conferences to help ex-Sammies land peacetime jobs. Scotty's own future wouldn't involve a return to Chicago.

9

Doc

The White Sox ended their 1917 campaign with a betrayal. Each player who'd earned a full share of World Series money received a check for nearly $3,700. Traveling secretary Joe O'Neill pocketed almost $1,700. Little-used infielder Bob "Ziggy" Hasbrook, who'd been with the club during the final weeks, got $1,000. But the split for longtime trainer Bill "Doc" Buckner was only $500, putting him among employees and mascots who got $100 to $300 apiece.

"This was the real surprise of the day, as the Sox conditioner was figured to share at least $1,000 of the big haul," George Robbins reported in the *Daily News*. Secretary Harry Grabiner said the players probably would make up the difference, and if they didn't, owner Comiskey undoubtedly would. It's unknown whether the Old Roman actually did so. "Buck has some real warm friends among the White Sox players, like Eddie Cicotte and Ray Schalk," Robbins wrote. "His friends were voted down."[1]

The slight made the Sox look racist and miserly. The *Chicago Defender* pointed to the New York Giants' contrasting treatment of their Black trainer, Ed Mackall. "The fans were bitterly disappointed when they learned that Buck received only $500, while Ed was given $1,000," the minority newspaper said. "The winners proved very cheap sports."[2]

Various white newspapers, whose sources perhaps weren't as good as the *Defender's*, said Mackall received $500, the same as Buckner. But even if such reports were correct, the Giants were still considerably more generous than the

Sox, since their World Series checks amounted to two-thirds of what Commy's men received.

The Sox had no financial motive to short Buckner. Indeed, they all had done quite well. A Broadway character called Diamond Joe had dealt briskly in precious stones after the World Series. "Most of the players purchased something in the way of diamond rings or pins for their wives even before leaving New York," Jimmy Crusinberry reported.[3]

The team also backed the current Liberty Loan drive by investing at least a hundred dollars apiece. Sy Sanborn wrote that Joe Benz kept only a bit of spending money for himself, deciding that "the bonds were just about the best investment he could think of for the remaining $3,600."[4] Why, then, had the team treated Buckner so shabbily?

In the wake of the subsequent Black Sox scandal, many fans and historians came to believe that the players had legitimate economic grievances against Commy's club. During the coming 1918 season a Chicago sports paper, *Collyer's Eye*, would declare it "a notorious fact that the White Sox payroll is one of the smallest in the league."[5] A narrative emerged about the parsimony of the club owner. Years later Chicago novelist Nelson Algren, in elementary school during the 1917 season, was among the believers.

"Comiskey so drastically underpaid his team that great resentment developed," Algren wrote as an adult. "He would make a fortune off his team, but had no intention of sharing it with the men who had been responsible for his financial success."[6] But no owner during the early twentieth century made his name or fortune by being magnanimous, and baseball historians have since largely debunked this damning narrative.

Commy undoubtedly was hard-nosed, wealthy, and influential, "known as a standpatter on holdouts," as Robbins wrote in 1919. "He made Ed Walsh come in as a supplicant when the Big Moose was out after a boost in his pay envelope and he has repeatedly refused to come to terms with recalcitrant players."[7]

Sportswriter J. B. Sheridan estimated that Commy had made $3 million during his baseball career.

"Thousands of young men are earning princely stipends every year playing the game Comiskey helped to make," Sheridan wrote after the 1917 World Series. "He makes more money every year than any man in baseball and his club makes more money every year than any club save the New York Nationals when they have a pennant-winning season."[8] But such success didn't necessarily also make him a pinchpenny.

"The accepted wisdom that Comiskey was a notably tight-fisted team owner is erroneous, thoroughly refuted by actual player salary data now readily available," writes Black Sox historian William F. Lamb.[9] He cites a landmark analysis of post–First World War salaries by SABR historian Bob Hoie, which reflects wartime payrolls equally well. The Black Sox, Hoie writes, "were paid the prevailing 1919 wage, and then some." Assertions of their owner's stinginess, he concludes, "were based on nothing more than an active imagination and a remarkable ability to suspend disbelief."[10]

Indeed, Harry Neily of the *Chicago Evening American* contradicted the harsh *Collyer's Eye* reporting in 1918. Neily, former secretary for Kansas City's defunct Federal League club, wrote that Commy sent his players new contracts "far in excess of those generally handed out by the owner of a world's championship ball club. If he had not done so, it is certain the Pallid Hose would not have signed so quickly."[11]

Clearly, Commy had prospered during 1917, despite multiple fears and uncertainties. His Sox had led the league in attendance, slightly bettering their figure from the previous season, when they'd also led the AL. "Toward the end of the season there was a falling off in attendance, but the interest in the game revived in October with the playing of the world's series," the *New York Times* said.[12] But the Pale Hose weren't a typical Major League club.

"Financially the year was not a good one for the major leagues, as only two teams in the National and four in the American made money for their owners," Sanborn wrote. "In the minor leagues it was a disastrous season and many circuits gave up the ghost soon after the Fourth of July."[13]

The Sox owner and his players had reason to worry about the coming 1918 season. Struggling with war-related restrictions and problems, only five of twenty-two Minor League circuits had completed 1917 intact. With the cantonments finally built and army training fully underway, conscription began cutting into rosters across Organized Baseball. The big leagues even considered cutting the schedule from 154 games to 140, causing disagreement between Ban Johnson and Commy. The AL prexy supported a reduction; the owner opposed it but agreed that other measures might be necessary.

"Pooling of players may become imperative to preserve anything like equality in playing strength," Commy speculated. "If the forthcoming drafts for the national army take half a dozen regulars away from others and none at all from some clubs, the result would be a runaway pennant race, which would rob the sport of all public interest early in the season."[14]

"In framing trades to strengthen their teams the clubowners [sic] now have to consider the eligibility of a player to the army in addition to his record as an athlete, his personality and his habits," Sanborn wrote, as assembling rosters grew complicated. "The owner who has under reservation a number of veterans too old to be drafted is quite likely to keep them, whereas a couple of years ago he would be figuring how to trade them for younger talent if they showed signs of slowing up."[15] Commy tried to reassure worried South Side fans.

"We will have baseball next year if the country wants it," he said. "It will make no difference how many of my players the government takes.... I am not worrying over the situation in baseball. All I am anxious about is for the United States to win the big game across the water. That is much more important than our sport at home."[16]

American League owners decided in December to retain a twenty-five player limit (later reduced to twenty-two or -three), continue spring training as usual, and retain the 154 game schedule. The magnates also announced that they would hold a day for the Griffith equipment fund in every AL city during June. They added that they would raise a new fund as well, to buy bats and balls for Canadian troops, popularly called "Tommies." The Sox, meanwhile, planned to leave Chicago for their Mineral Wells camp March 16, much later than usual.

"That war-time economy has hit the Sox organization is shown by the late date selected for the team's departure, the latest that a South Side team has left for its conditioning trip in many years," the *Daily News* said.[17] Buck Weaver later spoke about the economic pressure on South Side players that spring.

"I talked with President Comiskey about a contract for that year," he said in *The Sporting News*. "He told me about the bad war conditions. He said his chub would do well to make money owing to unsettled conditions. I signed a contract calling for the same amount of money I was receiving the previous season, when I helped win the world's championship, although I felt I deserved a boost."[18] Buck and others would remember those feelings throughout the new season.

Commy ordered Doc Buckner to pack the freshly washed uniforms as the Pale Hose readied for a second wartime season. "I wouldn't think of changing the color or the garments," the magnate said. "The same suits Buck packed to-day are the ones the Sox cavorted around in when they won the flag."[19]

Doc swallowed any resentment lingering from the fall. Commy praised him and denied persistent rumors that he was about to be deposed. "Buckner is the greatest trainer in the world," the owner insisted. "He's the boy that rubbed our men to a flag and he's going to repeat."[20] Buckner also looked after the team's bats and trunks and laid out fresh towels in the clubhouse as well. Neily said that the Sox without him would be "as flat as a mince pie without raisins." The scribe added that Commy's word was "equivalent to a contract and 'Buck' can consider himself hired again."[21] The club fired Buckner three days later.

William "Doc" Buckner, White Sox trainer. Courtesy of the Chicago Sun-Times/Chicago Daily News *collection, Chicago History Museum.*

"The announcement that 'Buck' would not go with the Sox this year came as a big surprise," Robbins wrote. "His friends supposed he was a fixture at Comiskey park. The devoted servant of the Sox took pride in helping get the team 'over the top.'"[22] Sanborn confirmed the dismissal. "Old Doc Buckner, the Ethiopian expert, who has massaged sore muscles for Comiskey's players for years and years, will not be with the club," he wrote. "Some time ago Commy intimated Buckner would be retained, but it seems he has changed his mind."[23]

The club hired a white masseur to replace Buckner. The man was well known around Chicago but had no particular expertise with ballplayers. The *Defender* sputtered its outrage.

"Just why Buckner was let out the fans throughout the city would like to have Charles Comiskey, the owner of the world's champions, explain, especially after such a beautiful article appearing in one of the downtown daily papers late last week, prior to the team's trip South," the paper said. The *Defender* blamed the Sox skipper for the firing. "Is Rowland really the manager of the White Sox, or are some of those southern crackers on the team running it?"[24] Robbins in the *Daily News* pointed instead to prominent Sox players.

"Friction between Eddie Collins, veteran second baseman, and Buckner was one of the reasons why Buck was cut off the Comiskey pay roll," Robbins wrote. "And midseason Buck had a run-in with Dave Danforth, a southern boy."[25] Looking back, Robbins went further after the season.

"Rowland was compelled to make the change to bring harmony to his team, he thought, although he wanted to keep Buck and would have done so if he had followed his judgment on the subject," Robbins wrote. He again pointed at Collins. "This temperamental ball player didn't like Buck from the time he joined the club. Collins kept after him persistently and was later joined by two or three other players. Clashes between these players and Buck became of frequent occurrence."[26]

Collins's biographer rejects the idea that the second baseman was involved. "Since Collins was still with the team when Buckner was rehired in 1922, the charges against him seem groundless," Rick Huhn writes. "In fact, Buckner served as trainer while Collins managed the White Sox in 1925–26."[27] Sanborn, writing for the *Washington Post* in 1923, pinned blame for the firing on Danforth. Sy clearly disliked the reliever and questioned whether he was worth all the trouble he caused for clubs and managers.

"In Buckner's medicine kit was a scalpel, razor sharp, which he prized highly," Sanborn recalled.

> One day on the bench he saw Danforth using it to whittle a stick, and instinctively called him down for it. . . . Danforth, who is a Southerner,

resented the call down, and started after the trainer with a bat. The outcome was a new trainer for the White Sox, as it then looked as if Danforth might be made into a good pitcher. After he was sent back to the minors [in 1920], Buckner again became trainer for the White Sox.[28]

The *Defender* applauded Buckner's rehiring. "Bill has been flooded with the letters and telegraph from all parts of the United States," it said, "congratulating him on his worth as a trainer, and his reappointment to the position of responsibility on the White Sox club."[29]

But that was all several years ahead, after damage had already been done. Many avid sports fans believe in fate, salvation, karma, and payback. Almost from the hour of their trainer's betrayal, the 1918 season went sideways for the White Sox.

10

Kid

Some pundits wondered if the big leagues should or even could play a full season in 1918. The financial situation looked dire. Attendance for Clark Griffith's club in Washington had dipped so low during 1917 that rumors said the capital city might lose its franchise. Brooklyn and other clubs had done poorly at the box office too.

"We intend to do better this season," Dodger owner Charles Ebbets said in the spring, "that is, if some of us do not go bankrupt."[1] Commy acknowledged challenges but backed the game.

"If there should be the slightest hint that baseball is not wanted during the war and that its discontinuation would serve our Government best, I would be the first to close the gates and turn Comiskey Park over to the Government if they wanted it," the magnate wrote. "I am not banking on the financial end of the game," he added, "although I see no reason now why the teams will not be patronized fairly well; but I do feel that the coming season will be an artistic success."[2]

The new season would be different in at least one noticeable way: No AL team would employ a drill instructor (nor any NL club either). Sergeant Smiley's B. B. N. G. was a memory.

"I was told by army authorities that the daily drills last season stimulated recruiting to a marked degree," Ban Johnson said. "There is no need of that now, because of the draft. We also believe the clubs will be changed about a good deal this season, as the players are called into the army, and we would not care to stage a poor exhibition."[3]

When Commy's players left for spring training in Texas, again from LaSalle Station, no soldier accompanied them. "Instead of the usual special train, the party was loaded into three Pullmans and hooked onto a fast train headed for Mineral Wells," Johnny Alcock wrote.[4] A band and a little more than a thousand fans saw the team off, less than a third the raucous throng of 1917. Unhappy news from the training site compounded the subdued departure.

"President Comiskey was distressed to hear of the accident that caused the discharge of Red Kuhn, one of his former catchers, from the army recently," Sy Sanborn reported.[5] Charles Kuhn had played 119 games for Chicago (1912–14). Drafted into the army and sent to Camp Travis near San Antonio, he'd lost sight in one eye during towel-snapping horseplay in his barracks. The injury was considered service-related but it might have happened in any clubhouse. The corporal received a discharge and small pension, his baseball career over.

"I'll come out all right," Kuhn said.[6] The Sox would soon encounter him working as a ticket taker, at an exhibition game with the local club in Dallas. Other portents dogged the White Sox. The previous season they'd avoided a train wreck in Texas by a few hours. This year saw them involved in another accident.

"Manager Rowland and the White Sox were dangerously near death when two wheels of the locomotive tender jumped the track near Weatherford," George Robbins reported. "The engineer threw on the brakes, jolting the whole party, emergency chains alone preventing the train from plunging twenty feet down a high embankment. . . . 'That was the nearest to a fatal accident we have had here in many a day,' said a trainman."⁷

The train stopped so suddenly, Sanborn added, that "the two steel sleepers which housed the players came near telescoping the regular day coach equipment ahead of them." The scribe credited the lack of injuries to "the proverbial luck that accompanies major league ball players on their journeys."⁸

The derailment delayed the team's arrival in Mineral Wells by three hours, costing them an afternoon's practice but nothing more. The good-news/bad-news scenario continued two mornings later as Eddie Cicotte, Ray Schalk, Joe Jackson, and Chick Gandil returned from a round of golf. An automobile shot out of a side street and smashed into theirs.

"I thought sure I was going through the windshield," Gandil said. "That's where I landed in a former wreck, but this seemed more dangerous and I was thoroughly scared. We were the luckiest bunch in the world."⁹

The trio practiced that afternoon, but the new trainer later put Cicotte to bed, suffering from shock and a lump on his neck. The crackup caused no serious injury but "narrowly missed wrecking the world's champion machine," Sanborn wrote. Commy was uncharacteristically angry—not with the other driver, but with the players. "Baseball is their game, and they are down here to get in shape to play baseball," he snapped. "Their place was on the ball field this morning if they were able to be there, not out experimenting with golf sticks and looking at scenery. . . . I am willing they should learn golf at someone else's expense."¹⁰

Troubles kept multiplying for the Sox. Joe Jackson went down with what newspapers called an attack of malaria. Buck Weaver's father died unexpectedly, following surgery, so the third sacker left the team temporarily. Eddie Collins suffered a "bad case of tonsillitis that threatened to develop into pneumonia," and would be sent back home to Chicago ahead of the team.¹¹

William "Kid" Gleason, White Sox coach. Courtesy of Library of Congress.

The greatest loss, however, was coach Bill Gleason. The Kid's knowhow, skill, and knowledge had benefited the club tremendously during the championship run. But he hadn't shown up this year and nobody knew why.

"Manager Rowland looked for a message . . . all day," the *Tribune* said in a dispatch during the rail trip South. "He figures the Kid will come along on a later train, believing he failed to make connections in Chicago."[12] Ten days passed with still no word. "The continued silence of Kid Gleason is causing a bit of worry in camp," Sanborn wrote. "Without him there will be no manager for the second team after tomorrow. As Gleason is well over 50 years old, there isn't a chance he has been drafted, and he never was a holdout in his life. Business troubles are the only explanation of his absence that sounds reasonable."[13]

Those troubles might have been related to a March 7 police raid on a Philadelphia poolroom located next to a church. During the offseason the Kid made his home in the City of Brotherly Love.

"Several patrol wagons were called and thirty-two men were sent to Central Station," the *Philadelphia Inquirer* reported. "Later the detective arrested two more, said to have been gambling in the rear room of the place." Philly cops said the coach was the proprietor of the poolroom but wasn't among the men hauled to the pokey. "We have suspected that gambling was going on in Gleason's place for some time," a captain said.[14]

The coach's continued absence gave "rise to rumors that he is a holdout," the *Chicago Examiner* said April 8, although adding that he was expected soon. "The 'Kid' is at his home here [Philadelphia] winding up some personal business affairs."[15] Gleason still didn't appear as the Sox prepared to start their season. South Side fans began asking his whereabouts.

"It was a question that remained unanswered," the *Daily News* said. "Rowland wanted the old order of things to prevail, but this was impossible, for the ever alert and peppery Gleason was among the missing."[16] Theories and gossip abounded.

"First, he was seriously ill [during the winter] and spent several weeks in a hospital, after undergoing an operation," a wire service reported. "Subsequently the Kid lost his world's series money in a private venture in Philadelphia. Because of this failure, he asked Owner Comiskey for a short leave of absence so that he could settle his affairs."[17]

"It generally was supposed that Comiskey and Gleason were not even on speaking terms," Jimmy Crusinberry wrote afterward. "In fact, Gleason refused to join the White Sox . . . as coach, a job he had held a number of years. It was rumored that he had a grievance against Comiskey."[18] The Sox owner disputed a later allegation that his coach hadn't received an expected payment.

"As to the report that Gleason quit because he didn't get a bonus promised," Commy said, "nothing was ever at any time mentioned as to a bonus, and he received everything due him from the White Sox."[19] A Baltimore sportswriter finally tracked the missing coach down in Atlantic City, New Jersey.

"The mysterious disappearance of Gleason . . . was one of the puzzles of baseball," the scribe remembered. "As usual he closed like a clam when questioned on the subject, but he told the writer that he had had no quarrel with Rowland. It seems that he and Comiskey must have had some words, or that some incident displeased Gleason, for it was not his way to hide himself."[20]

Whatever the whole tale, the pair never reached an agreement. The Kid didn't coach for the Sox or anyone else in 1918. His refusal to sign seemed to Robbins "cause for regret on the part of the scribes, as the Kid was a prolific source of stories."[21] The loss of his experience was far more detrimental to the club.

"Rowland kept the players on their toes and Gleason rammed baseball into their beans—an ideal combination," a Chicago scribe wrote. "But Rowland is no good on the latter half of the skit and unless Gleason shows up the Sox are due to lose a bunch of games in the absence of being told to do the right thing at the right time."[22]

The few highlights of the Texas trip mostly involved baseball-loving Sammies. The Sox took an interurban train down from Houston to Galveston for an April 1 game with the Eighth Marines stationed at Fort Crockett. The team appreciated the devil dogs' hospitality and dined in their messes as a camp glee club sang for them.

After lunch, Faber, Weaver, and a few others fired Lewis light machine guns off the seawall. Buck failed to bring down a single duck from a flock flapping above the Gulf of Mexico. The marines staged a bayonet drill for the club. Army coastal artillerymen also showed them a "disappearing" gun and mortar battery that protected the shore, but didn't shoot to avoid alarming the townspeople.

"For the benefit of the visitors a gun crew went through the motions of firing one of their ponderous pets," Sanborn wrote. "This was an uncommon distinction; civilians almost never are permitted to get near these big guns."[23]

Afterward, troops drove the players 3 miles by truck to a Texas League ballpark, where nearly all of Fort Crockett's 2,500 officers and men watched the game. The Sox easily beat a crack marine nine, 11–3. "The sea soldiers expected something of the sort and were not disappointed," Charley Dryden wrote in the *Examiner*. "From the way they supported him the pitcher must have thought he had a bunch of horse marines in tow."[24]

The Sox faced another military nine two days later at the Houston ballpark. Eddie Cicotte pitched well against Sammies from Camp Logan. Sanborn pointed out in their defense that the team from the Thirty-Third "Prairie" Division wasn't as strong as it might have been following the departure of Chicago's old Eighth Regiment, now designated the 370th Infantry. The Black outfit had been detached from other Illinois units and assigned to the segregated Ninety-Third Division, soon to win distinction fighting alongside French troops "over there." Doc Buckner's stepson, a sergeant in the 370th, would survive the war and return wearing a wound stripe on his sleeve.

The Prairie Division squad had "no star players since the Eighth regiment took away some of Rube Foster's [American Giants] performers," Sanborn wrote, though adding that "the men have been playing the game practically all winter and are in far better physical trim than White Sox ever were in their lives."[25] Eight of the white Sammies playing in the game were minor leaguers or semipros from the Windy City. All wore the new flannels donated by the Woodland Bards.

"The soldiers overflowed the grand stand and many of them camped on the field," Sanborn wrote. "They jammed the street cars and many of them came in trucks from Camp Logan. As each car or truck stopped at the park there was a yell, 'Thirty-fifth and Wentworth, all out,' for the crowd was made up largely of White Sox rooters, who called the players by their first names."[26] Proceeds from the contest benefited the all-white division's athletic fund.

The Sox demolished service squads of Sammies or devil dogs, but played poorly versus Texas League opponents while in Houston. "The attendance was small, and half of it composed of military men," the *Tribune* said after a game with the Buffaloes. "Houston apparently cares nothing for the White Sox, and you can't blame them after looking at the games."[27]

While there Cicotte, Gandil, and a pair of Sox prospects toured Ellington Field outside the city. An army flier recalled it as a "big factory, essentially human . . . where pilots and bombers, trained to the minute, were turned out for the vast air fleets that clouded the skies of Europe."[28] Risberg had once considered joining the Air Service.

"I always took a shine to aircraft and that kind of warfare appeals to me strongly," Swede had said. "There is something fascinating about an aeroplane."[29] But he didn't join his teammates in taking a closer look, perhaps having seen enough of the army while coaching at the Presidio. A former Chicago motorcycle cop died in a crash the day the Sox visited. "Those aeroplanes look like birds up there," Cicotte said afterward, "but that's no place for a pitcher."[30]

While on their way home to Chicago the Pale Hose stopped for a final service game at Camp Funston, Kansas. The Eighty-Ninth Division team was loaded with pro talent and had split two recent games with the visiting St. Louis Cardinals. The Sox beat the Sammies, 13–1, in front of a uniformed crowd of 10,000.

"Manager Rowland played as many as possible of the world's champions so as to give the boys in khaki a final look at them before going away from here," Sanborn wrote.[31] Proceeds again went to the division's sports equipment fund. The spring otherwise had been miserable for the South Siders.

"The training trip has been the least valuable the White Sox have ever taken, in spite of weather which has permitted work every day since they landed in Mineral Wells," Sanborn wrote, noting a catalog of the club's mishaps and misfortune. "Starting with a railroad wreck on the way to camp, things have gone wrong almost constantly.... It will require several weeks of championship combats to put the world's champions where they were last year at this time."[32]

The good news was that Commy's team remained largely intact. Seventy-six big leaguers in the armed forces had been missing when spring camps opened. Scores more would follow during the season. For the moment, the Sox lacked only Jim Scott and catcher Joe Jenkins, drafted soon after the World Series. With other positions covered, manager Rowland was eager to line up a third backstop behind starter Ray Schalk and Byrd Lynn.

The Sox had received rights to catcher Harry Lake of the Newport News club in the Virginia League during the winter. He hadn't arrived at Mineral Wells, or made any contact to explain his absence. The Sox first thought he'd enlisted in the navy, but later located him at a shipyard in Wilmington, Delaware, working during weekdays then playing ball for a company team on weekends. The Sox didn't appreciate his disappearance, but Lake could legitimately claim the job, having worked as an expert mechanic for shipyards during the off-seasons.

Catcher George "Speedy" Lees reported to Mineral Wells and was immediately regarded as Jenkins's successor. The club signed him in November following four seasons at Lehigh University in Pennsylvania. The *New York Sun* said Lees was "probably the best college catcher in the country last year."[33] The *Chicago Daily News* added that he "resembles Ray Schalk so closely that a fan in the grand stand yesterday was fooled into believing he was kidding the world's greatest catcher. Lee [sic], who is a modest chap, takes these compliments lightly."[34]

The rookie came north with the team with little expectation of seeing much playing time. But in mid-May, before ever appearing in a game, Lees received orders to report to the National Army. He wasn't the only Sox youngster lost to the armed forces. Several other prospects entered the services before their names ever appeared in a regular-season box score.

Two pitchers signed from the Western League were already wearing khaki and later served in France, George Payne with the 303rd Motor Transport Repair Shop and Earl Keiser in the 314th Infantry. ("This Keiser O. K.," a *Tribune* headline quipped later.)[35] Semipro pitching prospect Leo Constantineau joined the navy before spring training. First baseman Fred "Snake" Henry, who'd trained at Mineral Wells in 1917, was in the army too.

The club had hopes for pitcher Bruno Haas. A flop with the Athletics in 1915, when he'd walked a record sixteen batters during his debut, "Boon" also had trained with the Sox in Texas last year. Rowland's notion of shifting the southpaw into the outfield evaporated when Haas enlisted as a naval aviator. The list of other men the team lost to the armed forces lengthened over the summer. Hurler Charles Roberson, sent to the Minors before Opening Day, enlisted in the Air Service. Infielder Hervey McClellan, likewise sent down, also donned khaki. He later played six seasons for Chicago after the war, until his death in 1925.

Turnover and turmoil became normal in the Major Leagues. Rowland had managed twenty-six men during 1917. This season he would boss thirty-one, eleven new to the Sox roster. Of this near dozen, only one would return to the Sox in 1919.

11

Phil

Twenty-five thousand fans descended on Comiskey Park for the April 16 season opener. All were already familiar with the new 10 percent war tax, which they'd been paying at movie theaters and vaudeville halls since November. This was the first time it was due at the ballpark and there were problems.

Major League prices had been remarkably easy to handle until now. The previous season, seats had cost a quarter for bleachers, a half dollar for pavilion, six bits for the grandstand, and a buck for boxes. This year the clubs rolled the tax into the ticket prices rather than collect it separately. This boosted costs to 28 cents, 55 cents, 83 cents, and $1.10, respectively.

Dan Daniels of the *New York Sun* said the new prices caused "an ugly problem in making the required change and having so many coppers on hand."[1] The *Philadelphia Inquirer* added, "Already there is a greater demand for pennies than the supply will meet and the baseballers, beside not desiring to tackle the penny change proposition, believe they could not keep themselves in small change."[2]

Red Sox president Harry Frazee suggested rounding up the two most awkward figures to 30 and 85 cents and donating the extra two cents to the Red Cross or other approved war funds. But Dodgers president Charles Ebbets thought this solution would be unfair to fans.

"It will be an injustice to charge the public 85 cents for 75 cent tickets, or 30 cents for 25 cent tickets, simply because the addition of the war tax makes it difficult to make change," Ebbets said.³ He thought clubs instead should use a change-making device called a comptometer, which the *New York Herald* said "resembles a typewriter and is operated by the pressure of one or more keys that release the exact change, pennies and all, in an instant."⁴

The machine didn't work very well, however, and the Brooklyn boss soon realized how many pennies would be needed even if it operated perfectly. Ebbets relented, and the magnates adopted Frazee's suggestion for handling the tax. There were some exceptions.

Newsies, scorecard vendors, concession workers, and boys who retrieved foul balls didn't have to pay the tax. Neither did sportswriters, since their professional association issued their passes rather than the clubs. But the system covered nearly everyone else. Even folks who previously got into parks on free passes now had to pay a dime.

"Taking the capacity of Comiskey park as fixed by the national commission reports of the attendance at the last world's series, a capacity crowd there would net the United States in war tax more than $1,100 and an additional $400 for the Red Cross or some other charitable organization," Sy Sanborn wrote. "But 'capacity' crowds were not daily or even weekly occurrences at Comiskey park even in normal times, and they are expected to be more infrequent this year."⁵

Opening Day on the South Side still brought out a capacity crowd. Making change became a problem even without dealing with countless pennies.

"While the crowd was exceptionally well handled, the ticket sale was slowed up considerably by the necessity of making odd change at all box offices. . . . All ticket windows were plentifully supplied with small change at the opening game, but the unusual prices slowed up both the salesmen and the fans," the *Tribune* said. Some 2,000 fans missed seeing the first couple innings because of the backup.

The inexperience of Comiskey's workforce compounded the problem. No one who'd held a minor job at the park the previous season would still be working there in June 1918, "all of them having enlisted or been drafted into the national army," the *Tribune* would say. "This includes ushers, ground keepers, helpers, sweepers, 'butchers,' [candy or newspaper sellers] and score card peddlers."[6] The Sox wouldn't resort to hiring women, however, as the Cubs would do by introducing "usherettes" at their North Side park during the summer.[7]

Fans and employees both needed time to adjust to the extra nickel or dime needed to enter the ballparks. "Secretary Harry Grabiner of the White Sox has called for help . . . [and] requests all fans to bring the exact change in order to help themselves, the ball club and Uncle Sam," the *Daily News* said.[8] The Cubs made a similar appeal before their opener the following week. But all the extra change in the country wouldn't have helped Commy's team that first afternoon on the South Side.

The White Sox again opened versus Fielder Jones and the St. Louis Browns, this year at home. The weather was unseasonably mild and the crowd enthusiastic. "The impressive opening had a military coloring," George Robbins said in the *Daily News*. "There were jackies and soldiers sandwiched among citizens in street attire to be seen in all parts of the park."[9] Wild cheers erupted when the club and players contributed $25,000 to the third Liberty loan drive at home plate before the game.

The Browns under hurler Grover "Slim" Loudermilk quickly spoiled the mood by going out and swatting nineteen hits to hand the Sox a 6–1 defeat. "Barring the combat itself, everything was lovely," Sanborn deadpanned.[10] "Our champions were not in the running at any stage of the proceedings," Charley Dryden admitted in the *Examiner* after Captain Eddie Collins knocked in Chicago's only run in the sixth inning. "The rest of the time the Sox were being nipped in the bud just as they were on the verge of doing something handsome."[11]

Starter Eddie Cicotte took the loss, with Danforth, Faber, and Russell all in relief. "Jones, an expert in handling flingers, has five hurlers in condition to work," Robbins noted. "Rowland has only two of first rank—Cicotte and Faber."[12]

Felix "Phil" Chouinard, ex-White Sox utility player, Chief Yeoman, USN. Great Lakes Recruit.

Chief Yeoman Felix Chouinard, USN, led 400 jackies on a special train from Great Lakes to see the game. He'd once been a Sox himself, in 1910 and 1911, but hadn't played much. "Felix played with the Sox once and knows all about the club," the *Daily News* said. "A small cannon brought to the park by the jackies to boom when the Sox won boomed anyway."[13]

The papers didn't say whether manager Rowland personally greeted Chief Chouinard and his bluejackets. The two men had met when Rowland visited Great Lakes in late January. By one account, the skipper had intended only to take in the sights until he bumped into Chouinard and Washington third baseman Joe Leonard, also a sailor, at a navy bowling alley the pair managed during the winter. In another telling, athletic director Surgeon John B. Kaufman had invited the skipper up for a tour. Either way, Kaufman accompanied them around the station.

"Gangway!" Chouinard barked, clearing a path through jackies who recognized the Sox manager. "I see you have quite a bunch of former big leaguers up here," Rowland said. "Yes, and we have enough to challenge the White Sox to a game of ball," the chief replied. "The game is on," the skipper agreed.[14] Despite his and Commy's best intentions, though, the contest never happened.

A Chicago native, Chouinard was the son of a French-Canadian father and a mother of Irish parentage. His nickname, "Phil," was a diminutive of Felix. After high school he'd attended St. Ignatius College (Loyola University today). He'd not only played ball but acted and sung in student theatrical productions. After college and three seasons in the Minors he'd reported to the Sox in September 1910. *Tribune* columnist Hugh Edmund told fans how to pronounce his name: "Shinard—quick, just like that, and the CH soft as asparagus."[15]

Phil stayed with the Sox the following season but saw little action. During a bit more than a year with the Sox as a light-hitting utility player, he appeared in thirty-eight games at second base, in the outfield, and pinch hitting. He also enjoyed an offseason career as a vaudevillian. Unlike Buck Weaver and Jim Scott, who as entertainers were excellent ballplayers, Chouinard was "quite as much at home on the stage as he is upon the ball field," said a Wisconsin newspaper that applauded his "smooth, sweet voice."[16]

Chouinard returned to the Minors in 1912 and later played in the Federal League during 1914–15. When America entered the war in April 1917, he was managing a City League club back in Chicago. He gave up baseball that summer to enlist at Great Lakes and by August was a chief yeoman.

A chief petty officer (CPO) was a senior enlisted man who wore a different uniform from lower-ranking sailors. The *Examiner* noted that Chouinard stood out from his men in his "cheese cutter uniform, to-wit, brass buttons and a visored cap which is supposed to cut the cheese."[17] A yeoman, called a ship's writer during earlier years, was a clerk whose rating badge was a pair of crossed quill pens. A number of big leaguers enlisted as chief yeomen or yeomen first class (one step lower) following the 1917 season or the next year. Chouinard found a home in the navy at Great Lakes.

"Prior to the war it ranked athletically only on a par with some of the smaller midwestern colleges," baseball historians Harold and Dorothy Seymour wrote of the station decades later. "The war changed all that."[18] Over 900 sailors tried out for the station's baseball team that first war year. Surgeon Kaufman appointed Chouinard to manage the starting nine. A navy magazine thought the AD was lucky to have a man "gifted with the executive ability and power to commend men as Chouinard. Already he has shown that he is the right man for the post."[19]

Few pro ballplayers had yet entered the navy, and Chouinard's first aggregation was mostly amateurs. The season was "not one over which the sailors could waltz in ecstasy," a station history says.[20] But the team made a decent showing, mostly against semipro Chicago-area teams. The outlook was far brighter by March 1918. "The two strongest station nines in the country promise to be those of the Great Lakes and the Boston districts," the *New York Tribune* said, meaning the clubs led by Chouinard and former Red Sox player-manager Jack Barry, also a chief yeoman.[21]

"In any congregation of 20,000 or more youths averaging twenty years, there is bound to be at least 500 who have had liberal experience in manipulating the li'l ol' baseball," the *Great Lakes Bulletin* said. The navy newspaper added that Chouinard didn't want "any of the men on the Station with baseball ability to become discouraged because of the number of stars who will appear on the squad."[22]

His new roster included past and future big leaguers Joe Leonard, John "Paddy" Driscoll, George Halas, and several others. The *Tribune* said Chouinard "has enough talent at Great Lakes to almost put a team in a class A league," the penultimate rung on the Minor League ladder.²³ As the White Sox began their season at Comiskey Park, jackies at Great Lakes were building a multipurpose sports facility of their own.

"The baseball field probably will have a grandstand and bleachers with seating capacity of 10,000," the *Tribune* said. "A detail of 1,500 sailors will start grading the ball field this morning [April 1] under the supervision of Charley Kuhn, groundkeeper at Comiskey park."²⁴ The navy would dedicate their field the first week of August.

Cold and rain plagued the South Side club early in the season, disrupting the schedule at home and away. The owner reluctantly scrubbed an April 19 tilt with the Browns, "the first time in several years that a Saturday game had been canceled on account of cold at Comiskey park," the *Daily News* said.²⁵

"There are no radiators in the grand stand," Commy explained, "and I want my patrons to be comfortable."²⁶ Coats and scarves would be spotted in the park as late as July, when "it was a novelty for the fans to shiver in the cold."²⁷

Things never improved much for the Sox. Their first homestand ended April 23 with a storm washing out a game with the Tigers. "Comiskey's men have played only three out of the eight games scheduled for the home lot," Sanborn wrote of the one-and-two club, "and most of the time they have been unable to get any exercise to keep them anywhere near physical fitness."²⁸

More worrying news broke eight days later when outfielder Joe Jackson learned he'd been shifted into Class 1 of the draft, the highest classification. This meant the army probably would soon call the shoeless one's number, about the worst possible scenario for Commy's struggling club.

Jackson claimed sole support of his wife and a younger sister. His local board in Greenville, South Carolina, originally placed him in Class 4-A, common for men claiming dependents. "The District Board which met here today could not see it that way and put the Greenville boy in Class One," a newspaper in Greenwood, South Carolina, reported May 1.²⁹

Jackson didn't know why his case had shifted to the higher board 50 miles away or why his draft status had changed. He and the Sox got the news in Cleveland during a series with the Indians. "This is the first I have heard about Jackson being placed in Class 1," Rowland told scribes.³⁰ Jackson couldn't add much more.

"I'm ready to go whenever they call me. And I'll get me a few Boches too, if a good batting eye proves to be a good shooting eye," the slugger said, using slang for German soldiers. "Still I don't see how they could move me up to Class One when I married long before the war started."³¹

12

Shoeless

Scribes disagreed over Jackson's draft reclassification. Some applauded, while others shook their heads. E. A. Batchelor, for one, questioned its legality.

"I don't understand why Jackson was placed in class 1-A," said Batchelor, a former *Detroit Free Press* sporting editor soon to leave for France with the YMCA. "Joe is married and that automatically places him in class 4, as I understand it. There are many stars of the big league who are married and have many times the amount of wealth Joe possesses who are in class 4."[1]

Fritz von Kolnitz questioned the change too. Jackson's fellow South Carolinian and ex-teammate had left the Sox to work in industry, then enlisted as an army aviator. Following a crash, he worked with ground troops at Camp Gordon, Georgia. Von Kolnitz would be a major when he wrote to George Robbins about Jackson's plight in January 1919.

"I have known Joe for a long time . . . long before he was ever known in major league baseball," Fritz said. "I know his circumstances and I know the struggle he has had to attain the place he now occupies in baseball. I am aware of the dependence upon him of his mother, her two minor children and his wife." His defense of the slugger continued:

> During the draft period, I will venture, there were thousands of men walking the streets in civilian clothes with exemption papers in their pockets with far less claims than Joe. I know that Joe lost practically all of his savings a

few years ago in an unlucky investment. He is dependent upon his salary for the support of his family....

I have been in a camp where there were at least 12,000 draftees coming in monthly. I am fairly familiar with the personnel of our national army forces, and within the limit of my observation there have been no men drafted who had the family claims that Joe did. I have seen men discharged after having been drafted if they proved valid dependency claims and the dependency was never any greater than a mother or wife and children.[2]

The district board never adequately explained its actions. Jackson said half a dozen men with the same name lived in the country, leading to brief speculation that the board had reclassified the wrong person. Local officials enjoyed considerable leeway and any number of reasons might have led to the decision. Authorities might simply have needed married men to reach their quota, for example. A history of the rural South during the war points out that married men comprised a majority of the draft pool there—52.5 percent, far higher than in other regions.

"It was not really possible for southern draft boards to exempt all married men," author Jeanette Keith writes. She adds, "Some draft boards based exemption on virility: Men who had been married for several years without producing children might as well be sent to the front since, as the Caldwell County, Texas, board said, 'what use are they anyway?'"[3]

Perhaps, as some biographers have written, Greenwood board members thought Katie Jackson needn't rely on her husband's income, that Joe had ample resources to sustain his family while away. Perhaps they thought a professional athlete merited particular scrutiny in the name of fairness. Or perhaps, as George Robbins appeared to believe, Joe had an unknown enemy on the board.

"Any baseball writer who permits the elements of favoritism or of a grudge to enter into his scoring is a poor man to describe a ball game," Robbins wrote in *The Sporting News*. "And likewise any draft board that permits these elements to sway its decisions is a poor draft board. . . . Jackson contends his being switched from Class 4 to Class I was due to the action of his enemies rather than a desire to secure justice."[4]

Columnist Bob Pigue sensed something amiss too. "There is a measure of right in Joe's action," Pigue wrote, "for he had a family to support and was shifted from class 4-A to class 1-A without notice, on what appears to have been a case of hometown spite."[5]

Whatever the reason or rationale, Jackson found himself in the top draft class, although he wasn't required to report immediately. "As Jackson's number is far down the list, officials say it is not likely he will be drawn until after two more increments are furnished," the *Tribune* said May 3.[6]

More bad news for the Sox soon followed. A fall with a horse seriously injured Corp. Charles Felsch, brother of Hap, in training with the field artillery at Brownsville, Texas. Charles Felsch Sr. left his Milwaukee home to travel to his unconscious son's bedside. The outfielder left the team May 8 in Cleveland to join them.

"His enforced absence will cripple the club to some extent, as there is no one in the league who can go out and pull them down in abler fashion than Hap," the *Daily News* reported. The South Siders had left three men back in Chicago, their captain was sidelined by a bad knee, and Kid Gleason was still missing. "The Sox have only seventeen players, including Eddie Collins, with whom to battle the eastern clubs," the paper added. "The team is now on a war footing."[7]

Felsch missed eleven days before rejoining the team late May 19, "ready to play tomorrow if he has regained his land legs after his long journey to Brownsville, Tex., and return," Sy Sanborn wrote from New York. "He spent sixty hours on the way from Chicago to Texas to see his injured brother and seventy-two hours on the way back."[8]

Jackson's local board, meanwhile, had ordered him to report to the nearest draft board for a physical exam earlier than expected. "Jackson's number is 846, which places him for an early call for active service and unless he appeals from the action of the district board, he will be unable to finish the season with the White Sox," a Greenville newspaper said.[9]

Saturday, May 11, Joe appeared before Draft Board No. 6 at Twelfth and Pine streets, Philadelphia. After the physician found him fit, wire reports said the outfielder would be called for army service between May 25 and June 1. "I have been under the impression that I would not be called at this time," Jackson told scribes, "but I'm no slacker, and if Uncle Sam wants me, I'll be only too glad to go."[10]

Jackson played left field as usual that afternoon, going hitless in three at-bats during a 1–0 loss to the Athletics. The *Tribune* ran a boxed item that evening in which it cynically but accurately joked that Jackson "has arranged to enlist as a shipbuilder in the eastern shipyard if he is drafted, so as to escape being seasick crossing the Atlantic."[11]

The slugger had played in seventeen games during the rainy first weeks of the season, smacked one homer, and hit .354. Following their contest with the A's most of the Sox caught a fast train for a Sunday afternoon game in Ohio with the Indians, before dashing back again to finish the series in Philadelphia; Sanborn called this excursion "two tough nights in sleepers."[12]

Rowland said he'd given Jackson permission to skip the trip. The slugger himself told scribes he'd missed the train, and knew his season was over anyway. Monday, May 13, Sanborn reported that the Sox star planned to appeal his draft status. "If the appeal is denied, Jackson plans to enlist as a shipbuilder in one of the yards near Washington, if permission can be obtained," Sy added. "In any event he will not continue to drive out base hits for the world's champions much longer."[13]

"The Chicago camp followers say that Jackson and his wife left the Aldine Hotel yesterday morning in a taxicab and have not been seen since," Philly sports editor Bob Maxwell reported Monday evening. "Joe was not in the game yesterday at Cleveland either."[14] George Robbins gave a slightly different timeline later, reporting that Jackson had turned up at the team's hotel Sunday night.

"When Joe appeared he declared he had 'enlisted with an emergency fleet company,'" Robbins wrote in *The Sporting News*.[15] This was a reference to the United States Shipping Board Emergency Fleet Corporation, established by congress to oversee all wartime shipbuilding. But Jackson also seemed to contradict himself. "Well, the old boy will be out there slugging the Dutchman [Germans] pretty soon," he was quoted as saying sometime Monday. "And if I ever draw a bead on one of them birds, it'll be all off with him."[16]

Jackson and Katie then left town. Newspapers reported Tuesday that the outfielder had jumped the Sox for a job with the Harlan & Hollingsworth shipyard, on the Delaware River at Wilmington, 30 miles southwest of Philadelphia.

Joseph "Shoeless Joe" Jackson, White Sox outfielder. Courtesy of Library of Congress.

"This news puzzled White Sox fans not a little this morning," the *Chicago Evening Post* said. "Either one of two things actuated Jackson in making this move. He figured he could do his bit best by giving up a $5,000 a year baseball job to work in the shipyards for a half or a third of that amount. Or he figured he could evade the draft."[17]

Sportswriters pointed to Jackson's wife as the motivator behind his decision, which was almost certainly true. "Katie Jackson read and negotiated Joe's contracts, and her shrewd business sense helped Joe supplement his baseball salary," a biographer later wrote.[18] "Probably Mrs. Jackson, who is the boss of the family, has had some influence, also, in her husband's determination to take up ship building in preference to trench work," *The Sporting News* speculated.[19]

The *Philadelphia Evening Public Ledger* added that Katie had "helped Joe make his decision. She informed Joe, it is said by scribes with the White Sox, that he must get some kind of Government work right away. Joe followed instruction."[20]

Harlan workers, like the male employees in many other wartime industries, generally received exemptions from military service. Jackson's illiteracy was no barrier to his employment. The company not only hired the Sox star as a painter, but according to one report from Philadelphia made him an inspector.

"If Jackson should stay at the shipyard as an employe [sic] he would be eligible to play in the Bethlehem Steel Baseball League as a member of the Wilmington team," a wire service added. "This organization has teams at Bethlehem, Lebanon and Steelton, Pa., Fore River, Mass., Wilmington, Del., and Sparrows Point, Md. It is outside of organized baseball and has in its ranks many players formerly in the major and minor leagues."[21]

Sportswriters noted that Harlan manager Fred Payne was a former catcher who'd played for the Sox during the 1909–11 seasons and the Tigers before that. The skipper certainly was eager to land Jackson for his club.

"Payne has done only what athletic directors of nearly every cantonment in the United States have done—brought athletes of ability to their camps,"

Robbins wrote.[22] The Steel League and other industrial circuits also employed agents, who circled Major and Minor League parks like vultures and swooped in to convince players to jump their clubs for industrial jobs.

"The pitch was easy, something most likely along the lines of: 'Join the shipbuilding trade, earn a sizable paycheck, and continue to play ball on the weekends,'" Jackson biographer Tim Hornbaker writes. "And most important of all: 'You'll never set foot on a foreign field of war.'"[23] The pitch worked with Jackson.

"When the whistles blew at 7 a.m. this morning [May 14] in the Harlem [sic] & Hollingsworth Shipbuilding company, Joe Jackson stepped up, punched the time clock and started work as a painter," the *Tribune* said in a Tuesday dispatch. "From Greenville, S. C., Jackson's home, comes word that his employment in a shipbuilding plant will not exempt him from the draft. He will be called in his turn sometime this month."[24]

Jackson's actions played poorly in Chicago and elsewhere, especially with Felsch still away from the South Side club. He'd apparently deserted his club for a safe berth in a shipyard when faced with induction into the army. Jackson denied any such intention.

"All this talk about my coming here to avoid the draft is untrue," he told a Wilmington paper. "Two months ago I applied for a job at the Harlan plant, because during the winter months I have been working at odd times about shipyards and last winter spent some time at Jacksonville, Fla." Joe continued his lengthy justification:

> I made arrangements to locate to this city, and Clarence Rowland, the White Sox manager, knows it. He knew that the next time we came East I was going to drop out in Philadelphia and quit the big game. Anyone who does not believe this can ask him.
>
> The Sox finally reached Philadelphia. I came to Wilmington on a Friday night and made arrangements to start work here on Monday. On Saturday

I was told to report for physical examination in the draft. That's how close it was to my signing up to work and my being called to take the physical examination. But the preliminary details had been made two months before. . . .

I have not received any word from the South Carolina draft board, although I have telegraphed to know where I stood. I have not received any word from the board stating that I have been put in a deferred class in order that I might work in a shipyard. All I know is what I have read in the newspapers.

I have been married ten years and have a mother and a crippled sister to look after. There are a couple of brothers, but my mother does not depend on what they give her. For my sister I always send home $25 a month. All this talk about my joining the shipyard making me unpopular after the war, I want to say that I am not going back. I have taken up shipbuilding and am going to stick to it.

People have a misconception about what I have made out of baseball. I haven't made as much as they think I have. What I earn here is my only income.[25]

Jackson's case was "a complex one," Robbins wrote. "It is subject for keen debate and those on the soap boxes hold divergent views."[26] Almost nobody, though, believed that Jackson was through with baseball.

"There is going to be enough done around the shipyards to keep Joe busy for quite a while, and maybe he will have time to change his mind," *Daily News* columnist David Rotroff wrote.[27] *Collyer's Eye* said the hole the slugger had left in the White Sox lineup was "a good example of what war times can do to a baseball club."[28]

Jackson spoke well of Rowland, who in turn said little about his outfielder except to wish him good luck. Early Wednesday morning, the skipper got a long-distance call from Jackson at Washington, asking for someone to send him his game shoes. "He told the boss he thought he was doing the right thing and turning painter to protect his family," the *Tribune* said.[29]

Shoeless Joe felt he couldn't exchange his $6,000 White Sox salary (arguably a poor deal) for only thirty dollars a month as an army private. His Harlan deal was never revealed, but shipyards and steel mills paid well, and athletes earned more than the base salary.

"Ball players on East Coast shipyard teams . . . did well financially, earning as much as $500.00 a week," the Seymours wrote long afterward.[30] But in his jump to the shipyard Jackson ignored a common American belief that sports icons also should be military heroes, regardless of circumstances.

The suddenness of Joe's departure and his lack of candor beforehand exposed him to an avalanche of criticism. Commy and Rowland uncharacteristically kept mum, but Ban Johnson didn't hesitate to express deep unhappiness over Jackson's desertion, if without naming him directly. The prexy said his circuit didn't want to impugn any player who left the diamond for industry and added that some had patriotic motives for doing so.

"But if there are any of them who are in class 1A, I hope Provost General [Enoch] Crowder yanks them from the shipyards and steel works by the coat collar and places them in cantonments to prepare for future events on the western front," Johnson sputtered. The AL had lost seventy men to draft or enlistment, Ban added, expected to lose others, and "does not approve of players trying to evade military service. Some of them apparently have been badly advised."[31]

Fans in every part of America could see good industrial baseball in 1918. Mills and shipyards fielded seventy-four teams in thirteen circuits, providing much-needed recreation and entertainment for wartime workers. Although many scribes derived the circuits as "paint and putty leagues," the games proved popular with employees and outsiders and were often covered on local sports pages.

Every industrial league attracted professional players, sometimes in large numbers. Critics called the Bethlehem Steel League the "Steal League" for its aggressiveness in recruiting Major Leaguers. Criticism, complaints, and investigations mounted throughout the summer, with the first star to jump to a paint and putty club taking more heat than anyone.

Washington Times sportswriter Louis A. Dougher slapped Jackson with a nickname that stung and stuck: "Joe the Painter."[32] Another scribe slammed the star in prose: "Joe Jackson very hurriedly a shipbuilder became when they asked him to head toward battlefield fame, and thus he pointed the way for others to tread, if they, too, were afraid to go over there and crack the Hun head."[33]

A *Boston Herald* columnist thought the Emergency Fleet Corporation shouldn't allow Jackson's employment when the army was about to summon him. "It has too much the look of ducking duty on the part of the athlete and too much the aspect of favoritism on the part of the shipping board, or of some official under the jurisdiction of that board," he wrote.[34] The *Chicago Tribune* didn't think highly of Joe's action either.

"Joe Jackson, until recently of the White Sox ball team, besides possessing extraordinary athletic talents, is a man of unusual physical development," the *Trib* editorialized. "Presumably he would make an excellent fighting man. But it appears that Mr. Jackson would prefer not to fight."[35] At least one reader agreed with that assessment.

"After this vaunted athlete and physical giant had been put in class 1 of the draft—so the newspapers again report—he gets out of danger by getting a job as a painter in a shipbuilding plant," the Chicagoan wrote. "Why cannot any draft man in class 1 follow the example of Jackson and keep out of danger, and out of the army, at the same time?"[36]

The ex-Sox outfielder reported for work at the shipyard and tried to keep his head down. Continuing uncertainty about his draft status hung over his head. Joe said he'd spoken with a marine recruiter but denied he'd signed up as a devil dog.

"Jackson is in charge of a bolting-up gang on a ship that is to be floated at the Harlan plant this week," a Wilmington paper said his second week on the job, contradicting earlier reports about painting.[37] "Yea, and now he is known as a bolter by his fellow-workmen," a Pennsylvania sports editor sniped.[38]

It remained far from clear whether Shoeless Joe's employment would result in a draft exemption. The army might yet call, with the full weight of the Selective Service, the war department, and public opinion behind it.

"In the case of Jackson he has not received any word from his draft board to report for service," a Wilmington paper said. "He has heard the rumors to the contrary and last night made efforts to learn if such demands had been made for him, but failed to ascertain anything definite."[39]

The local draft board in Greenville received no appeal. People close to Jackson believed they knew why he hadn't filed one. They made a rare public admission about the slugger's limitations.

"Jackson can neither read nor write, and his friends say that he made no attempt to appeal from the decision of his local board, being totally ignorant of the usual method of procedure," a wire report said.[40] The board issued an order May 18 for Jackson to report immediately for army service.

"Large groups of men are being sent to camp at frequent intervals by Local Board No. 2, and it is probable that the famous baseball player will go with one of the next few groups to be sent off," a Greenville paper said.[41] Editor Bob Maxwell was sharply critical of Jackson and called the report "the most pleasant piece of news we have seen for some time. . . . In other words, Joe has no chance to work that old stall regarding 'war work,' and his new job is spurious."[42]

Ironically, the army wouldn't have accepted someone who couldn't read before America entered the war. A childhood spent working in textile factories had left Jackson no time to get an education, a plight that wasn't unusual where he came from. "The number of illiterate men of draft age in South Carolina is positively appalling," the state's Federation of Women's Clubs said.[43] Many parts of the country weren't much better.

Jackson might legitimately have feared that his inability to read orders or instructions would endanger himself or others in the army. But the company employing him now wasn't some little mom-and-pop outfit turning army belt buckles or collar insignia, either. It was an enormous, occasionally dangerous industrial concern. The Harlan yard was a subsidiary of Bethlehem Steel that built naval and cargo ships urgently needed for the war effort.

Charles M. Schwab had headed Bethlehem until April, when President Wilson appointed him general director of the Emergency Fleet Corporation. The shipyard valued Jackson both as a worker and a weekend player on one of its ball clubs. "The Wilmington concern wants to keep Jackson and probably will put up a fight for his services," Robbins wrote.[44] South Carolina officials stood no chance against such powerful forces.

The ex-Sox outfielder "has been certified to the local draft exemption board, which had ordered him to report for military duty, as being in the employ of the Emergency Fleet Corporation," a wire service reported May 21. "This certificate stays the order of the local board calling Jackson and places him in the classification of necessary employes [sic]. As he is employed in shipbuilding on the Delaware, he probably will not be subject to the draft."[45] In fact, Jackson would work at Harlan for the rest of the war.

Prospects for the White Sox again winning the pennant in 1918—assuming there was a pennant to be won—grew even dimmer. Urban Faber was leaving too. He'd passed his draft physical in April but didn't expect to be called right away.

"While undergoing the test, 'Red' said the medical sharps never looked at his feet, and he has one flat wheel, deflated in a jumping contest at Cascade, Ia., many years ago," the *Examiner* joked. "Maybe the doctor who conducted the examination was present at the world's series game, the one in which 'Red' stole third base while Weaver was occupying that bag."[46]

Faber announced June 4 that he wouldn't wait to be drafted. He would instead enlist in the navy and join Chief Chouinard's team at Great Lakes. Commy congratulated his hurler, as he had Jim Scott, and kept any misgivings to himself. A week later, pitcher Lefty Williams and catcher Byrd Lynn contributed to the mounting chaos by telling the Sox magnate they were leaving too—not to enlist, but to join Jackson at the Harlan plant.

"Williams was a chum and inseparable companion of Joe Jackson and no doubt Joe had much to do with influencing this pair to join him in the Wilmington ship yards," the *Daily News* said June 11.[47] The two men were married and Lynn had two children. Both faced the same decision Jackson had. This time, however, the Old Roman exploded. He ordered the pair to hand in their uniforms and get out, telling the *Chicago Tribune* in a fury:

> I don't consider them fit to play on my ball club. I would gladly lose my whole team if the players wished to do their duty to their country, as hundreds of thousands of other young men are doing, by entering the army or the navy, but I hate to see any ball players, particularly my own, go to shipyards to escape military service.
>
> There can be no other reason for their act, as they cannot honestly earn as much building ships as they can playing ball.
>
> I don't want to be considered unpatriotic. I had the greatest respect for Jim Scott when he quit the team last summer to become an officer. When Urban Faber gave up baseball to join the navy I congratulated him and was glad of it, although mighty sorry to lose him.
>
> I feel the same about any other players who have or who may quit my team to serve their country.[48]

"By inducing two of his pals to join him, Joe Jackson probably thinks he has squared accounts for all the mean things said about him when he 'jumped' to the painter's league," the *Tribune* said.⁴⁹ The paper later added, "There was an unconfirmed report that Comiskey ordered the uniforms disinfected for fear some of the Schwab germs which infected Jackson, Williams and Lynn might have crept into the other players' suits."⁵⁰

"These are dark and stormy days for the good ship 'White Sox,'" Robbins observed in the *Daily News*. "She is being tossed and battered around by the angry waves and dark, foreboding clouds are discerned in the offing. . . . Now his champion ball club has suddenly been shattered by enlistments and desertions."⁵¹

The deterioration continued as the Sox dropped a June 24 game in Detroit. "The result shoved the Rowland outfit into the second division," Jimmy Crusinberry wrote, "which is rather humiliating for boys who won world's championship emblems."⁵²

13

Red

Prospects for the Sox or anyone completing the season had dimmed after Provost Marshal General Crowder issued a "work or fight" edict May 23 in Washington. New federal regulations "may require professional base ball players either to engage in some useful occupation or to join the Army," the *Washington Evening Star* had reported. "Base ball players, as well as jockeys, professional golfers and other professional sportsmen . . . will be affected by the regulations if strictly enforced."[1]

Crowder said he'd rule on specific cases once they reached him from local boards. The baseball world "trembled for a while today," the *Chicago Daily News* said. "The interpretation first put on the message was: 'Baseball is ruined for the period of the war.'"[2] Magnates were shocked but found reason for optimism.

"All was confusion among the Chicago players of the Cubs, who are at home, and among the officials of both Chicago clubs," the *Tribune* said the next day. "Until they obtain more definite knowledge of the intentions of Gen. Crowder in issuing his edict . . . they are living in hope that the national game will be counted among the vocations classed as useful."[3]

Charles Comiskey said he would wait for a definitive order but would do anything the government suggested. He also pointed out how much money Major League teams had raised or contributed to the Red Cross and Liberty Loan drives, not to mention the Griffith fund and other war charities. President

Johnson chipped in too, but his response wasn't entirely applauded by Commy or others.

"I do not believe the government has any intention of wiping out baseball altogether." Ban said. He then added, however, that if he'd had his way, "I would close every theatre, ball park and other places of recreation in the country and make the people realize that they are in the most terrible war in the history of the world."[4]

Baseball headed into a period of gloom and uncertainty. Red Faber, at least, knew his future. He was bound for the navy.

Faber had last worked in a 3–2 Memorial Day loss at Cleveland, "and hopes his next battle will be with the enemies of Uncle Sam in the briny deep," the *Daily News* said. "Red is an expert on engines and hopes to run one in chasing down the enemies' craft."[5]

The hurler was nursing a bum shoulder and delayed taking his physical exam, wanting to enter the service in top shape. A newspaper in Cascade explained that he hadn't wanted to be drafted into the army. "His number was likely to be called very soon," the weekly reported, "hence his decision in resigning his position on the pitching staff of the White Sox."[6]

Faber signed his enlistment forms Friday, June 7, and received orders to report a week later. He would enter the navy as a chief yeoman, the same rank as Phil Chouinard. Tuesday afternoon, hours after Williams and Lynn had handed in their flannels, Faber, still a civilian, helped a battalion of sailors hoist the 1917 AL pennant at Comiskey Park.

The Sox hadn't raised their league or championship banners any earlier partly from superstition and partly in hopes of drawing a big home crowd later in the season. Many fans and scribes thought they waited too long. "Let's have a look at those pennants early in June after the White Sox get back from the east," Sy Sanborn had suggested in May. "Perhaps it will change their luck, which has been rotten all this spring."[7]

The Sox accepted his idea, although the attendance of 3,800 wasn't nearly what the club had hoped. Commy's navy-bound pitcher helped hoist the flag, then surprised many by taking the mound to face Boston.

"Red Faber, who already has enlisted at Great Lakes naval station and did not expect to pitch again for the Sox, asked for his uniform when he learned of Manager Rowland's plight for slabmen," Sanborn reported. "What's more, Faber pitched a brilliant game, enabling his pals to lick the Red Sox, 4 to 1."[8] The Sox paused the contest before Red's first at-bat for Eddie Collins to present him with a wristwatch.

South Side fans who now thought they'd surely seen the last of the hurler were mistaken. Faber took the mound for the last time Saturday, June 15, after the navy moved his induction to Monday. "Red offered Boss Rowland his services during the interval, besides expressing a willingness to pitch on any day the White Sox are at home and he has 'shore leave,'" the *Tribune* said.[9]

Faber was serious about throwing again for the Sox again while in the navy. Major Leaguers in khaki or blue did occasionally don flannels for a game or two with their old clubs while on furlough or leave, usually with military permission. The navy would abruptly transfer pitcher and Chief Yeoman Bob Shawkey to a battleship after he skipped service games to take the mound for the Yankees.

Red wouldn't throw again in 1918 for the White Sox, however. The *Tribune* later explained that "the authorities at the Great Lakes Naval station didn't favor it."[10] But he did pitch all nine innings for the Sox today, falling to the Senators for his first loss of the season after four victories.

"You wouldn't blame Yeoman Red Faber, if you saw yesterday's game, if he never came back to pitch another battle for the White Sox the way his old pals treated him in the second chapter of the Washington serial," Sanborn lamented. "He pitched a shutout game, yet Washington won, 3 to 1. All three of the enemy's tallies were handed out by Faber's backers, and they were quite as weak offensively as they were on the defense."[11] The new sailor then reported to the navy June 17.

"Urban Red Faber, White Sox slab ace, and Albert Bernoudy, a nephew of President Comiskey of the Sox, were initiated into the Great Lakes naval station yesterday, the Old Roman accompanying them to the station," the *Tribune* reported.[12] George Robbins added that the owner gave Faber "a kit of valuables" to take to Great Lakes with him. "Commy has a warm spot in his heart for his World's Series hero, also for Scotty [Jim Scott], who volunteered in the Army service."[13]

Urban "Red" Faber, White Sox pitcher, Chief Yeoman, USN. Garrett Price, Great Lakes Bulletin.

The navy made Faber an athletic instructor rather than a clerk. The *Great Lakes Bulletin* scooped the big metro dailies by reporting how the jackies had landed him. Early in the season the Sox star had spied Yeoman Sol Grabiner, brother of Sox secretary Harry Grabiner, sitting in a box seat at Comiskey Park. "See me in the club house after the game," the pitcher said. "I like the looks of that uniform."[14] Red liked what he heard from him about naval life just as much.

"Faber's White Sox pals should see him now in his Chief's uniform," Chicago sportswriter Jimmy Corcoran, also in the navy, wrote after Red's induction. "He's a military masterpiece who will command as much respect here as he did with American League batters."[15]

Anyone entering the services normally first spent time in a "detention camp," to prevent the spread of diseases to thousands of others already in training. "For twenty-one days he'll wash dishes and peel spuds, just like Hank Spreckels from Six Corners, Neb.," Corcoran wrote of Faber.[16]

But after only three days in uniform, Red hit the road to pitch for the jackies. He started versus a team of Sammies from Camp Grant, Illinois, in an exhibition at Palmyra, Wisconsin, west of Milwaukee. He returned to Great Lakes with his throwing hand wrapped in bandages after a fourth-inning line drive nearly broke a finger.

"Chief Faber says it was the first time in his life that he ever tried to spear a line smash with his meat hand," Corcoran wrote. "And the prize at stake was less than in one of our Regimental League games. Can you beat it?"[17] The soldiers clobbered the gobs, 18–8, scoring nine runs in the ninth.

Faber turned out in his new navy uniform two days later, June 22, to lend a hand as the White Sox finally raised their championship banner. He stood at attention with other sailors from Great Lakes and soldiers from Fort Sheridan as Old Glory rose behind right field. The chief then led the Sox to the pole in deep left and "helped hoist to the cool zephyrs the emblem that he had won for Chicago in the historic clash with the Giants last fall," Robbins wrote. "The Cleveland club trailed behind the champions and four companies of jackies from the Great Lakes, led by their band, followed."[18]

A championship banner usually was purple and gold. This wartime version, however, was red-white-and-blue, the white being a stocking. The Sox then spoiled the celebration by losing to the Indians, 4–3. After the game a fan mistook Faber's uniform outside the park and asked him, "Can you get me a taxi right away?"[19]

The loss dropped the South Siders to twenty-seven and twenty-six, one game above .500. Gamblers figured the odds of them winning the AL pennant were now one-to-four. "To grouchitis—a sort of mental mumps—is attributed the sorry showing of the champions," *Collyer's Eye* said. "The players are sore on the management, disgruntled over the failure of Kid Gleason to return and there is discord among the players."[20]

The feeling at Great Lakes was exactly the opposite. Once his injured digit mended, Chief Faber became the cornerstone of a tremendous baseball team. Corcoran later wrote that the station had enough stars for two clubs, "and it has taken the expert judgment of Manager Chouinard to select the best nine men for the representative station team. He has had nearly ten years league baseball experience so the sailor rooters undoubtedly will approve his selections."[21]

The bluejackets definitely did approve them. With Chouinard both managing and playing, the Great Lakes nine began dominating their service, semi-pro, and industrial opponents.

While his hand healed, Chief Faber inspected the navy athletic field under construction, surprised to find so handsome a facility at a military station. "Why, this diamond is fully 100 per cent better than I had imagined it would be," he said. "I have played in every park in the American League and in some of the homes of the National League clubs, and I really believe that this field is as good as any new diamond I have ever seen."[22]

"With 'Red' Faber on the hurling mound and the personnel of the classy Station machine unchanged," the *Great Lakes Bulletin* said, "Surgeon Kaufman believes the bluejacketed tossers could give the big league fellows a regular fight from start to finish and he even admits harboring a wee bit of hope that our sailors would be returned winners."[23] Faber missed five weeks with his bad hand before returning July 25 to face the Naval Auxiliary Reserve Officers' Training School from Municipal Pier, Chicago.

The opposing pitcher on the new field was ex-Brooklyn pitcher Jeff Pfeffer. A week earlier Pfeffer had rejoined the Dodgers for an afternoon on the North Side and two-hit the Cubs for a 2–0 victory. Faber got off to a rough start this afternoon, walking two batters and hitting another with one out in the first inning. "'Red' tightened up, however, and brought the 10,000 fans to their feet by whiffing [two] with some of the prettiest hooks seen this year," the Great Lakes paper said.[24] The *Tribune* added that Faber "held the embryo officers to five hits during the seven innings he worked," during the 7–0 Great Lakes win.[25]

Scribes everywhere appreciated the brand of ball that service teams were capable of playing, especially with the future of the Major Leagues so uncertain. "Fans want and need baseball more in time of war than in time of peace," Robbins wrote the following week. He added that if the big leagues "fail to grasp their golden chance to give the fans some brand of baseball service teams will step in and take their place."[26]

Chicago fans eagerly awaited a three-game series between Chouinard's jackies and the Atlantic Fleet team slated to begin Saturday, August 3. Thanks largely to the disbandment of Chief Jack Barry's excellent team in Boston, the eastern club now included Major Leaguers Walter "Rabbit" Maranville, Del Gainer, and Lawton "Whitey" Witt.

Great Lakes had defeated the Atlantic club back east, 2–0, under a security blackout Independence Day, reports of the game emerging only later. Game One of the big new series was also the formal inauguration of Great Lakes' stadium. Faber opposed Dick Durning, who'd briefly pitched for Brooklyn earlier this season and last.

Over 13,000 sailors cheered the game on an afternoon when the White Sox drew barely one-third as many while splitting a doubleheader with the

Athletics on the South Side. Faber "came through with high honors after his mates turned defeat into victory by a five tally rally in the sixth round," the *Tribune* said of the 6–2 Great Lakes win.[27]

The Atlantic boys evened the series Sunday with an 8–7 win before a navy crowd of nearly 15,000, Maranville and Witt both smacking triples. The Great Lakes loss set up a rubber match Monday, August 5, in a benefit game on the North Side. "Why worry whether or not the majors play a world's series?" the *Daily News* asked. "If it's championship baseball you want, just hop a car and journey up to the Cubs park this afternoon."[28]

The fleet once again started Durning. Great Lakes sent out a hurler once drafted by the New York Giants. His name, appropriately, was John Paul Jones. This Jones did give up the ship, however, and soon handed the ball to Faber in relief.

"John Paul Jones struck a heavy swell when he started and in the second his periscope disappeared, when Red Faber injected his world series smile into the battle," the *Great Lakes Bulletin* said. "After that there was nothing to do, but for the Navy Relief Society to count the receipts."[29] Chouinard's nine won easily, 11–6.

"These contests are of no small importance," Faber's hometown weekly newspaper observed of the series, "as most of the men are former major league players, now enlisted men."[30] The *Tribune* expressed disappointment at the crowd size, only about 7,000, but added, "The result gives Great Lakes undisputed possession of the championship of the east and middle west. It might be called the championship of the entire United States navy, but out at Mare island in San Francisco bay they have a nine of ex-major leaguers that rates too highly to be passed without consideration."[31]

Following his wins over the fleet, Faber briefly entered a navy hospital suffering from a heat-related illness. Lingering weakness might have accounted for his 2–1 loss August 10 to the Camp Grant nine behind Pittsburgh Pirate hurler Hal Carlson. The ex-Sox star recovered his form, twice defeating the formidable Fairbanks-Morse industrial team later that month at Beloit, Wisconsin. The Cubs then provided what the White Sox had promised but hadn't delivered, an exhibition game at the station's new park, August 27.

"The game was attended by so many jackies you could not count them," Sanborn marveled. "The new stands were packed to overflowing and the field was surrounded by sailors in white many rows deep."[32] The station newspaper estimated the crowd at 20,000. "The Great Lakes team ought to be proud of a following like that," Cub manager Fred Mitchell said. "I wish we had a crowd so full of enthusiasm to follow us around all year. It would make an immense difference in the work of the club."[33] Faber, however, was again off form and lost to Cub starter Phillip "Shufflin' Phil" Douglas, 5–0.

In mid-September, the Great Lakes aggregation traveled to Rock Island, Illinois, to take on Rock Island Arsenal. "When Faber marched out to the mound the crowd cheered, someone in the crowd then yelled, 'hurl 'em like you'll sink the subs in a few more months.'"[34] The locals played a good game but fell to Red and the jackies in ten innings, 3–2.

Faber "may pitch in another world's series before snow flies," Robbins wrote in early October. "The games will be for the championship of the United States navy, which means the 'naval baseball championship of the world.'"[35] The expected opponent was Mare Island under Duffy Lewis. But the Spanish Influenza pandemic then sweeping the world halted baseball both at Great Lakes and across the navy.

Faber took charge of the station athletic storeroom from Sol Grabiner and awaited new orders. Later that month, he climbed into flannels to pitch a couple of Sunday games for the Garden City semipro team, winning one and losing one. The armistice signed November 11 in France changed whatever subsequent plans the navy had for him.

"Red was about to leave the Great Lakes on a grand submarine hunt and was given a short furlough to visit his folks at Cascade, Ia., before his departure to sea," a Boston paper said. "Then came the blowup of the whole Kaiser works and now Red is thinking of home and major league baseball."[36]

The chief yeoman pitched in nine games during his time at Great Lakes, winning six and losing three. Chouinard's club triumphed in thirty of thirty-eight contests, at one point winning thirteen in a row. "Faber was the mainstay hurler of the 1918 'Varsity' baseball team and holds the same distinction on the White Sox pitching staff," the *Great Lakes Bulletin* said. "He twirled that sort of high class ball for the Station nine that he has pitched for the Hose de Comiskey in the past several seasons."[37] His club's shining season was no small accomplishment.

"The colossal system provided for the greatest naval team at the greatest naval station," *Spalding's Official Base Ball Guide* declared. Great Lakes athletics "permitted hundreds of youths to participate in play, and it entertained thousands of Bluejackets while they were training for 'the big job.'"[38]

14

Hap

Stormy baseball seas had grown steeper for the White Sox since June. Disheartened fans sometimes cheered louder for visiting players than for their own. Many were especially glad to see forty-one-year-old Washington coach Nicholas Altrock at the South Side park June 16. Known now mostly for his antics along the lines, "Old Uncle Nick" had won twenty games for the champion Sox back in 1906. The southpaw had appeared in only seven games in recent years, none during the past two seasons. But he took the mound Sunday for his second appearance of the month for the hard-pressed Senators.

"Until Manager Griffith roiled the fans by his [Cicotte] shine ball kick the crowd was rooting harder for Washington than for the Sox which was a great demonstration of affection for Altrock," the *Tribune* said. "After that kick the majority of the rooters were for the Sox."[1] Sy Sanborn added, "Some of them didn't know whether to be glad or sorry that Chicago beat Washington, 3 to 0."[2]

Denman Thompson in the *Washington Star* said interest in South Side baseball had fallen far below normal, with gate receipts down by about half. He mentioned as factors the drain of young male fans into the armed forces and the club's recent poor play. Unseasonable cold had greatly reduced the crowd Friday too. "But Saturday, with good weather, barely 9,000 turned out, and yesterday, warm and clear, but a few more than 10,000 paid their way into the park," Thompson wrote. "Last season and prior to that on any Saturday or

Sunday there would be 15,000 or 18,000, and not infrequently nearly 25,000, in the stands."[3]

The scribe didn't mention another factor perhaps keeping crowds away. Fans simply didn't know if other Sox players might soon jump to Delaware and join Jackson, Williams, and Lynn in the Harlan shipyard. Some surely wondered about Oscar Felsch, who'd patrolled the outer gardens beside Shoeless Joe.

Oscar "Happy" Felsch, White Sox outfielder. Courtesy of Library of Congress.

The popular centerfielder had been reared fewer than a hundred miles north of Chicago, on Milwaukee's working-class north side, one of twelve children of German immigrant parents. "Felsch's easygoing nature and wonderful smile made the family nickname 'Happy' a perfect fit," writes his SABR biographer, Jim Nitz.[4] Felsch was unhappy now, though, as the White Sox continued to disintegrate. He abruptly joined the exodus July 1, his departure apparently hinging on the implementation of the work-or-fight rule that day.

"Many believe that it was fear that he would be classed as a nonessential, as one engaged in a nonproductive vocation, that caused Happy Felsch to administer the crowning, the crushing blow to the hopes of the White Sox by deserting without a moment's notice," sportswriter Bill Bailey wrote in the *Chicago Evening American*.[5] Felsch wasn't jumping to the Wilmington shipyard, though, but to the nearer and safer Milwaukee Gas Light Company.

"His going came as a surprise to the baseball world, no intimation of his intention having circulated about," Malcolm MacLean wrote in the *Chicago Evening Post*.[6] Besides working for the gas company, Hap planned to suit up Sundays and holidays for the Kosciusko club in Wisconsin's four-team, semipro Lake Shore League. Rowland delivered the bad news at the South Side park.

"Well, I hope he hits better in that league than he has been doing in ours for the last month," Commy snapped, "and I hope he has his mind on his work."[7] But he was more mystified than angry, telling his manager that Felsch hadn't complained about his contract.

"When players get those foolish ideas in their heads I don't care to talk to them," the Sox owner said. "I thought I was dealing with members of a world champion club, not members of a kindergarten."[8] Commy wasn't entirely surprised, however.

"It has been apparent Felsch has been worrying for some time, for he hasn't been playing his regular game at all," he added. "He looked like one of the greatest a year ago, but something has been on his mind for the last few weeks. At least his mind wasn't on the ball game and he wasn't doing us any good."[9]

The outfielder's actions baffled even papers in his hometown, where they knew him best. "Hap, it will be remembered, left the Sox flat last summer under mysterious circumstances which never have been cleared up because of the silence maintained by both sides," the *Milwaukee Evening Sentinel* said months later.[10] Commy's comments to the *Tribune* around the same time didn't go much further toward unraveling the story.

"Felsch was promised an additional amount if he would refrain from drinking, and although he violated this agreement, and so admitted himself, nevertheless he received the additional amount," the Old Roman said. "When Felsch left the White Sox on July 1, the only reason, as he is supposed to have said, was due to some trouble that he had with Eddie Collins. After he left he conferred with a club official and gave no reason for leaving, but promised to return, and gave his word to that effect, but his word did not hold."[11]

An article published in several Wisconsin newspapers July 3 offered one plausible explanation for Felsch's defection. Hap had been "discontented ever since he took the trip down south to visit his brother, who was severely injured in the army," the report said. "The Sox owners frowned upon the idea of letting Hap go, it is said, but in spite of this, he took leave just the same. When he returned to the club, the Sox management severely reprimanded him for his act, and this, it is claimed, started the trouble, for things were made unpleasant for him since that time."[12]

The problem with this scenario was that some people didn't entirely believe Felsch's account of visiting his injured brother. Reports in Milwaukee said that neither the White Sox nor his family had known Felsch's whereabouts after he'd left for Texas. The player disappeared "as absolutely as if the earth had opened up and swallowed him," according to a local column. "It seems that brother Felsch was simply evidencing and enjoying his rights as star performer. He figured that he had to get away a little while to see his brother and naturally he figured that a little mystery about the matter would not hurt his reputation as a star performer."[13]

Collyer's Eye in Chicago, however, attributed the affair to the continued absence of Kid Gleason. "Jackson quit because like all great and near-great artists he has the 'artistic temperament' and Felsch quit because with no Gleason to kid him and praise him he deteriorated into his natural class," the

Eye said, "which, as shown by his record this year, is a mere ordinary fielder and a natural .260 batter."[14]

Commy took no legal action to retain his wayward player. Hap cobbled together a reasonable living in his hometown, but the shift still clearly cost him.

"Felsch, working for the gas company in Milwaukee, will receive $125 a month, and in addition plans to add $200 [$50 per game] to his income by playing the national game on Sundays," Bailey reported.[15] Hap later told a local paper he had no intention of jumping to the Steel League but didn't plan to rejoin the White Sox either. "He is willing to return to the American league, but wants to be traded to some club other than Comiskey's organization."[16]

Although he didn't join a shipyard team himself, Felsch did play against the Manitowoc Shipbuilders in the Lake Shore circuit. It's unclear whether working for a public utility exempted him from the draft; Commy said it didn't. Industrial clubs tried to lure Hap away with wartime employment, but he stayed put and was neither drafted nor warned to change jobs. The Sox, meanwhile, immediately felt the effects of his jump.

"Felsch isn't the only star who has had the work or fight order upon his mind," Bailey wrote. "Officials of the St. Louis Browns yesterday declared that their men didn't know whether they were playing baseball or checkers. This may be taken with a grain of salt, since they stepped upon the field at Comiskey Park and humbled and humiliated the world's champions in both games of a [July 1] double header."[17]

The season was half over, and the *Daily News* figured the Sox had lost eight players: Felsch to Milwaukee; Jackson, Williams, and Lynn to Harlan; Faber to Great Lakes; and little used first sacker Ted Jourdan, rookie catcher George Lees, and rookie infielder and pinch hitter William "Pat" Hardgrove to the army. With only Ray Schalk left to work behind the plate, Rowland badly needed another catcher. Pants remembered his seasons managing in the Illinois-Indiana-Iowa League and his pal Otto Jacobs.

Jacobs had never made the Majors, but in Rowland's opinion was the best backstop the Three-I circuit had seen in years. He was working as a bricklayer now and playing semipro ball for a club in Joliet, Illinois. When Rowland tracked him down the twenty-nine-year-old catcher said he wasn't interested in signing with the Sox.

"We need you down on the south side and you'll pull us out of a hole, old man," the skipper persisted. "Just lay aside the trowel and come down and talk turkey to Mr. Comiskey." Jacobs eventually gave in. "Well, Clarence, if you need me that bad I'll go along and give you the best there is in me," he promised his pal. Before his first game Jacobs amazed Sox veterans by leaping up when the skipper asked for a volunteer to coach first base. "Go on out there," Rowland said, "you're just the man I need, and don't fail to help us put one over."[18]

The signing proved especially wise a month later when Schalk hurt his throwing hand. Jacobs would catch twenty-one games altogether and pinch hit in eight more. The sole concern, as with so many players, was his military status. "Otto Jacobs has received word from his draft board in Chicago to appear and show why he should not be placed in class 1," the *Tribune* said in mid-July. "As he has a wife and two children, it probably is some matter of minor importance to fix up."[19]

Without Capt. Jim Scott or jumper Lefty Williams, Rowland also had pitching woes. He relied more than he'd have liked on rookie Frank Shellenback, a tall Californian out of Hollywood High and Santa Clara University. The righthander was only nineteen, under the draft age. Youth was an asset to any team now, especially since "Shelly" also could play in the outfield. He would end the season with a 2.66 ERA and nine wins versus a dozen losses.

The club tried to bolster the staff further in July by acquiring hurler John Pincus "Jack" Quinn, who'd first played in the big leagues in 1909. He'd been pitching for the Vernon Tigers when the PCL closed its gates that summer. The shuttering was no surprise; of the ten minor circuits that had begun play that year, only the reorganized International League completed its schedule. Quinn's signing seemed routine for a wartime season, but would lead to the end of Commy's long relationship with Ban Johnson.

"Quinn was released by the Los Angeles club, and as his home is in Chicago, he came here," Jimmy Crusinberry wrote. "Immediately he was wanted by the Sox to finish the season and came to terms with the south side boss. He followed by turning out some excellent slab work."[20]

The pitcher reported August 1 and won five of the six games he pitched, helpful to the struggling Sox. Commy thought he could dicker with Vernon to keep Quinn into 1919, but August 24 the National Commission awarded him instead to the Yankees, under circumstances it called "peculiar and unfortunate."[21] Unable to use his hurler again, Rowland sent him home to Chicago. The Sox owner was outraged.

Commy believed he'd received a go-ahead for the Quinn deal from Cincinnati Reds president August "Garry" Herrmann, one of the commission's three members. Johnson was another member, and Comiskey blamed him for the reversal. "Johnson's actions in the matter can only be attributed to a desire to take advantage of the opportunity to inflict injury upon the Chicago club," Commy wrote years later, "and at the same time curry favor with the New York owners."[22]

The dispute hinged on timing. The commission had ruled earlier that players could sign elsewhere if a minor league shut down, but they would revert to their original clubs once play resumed after the war. There was a complication in the Quinn case, however. The Vernon and Los Angeles clubs had scheduled a championship series after the PCL folded, and Vernon's owner had notified the commission that he retained rights to his players until play concluded.

"This extension of the season meant that Quinn was still a member of the Tigers on July 18, when the White Sox signed him—and not a free agent,"

Quinn biographers Lyle Spatz and Steve Steinberg explain. "That same day the New York Yankees reached terms to acquire Quinn directly from [the] Vernon owner."²³

The commission acknowledged that in following its advice Commy "probably may have lost the opportunity to deal direct with the club and thus may have secured the player's release previous to the time that the New York club commenced to negotiate for him." Quoting this language years later, White Sox historian Warren Brown called the ruling "some kind of a record for confused expression." He added that it constituted "the final destructive blow to any hope of a reconciliation between Comiskey and Johnson."²⁴

Many sportswriters and owners thought the commission nonetheless had reached a sound business decision. Quinn would have preferred staying with the Sox but felt obligated to negotiate with New York instead. Comiskey cited new evidence in filing an appeal to the ruling at the end of January 1919. The commission denied it. "Rejection of the appeal was based on the national commission rule that an appeal must be taken within ten days after the original finding," the *Tribune* said.²⁵ The AL president realized the cost of the quarrel.

"Charlie Comiskey, starting out as my friend, had become my enemy," Johnson wrote long afterward. "Many explanations have been offered by outsiders. . . . The real cause of the break, however, was a decision of the National Commission in the case of Pitcher Jack Quinn. Comiskey felt that he was entitled to the player and never forgave me for refusing to side with him."²⁶

Hap Felsch meanwhile had kept his head down in Milwaukee. He'd made news only on the diamond, starring for the Kosciuskos. With Philadelphia Phillies first baseman Fred Luderus, he played a couple of games in mid-September for a squad called the Allprofessionals [*sic*]. A month later the two big leaguers took an All-Star team to face the Albany Park semipro club in Chicago.

"Hap Felsch, who made his first appearance in the Windy city [*sic*] since quitting the White Sox in midseason last summer, was the star of the game," the *Milwaukee Sentinel* said of the 13–1 walloping.[27] The Chicago papers largely ignored him, the *Daily News* covering the game and his return in a sentence: "Happy Felsch's All-Stars from Milwaukee found the going easy against Albany Park."[28]

The club canceled the rest of its schedule because of the influenza pandemic. The *Tribune* reported in December 1918 that Felsch was making a bundle through a monopoly of the Christmas tree market on Milwaukee's North Side and wasn't worrying about ever again playing Major League ball.

"If the Sox don't want me I can make about as much on part time working in the big games of the Lake Shore league," Hap said. "So I should worry what Comiskey says.'"[29]

15

Cocky

The White Sox were two games below .500 at thirty and thirty-two when Hap Felsch quit the club July 1. That afternoon Danforth and Benz lost a doubleheader on the South Side to the Browns, dropping Commy's boys into sixth place in the American League. The timing was lost on no one.

"On the first day when a fellow was supposed to work or fight," Jimmy Crusinberry wrote, "the White Sox players found themselves unable to do either."[1] Five Canadian troops sat among fans in the grandstand and saw the dual losses. Four of the Tommies were missing an arm and the other a leg. Capt. Jim Scott, on his way back to Washington state from Camp Perry, watched his old teammates lose too. Only 4,000 others turned out for the twin bill.

"It's quite possible many worked six hours during the morning and others expected to work all night," the *Tribune* said.[2] Attendance stayed abysmal. A doubleheader with the Tigers on the Fourth of July drew only about 14,000 as the afternoon threatened rain. Things got worse July 19 when Secretary of War Newton D. Baker sent shockwaves through both Major Leagues by ruling that baseball was a nonessential occupation during wartime. "I have decided that the work or fight regulations include baseball," Baker said.[3] Many Sox feared their season might be over.

"Some hinted they rather expected an unfavorable decision regarding baseball, and had made preparations for jobs in essential work before starting on this trip," the *Tribune* said.[4] The paper thought Eddie Collins and Buck Weaver had already made decisions but weren't yet ready to announce them.

The team left Philadelphia for Washington and a four-game series with the Griffmen. As the train huffed past shipyards along the way, the *Tribune* said, players "gazed interestedly at hundreds of men with saws and hammers and paint brushes at work on some big boats."[5] The timetable for implementing the work-or-fight order remained unclear, giving hope to Ban Johnson and others that they might keep the game going a while longer. Clark Griffith and his club president met Secretary Baker and Provost Marshal General Crowder July 20 to seek a compromise, but uncertainty dragged on.

"Tip O'Neill, acting traveling secretary of the White Sox, was much relieved when Manager Rowland received word to keep on playing ball until notified to quit," the *Daily News* said two days later. "Tip wants to see the boys keep on playing."[6]

"Play in the American league is going right along as if nothing had happened," Rowland told his Sox in the lobby of their hotel that evening. "We had just been told that baseball was a dead issue," Nemo Leibold piped up. "It's very much alive—the league is going right on through the season," the skipper assured him.[7]

Rowland was partially correct. Secretary Baker later decided that the work-or-fight rule would apply to ballplayers starting September 1—which effectively meant the third, since September 2 was Labor Day. "This is extremely favorable," Commy said July 26, as fans cheered the news while the Pale Hose beat the Red Sox, 7–2, at Comiskey Park. "It gives us time to arrange our affairs, plan for a shorter schedule and probably put on a world's series. The government has made a sensible concession."[8]

Not everyone agreed, and Baker's announcement set off a new round of questions and angst. The National League wanted to play until September 1, although it was unclear whether a World Series would then be possible. Ban Johnson suggested August 20 as the last day of the season, with the World Series to follow and end before the deadline. Commy and Griffith agreed with the NL, opposing their president.

The Sox and Senators played another series in Chicago the last three days of July and the first of August. Griffith told scribes there that the notion of shutting down on the twentieth was foolish. He added that the government wasn't against baseball or trying to shut it down. "Secretary of War Baker simply got Sept. 1 as the day on which those in the deferred classifications would have to seek other occupations," Griff said. "They are given seven days in which to make all arrangements."[9]

"The fans in the east want baseball and need it," Commy added, likewise bucking a shorter schedule. "There is where we are drawing the crowds. The many government plants there employ thousands of men, many of whom work nights. We are drawing the largest crowds in several years in the east and we'll give the east its part of the schedule just as it was originally mapped out."[10] Not everyone agreed, even in Chicago.

"It was expected that the war department's reprieve to Sept. 1 would tend to restore baseball with the fans and draw reasonably fair crowds for the balance of the races," Johnny Alcock wrote in the *Tribune*. "Such has not been the case. On the contrary, the attendance appears to be dropping rather than improving. Under such conditions, the sooner the magnates toss up the sponge the smaller will be their losses."[11]

Johnson attended the July 30 game on the South Side as the sportswriters squabbled over the possible August 20 shutdown. He sat talking with Commy, "probably regarding the plans for the remainder of the season," according to the *Tribune*.[12]

All the AL magnates then met August 3 at the Hollenden Hotel in Cleveland. Pittsburgh Pirates owner Barney Dreyfuss also attended, representing the National League. Dreyfuss said his circuit wasn't interested in playing a World Series before September 2. Commy and Griffith agreed, but the AL president believed the other six clubs backed his plan for an earlier closure. He was mistaken. The Red Sox and another club, thought to be the Yankees, joined the Sox and Senators in supporting the NL, leaving Johnson short of a majority.

"American league club owners in special session here today defied the wishes of President B. B. Johnson by voting to continue their playing season through Labor day and to play a world series after that date unless the war department interferes," the *Tribune* reported from Ohio.[13] The *Trib* and many other papers also printed a statement sharply critical of Johnson, attributed to Commy, Griff, and Red Sox owner Harry Frazee.

"He has tried to close our gates several times this season, but from now on he is through spending our money," the document said. "From now on, the club owners are going to run the American league.... We have nothing against him personally, but from now on we intend to take a hand in the management of the league. His rule or ruin policy is shelved."[14]

The denunciation shocked many and offended some. Ed Bang of the *Cleveland News* thought the South Sider had scuttled Ban's plan so his Sox could make the East Coast swing that otherwise they would have abandoned.

"Commy always did and always will like the mazuma and he sees a chance to rake in a few more shekels, down east," Bang wrote.[15] "In the ultimate pinch Ban Johnson proved bigger and braver than those who have sat at his feet but now have his shoulders pinned to the mat," Louis Lee Arms added in the *New York Tribune*.[16] The rebellion damaged the AL prexy's power within his circuit.

"It would not be surprising if Johnson was deposed as head of his league before another year," the *New York Times* speculated. "Johnson, it is stated, has wanted to get out of baseball to go into another business for some time."[17] Ban left Cleveland to spend several days in Indiana before going home to Chicago. He arrived to find letters waiting from Comiskey and Griffith in which they denied signing the inflammatory declaration. That left Frazee as the probable author.

"I never saw any such statement," Commy insisted. "I doubt if there was any such statement. All my talking was done behind closed doors at the meeting. ... We decided to go through till [sic] Sept. 2, then play the world's series. That's all I had to do with the matter."[18] But Hugh Fullerton wrote that Griffith, at least, *had* attacked Johnson. Fullerton also alluded to evidence that "all three club owners did criticize Johnson violently in the hearing of reputable witnesses."[19] Others defended Commy.

"Comiskey was a game person and a good sportsman," George Robbins later wrote. "He refused to desert the sinking ship. When others wanted to close up shop Commy, in the most impassioned speech of his long and eventful career, insisted on going through to the bitter end and he helped save baseball by keeping the old machinery moving."[20]

A World Series would indeed quickly follow the season's close September 2, with both teams' players granted extra time to comply with Baker's ruling. Commy suffered personally, however, for butting heads with the man who'd once been his friend—and with the Quinn debacle yet to come.

"Since the last feud of many years ago between Comiskey and Johnson, in which Johnson emerged victorious, the American league has been known as the 'happy family,' with Johnson as czar," the *Tribune* reported from Cleveland. "Developments today promise domestic discord in the future, with the first skirmish decided in favor of the rebels."[21]

The Old Roman likely was unhappy long before the AL conclave began. Robbins had written days earlier about indications that Commy was disheartened. "The desertion of Joe Jackson was a hard blow from which he has not recovered even yet," the scribe wrote. "Then the departure of Lynn and Williams followed by the astonishing desertion of Happy Felsch, depriving Rowland of his punch, were hard raps for the Sox owner. The enlistment of Urban Faber in the United States navy deprived him of his world's series hero."[22] Commy found little cause for optimism as the season wound toward its close. His club drew only 10,500 fans for the weekend games July 27–28 with Boston.

"Either Chicago's loyal fans are too busy or have lost interest in the Sox," the *Tribune* said after 4,500 attended Saturday.[23] Despite sunshine and a league-leading opponent, the next day's game drew what the newspaper called "one of the smallest Sunday crowds in ten years at Comiskey park."[24] The White Sox won three of four contests but still trailed the Red Sox by ten and a half games.

"By the end of July the Sox looked more like a club in the Three-I league than a major aggregation," Robbins remembered.[25] The Sox ground through their lengthy homestand with no bump in fan interest. "Gents who now thrill over the stories about the White Sox will find the mortuary columns a dandy substitute," Ring Lardner Sr. said in the *Tribune*.[26] Jimmy Crusinberry shook his head following a doubleheader split with Connie Mack's Athletics the following Saturday.

"It's hard to tell what the Sox and Macks are playing for, but in this instance they did furnish a few thrills to about 5,000 of the 15,000 or more Chicago fans who formerly visited the south side park on Saturday afternoons and cheered themselves hoarse," Crusinberry wrote. "The Macks are trying to get out of last place and the Sox are trying to keep in the lead of the second division, so the incentive for baseball prowess is not of the keenest brand."[27]

Nothing improved during the long road trip that followed. The South Siders split four games at Cleveland, getting drubbed in the last contest August 12.

"The White Sox perpetrated something new in baseball today," the *Tribune* crabbed. "Nothing like it was ever seen before. It is rather difficult of description, being sort of a cross between a farce and a burlesque of the national game."[28] With the 11–2 loss eliminating the Sox from the first division, their star second baseman finally had seen enough.

Edward Trowbridge Collins possessed what SABR biographer Paul Mittermeyer calls "self-confidence and good breeding that at times seemed as though it belonged more in a ballroom than a baseball clubhouse."[29] The assurance led to a nickname, "Cocky." The awful 1918 season hadn't shaken him but it did get him thinking about military service.

The second sacker had considered enlisting the previous summer, around the time that Jim Scott had signed up. Collins was then thirty years old, married with two children, and pulling down a salary most big leaguers only dreamt of earning. The nation's first draft call passed, leaving him and most teammates still civilians, but several times during the 1917 season rumors emerged from the clubhouse that Eddie wanted to join Uncle Sam's forces. No word of this reached fans until the winter after the championship, when wire services had Eddie nearly ready to enlist or enter the army via the draft.

A San Francisco paper in November cited Ban Johnson in reporting that "no less than fifty-six of the major performers, including Eddie Collins . . . , have declared their intention of 'getting into the scrap' before the next [draft] call."[30] Other papers repeated the number, one dispatch even saying that Collins already *had* joined the army.

"I have not enlisted, and my military status is the same as The [Philadelphia] North American described it two Sundays ago," Eddie said, correcting the report. "I am waiting to see what the next draft brings out, and until then I have nothing to say." The article added, "Friends of Collins' say that it is a pretty safe bet that he will join the service."[31]

As Christmas 1917 approached, the AL president reiterated that Collins was indeed considering enlistment. "According to Johnson, Comiskey's star player is most serious in his plan," the *Tribune* warned, "and Johnson said he would not be surprised if Eddie was in some branch of the service within the next few days."[32] The winter passed with no resolution, an indication, perhaps, of how difficult and personal such a decision could be, whether for a clergyman, cobbler, or ballplayer.

The spring and summer of desertions had followed. Crowds were small and losses tough on the South Side. Eddie played into the dog days and saw two more teammates desert the White Sox.

Swede Risberg and Fred McMullin left Chicago the evening of August 7. Both said they were going home to California to join the colors. Their comments were a bit unusual, since both were married and neither was in Class 1 of the draft.

"They haven't formally enlisted with Uncle Sam, yet they intend to do so soon after reaching the coast," the *Tribune* said. "McMullin expects to land with the navy, desiring to be placed at the submarine base at San Pedro, while Risberg hankers for the army and intends to offer himself at the Presidio just outside of San Francisco. . . . Risberg held a baseball coaching position at the army camp out there last winter and has wanted to get back to it all summer."[33]

Commy said he was proud of both men, as he was of every Sox player who'd exchanged flannels for khakis or blues. "As a matter of fact when I saw McMullin and Risberg thought they ought to enlist, I arranged for their reservations to the coast," the magnate added. "I am delighted that the White Sox club was fortunate enough to include men of this caliber."[34]

McMullin hailed from Los Angeles, a Kansan whose family had moved west while he was a teen. He'd worked as a blacksmith's apprentice before playing one game with the Tigers in 1914 then returning to the minors. After landing in Chicago from the PCL in 1916, the capable infielder averaged fewer than seventy games per season for the Sox.

Navy officers expected McMullin to enlist at the sub base. At least one Los Angeles newspaper said he'd already done so. The San Pedro team was stocked with Minor and Major Leaguers and played in the Southern California War Service League, which included military, industrial, and civilian clubs. All reports of McMullin's enlistment were wrong, however.

The *Los Angeles Herald* said late in August that Fred was "busy every day with essential work, and it is doubtful if he will join the Submarine Base for some time."[35] The paper later reported that McMullin was working for the Southern Pacific Company. By late autumn the ex-Sox was covering the infield for the pennant-winning Pasadena Merchants club, playing in the same circuit as the submariners he'd spurned.

Risberg didn't join the armed forces either, or coach any army team as he had a year earlier. Swede instead returned to Northern California and went to work for the Union Iron Works at Alameda, across the bay from San Francisco.

He also played first base for the company team in the area Shipbuilders' League, although few were inclined to compare him to Jackson, Williams, or Lynn.

"Risberg has made a big difference in the entire bunch of players of the Alameda Bethlehem club," the *Oakland Tribune* said. "They all seem to have the spirit the same as Risberg, who always puts pepper into the game."[36] The ex-Sox got too peppery when he then slugged an umpire in late October. He received a roasting from the league's directors but no more, lenient treatment even by paint-and-putty standards. "Shipyard moguls in California don't seem to care much about baseball umpires," Louis Dougher wrote in the *Washington Times*.[37]

The actions of McMullin and Risberg on the West Coast couldn't have pleased Charley Comiskey, although he said nothing. They'd both clearly jumped the South Side club, like the others, no matter their intentions when leaving.

The remaining Sox had been considering their futures too. "As soon as the season's over I intend to get into some line of essential work myself, though I am above draft age," manager Rowland said the day after the pair's departure. "Perhaps congress will pass the new bill before I get back, compelling me to work."[38]

Eddie Collins reached his limit two days later. The big Allied offensives in France wouldn't begin for another month, and the war seemed likely to last a good while yet. Collins told Commy he'd leave the Sox the following Thursday, August 15, at Boston during the last long eastern road trip. The Sox captain wanted to return home to Lansdowne, Pennsylvania, before joining the marines at nearby Philadelphia.

"Collins at first intended to quit with Risberg and McMullin, now on their way to the coast to enter the service of Uncle Sam, but later decided that he owed it to Mr. Comiskey to give him longer notice," Robbins reported. The Sox were playing the Indians, then the Red Sox, "and since both are pennant contenders Collins did not want to display favoritism by playing against the one club and not the other."[39]

Edward "Cocky" Collins, White Sox infielder, Private, USMC. Philadelphia Inquirer.

The White Sox owner again graciously lost a valuable man to the armed forces. "Collins and I talked over the matter for a long time before he left," Commy told writers. "He carries with him my very best wishes. If the rest of the club had acted as Eddie has done instead of running to paint and putty jobs we'd be up there now fighting for the pennant."[40]

"Comiskey insisted that Collins accept a check for as long as he wanted to remain with the club," the *Tribune* added.[41] The rest of the Sox told Rowland they'd stick with the team through the rest of the schedule. "The departure of Eddie Collins to the marines was really welcomed by Rowland," Robbins wrote. "It enabled him to try out some fresh material and helped clear the club of the charge of attempting to dodge the draft."⁴²

General Crowder had ordered draft boards to bar men from enlisting in the navy or marines because the army needed them more. But Collins had beaten the deadline and believed he'd done the right thing. "I didn't feel right when playing, so I just stepped out and enlisted," he said. "At that time I made up my mind to forget all about baseball until the war was over, and then if I still was wanted I would try it again."⁴³ The Sox captain played his last game as announced at Boston.

"Collins, playing with abandon, playing as if there were no tomorrow for him, flashed one of the brilliant games of which he is capable," the *Tribune* said.⁴⁴ Eddie went two-for-four at the plate in a 6–2 Chicago win. The game ended with a grounder to second, which he scooped up and threw to first base for the out. He then retrieved the ball and stuck it in his pocket as a souvenir.

"I was wending my way off the field not to return to baseball until the big fight was over 'over there,'" Collins remembered. "Then came [umpire] 'Silk' O'Loughlin rushing across the field. I just happen to recall it now, that he was the last person in baseball to wish me the luck of 'beaning' the Kaiser.'"⁴⁵ The moment would seem especially poignant that winter when O'Loughlin died during the influenza pandemic.

The second baseman enlisted the afternoon of August 19 at the marine recruiting office at 1409 Arch Street, Philadelphia. "Eddie Collins is now a Teufel Hund. . . . Some time ago Eddie had a chance to go overseas as a Y. M. C. A. secretary, but he couldn't see that. He wanted to get into a more active branch of the service," the *Philadelphia Evening Public Ledger* said on its front page.⁴⁶

"He entered the marines' office without an air of importance," the *Inquirer* added, "and in a short space of time had filled the necessary papers which turned him from a tax-paying citizen of Lansdowne, Pa., into a fighting unit of Uncle Sam."⁴⁷ The Sox were then in New York, battling the Yankees for fourth place. "With Eddie Collins gone," the *Tribune* said, "most of the driving power of last year's champs has disappeared entirely."[48]

Marines usually reported to boot camp at Parris Island, South Carolina, but Collins remained in Philadelphia. He played baseball for the Leathernecks several times on orders from his commanding general but didn't have much fun otherwise, even after the armistice. "Mostly it was drill and exercise and guard duty on the wind-swept piers of the Philadelphia Navy Yard in the dead cold of winter," he recalled long afterward.[49]

"Since that August afternoon he has been stationed in the depot supplies base at Broad street and Washington avenue, doing his work like the other marines, has not tried to use his influence to get a commission and is known as 'Private Collins,'" Bob Maxwell wrote in December. "Many of his pals do not know it is the illustrious Eddie who is wrestling big boxes and pushing a truck from 7:30 a. m. to 4:30 p. m. six days a week. . . . He has received less publicity than any ball player in the service and, strange as it may seem, never looked for any. He has been on the job every day, and only once asked for an afternoon off."[50]

Collins decided he'd play ball again following the service but made no effort to get a quick discharge. "I'm in the game until the marines have no more work for me to do," he wrote a week before Christmas. "I hope to get back into the baseball harness later. Why not? It's my profession."[51]

Eddie left the marines the first week of February, still a private, and went home until the Sox started for spring training at Mineral Wells. "I expect 1919 to be one of my best years on the diamond," he said.[52]

16

Cracker

The remnants of Commy's team won seven games and lost eleven during their last long road trip to Cleveland, Boston, New York, Philadelphia, and Washington. "That they are living in war times and must adjust themselves to unsettled conditions once more was brought forcibly home to the White Sox here to-day when each one received a notice terminating his contract obligation on Sept. 2," George Robbins wrote from Philly.[1] The players concluded the eighteen games Monday, August 26, not knowing their next destination.

"That the Sox and Secretary O'Neill didn't know where they were going after the game yesterday was literally true," Robbins said in a piece filed Tuesday from a train in western Maryland. "Word was awaited from President Comiskey, but a delay, due to the heavy strain of the telegraph wires, put the club up in the air."[2] Word finally arrived confirming that the team was expected for a Thursday exhibition in Toledo, Ohio. The Sox got no farther than Akron before plans changed.

"This is a sad life for the White Sox," the *Tribune* said. "Told they would have two days of rest and could sleep until noon, a porter came along and rousted them out at 6 in the morning with an order to go to Massillon, O., for a game Wednesday. They are surely a grumpy, complaining, discontented bunch."[3]

The Sox abandoned their Pullmans to ride an interurban line 25 miles south to Massillon. When their game with the semipro Agathon club was washed out, they turned around and went back to the Rubber City to board another westbound rattler. The following afternoon they played the Toledo Railways &

Light Company amateur club, which they'd beaten earlier on the way east. This time the Rail-Lights racked reliever Dave Danforth for a 4–3 walk-off victory.

"The White Sox played miserable ball at times in the field," a Toledo paper said. "They booted 'em around in grand shape and looked like a bush league organization in several innings."[4] Once back in Chicago the dispirited Sox spent their final free day Friday at the Reds-Cubs game on the North Side. They then dropped two single games over the weekend to the visiting Indians to end their home season. "A fistful of fans gathered at Comiskey Park yesterday to see the last local American League game until it's all over, over there, and beheld the world's champions retreat faster than the Crown Prince's Army ever thought of doing," the *Chicago Herald and Examiner* said Monday.[5]

"When the small crowd had departed, Owner Comiskey, accompanied by two or three close friends, walked quietly to his home, it being a motorless day," the *Tribune* added. "The old Roman was retrospective, telling of his forty-three consecutive years in baseball, and he wound up with the words: 'What shall I do now?'"[6]

The Sox dashed east again for the Labor Day doubleheader at Detroit that ended their 1918 campaign. Rowland took only fourteen players to the Motor City. "Chicago's once famous White Sox wound up the season here today by losing two farce ball games to the Tigers, Detroit taking the first, 11 to 5, and the second, 7 to 3," the *Tribune* said. "Both Dave Danforth and Eddie Cicotte were slaughtered."[7]

Between the contests, army aviators from nearby Selfridge Field entertained fans by flying above the ballpark. "Several daring flyers [sic] did tail spins, looped the loop and performed other tricks," the *Daily News* said. "One flyer almost grazed the top of the grand stand."[8]

The second game provided comic relief as Sox rookie third baseman Ralph "Babe" Pinelli, a big leaguer for only a month, pulled the hidden-ball trick on George Harper. Ty Cobb, soon bound for France as a captain in the army's Chemical Warfare Service, added to the levity by pitching a couple of innings before moving on to third base.

"When it was over and the crowd passed out of the gates the single expression, 'It's the last of base ball for a while,' was heard," the *Detroit Free Press* said. "Where the next year will bring us is a problem that time only will solve."[9] After winning the championship a year earlier, the Sox weren't within a long fly ball of making the postseason. They ended with a 57–67 record, good only for sixth place in the American League.

"With a shattered and battered team of minor leaguers, amateurs and a smattering of the old club untouched by the draft, Clarence Rowland ended the season lucky to finish out of last place," Robbins later wrote.[10] The skipper shared the disappointment. "It was cause for keen regret on my part," Rowland wrote, "that Mr. Comiskey was compelled, on account of circumstances beyond his control, to relinquish the right to compete for the world's flag this season."[11]

Worse for a keen businessman like Comiskey was his club's abysmal home attendance. It had plummeted from a Major League best of nearly 685,000 in 1917 to fifth in the AL at 195,000 in 1918. True, the Sox had played thirty fewer games, and attendance was down all across the big leagues. But lopping almost one-fifth off the schedule didn't account for a fan drop of over 70 percent, especially since the circuit's overall decline was 40 percent.[12] Small crowds and bad weather also pummeled Commy's charitable contributions. He'd delivered more than $17,000 to the American Red Cross during 1917. This season he wrote a single publicized check, September 10, for $5,000.

Once back from Detroit, the Sox quickly scattered to conform with the work-or-fight rule. Chicago papers took little note of their comings or goings, focusing instead on the NL champion Cubs, who would face the AL Red Sox in the World Series. But the South Side still hosted Chicago's share of the games. The reason was simple: Comiskey Park had twice as many seats as Weeghman Park on the North Side.

Owner Charles Weeghman accepted Commy's offer to use his larger facility; although, as Louis Lee Arms quipped in the *New York Tribune*, "the Cubs doubtless prefer to use their own ball team."[13] Demand for seats wasn't high, the Cub secretary said, "but it is big enough. Harry Grabiner declared that if we obtained one-tenth of the requests that he did last year we would have plenty."[14]

The 1918 World Series adopted a unique format, a single home stand in each city. Game One in Chicago drew fewer than 20,000 fans, about two-thirds the capacity of Comiskey Park. But all in all, Commy thought that wasn't too bad.

"When you stop to think that most of our boys between 21 and 31 years of age are gone, and most of those at home too busy to get away, I think the attendance was large," the magnate told Jimmy Crusinberry. "Then, too, there are few out of town patrons because of the high railroad rates and busy times. I don't know that there has been as big a crowd as that present at a ball game in Chicago this year."[15]

The series was dispirited, marred by disputes and a brief players' strike that brought a cloudburst of criticism and condemnation. The Red Sox won the flag in Game Six in Boston. Attendance during the half dozen games, the same number as in 1917, was down nearly one-third.[16] Fans who believed in omens wouldn't have been surprised if they'd somehow divined that Boston wouldn't repeat its triumph for eighty-six years, or that Chicago would wait ninety-eight seasons to hoist its next Major League championship.

Commy's share of the Chicago gate wasn't disclosed, but his park workers benefited from the additional wages. Weeghman sent a letter of thanks to the owner and the Woodland Bards. "Although of different and rival leagues," the Cub magnate wrote, "the wholeheartedness of your invitation and the many courtesies extended to us during the series have added to your nation-wide reputation for good sportsmanship and to our admiration of you."[17]

Joe Jackson played in a World Series of sorts too. He'd performed well for Harlan & Hollingsworth, topping the Bethlehem Steel League with a .393 batting average after a nineteen-game season. Finishing third in the standings after a nineteen-game season, the shipyard then shifted Joe onto its second club, which played in the eight-team Delaware River Shipbuilding League. This Harlan nine suddenly jumped into a first-place tie in its circuit after an eligibility committee controversially stripped victories from two other clubs.

Such machinations raised the eyebrows of sportswriter Edgar Forrest Wolfe, who wrote a popular column in the *Philadelphia Inquirer* under the byline Jim Nasium. One of the demoted squads, Wolfe growled, "must have committed murder if they were found guilty enough to have their games thrown out, while the acts of Harlan in reinforcing its team with players from another league solely for the decisive championship contest can be considered innocent."[18]

The Delaware River circuit scheduled a playoff between Harlan and the New York Ship club on a neutral diamond August 28 in Philadelphia. Marine Pvt. Eddie Collins got to the park in the eighth inning to watch his old teammate play. "The fans came close to breaking up the game, flocking to see him in his natty new uniform," the *Washington Times* said. "Joe Jackson, . . . now known everywhere as 'Joe the Painter,' spied his former captain and shook hands with him. Then he went to bat and FANNED. Wonder if Joe the Painter was worrying any."[19]

Harlan won handily, 5–0, center fielder Jackson getting a walk and a hit beside the strikeout. The win propelled his team into a best-of-five series for the championship of Atlantic Coast shipyards. The opponent was Standard Shipbuilding of Staten Island, champions of the New York Shipyard League.

Over 5,000 fans saw Game One at the Philadelphia Phillies' ballpark September 7. Harlan trailed 2–1 in the ninth when Jackson pinch hit. Although suffering from an injured right foot he laced a single down the first base line to begin a rally that brought Harlan a 3–2 victory. The clubs played Game Two the next day in a steady drizzle before 4,000 fans at the Polo Grounds in New York. With Jackson out of the lineup, the old Sox battery of Williams and Lynn held Standard scoreless for a 2–0 victory. Harlan completed the sweep September 14 in Philadelphia before 4,500 fans. Jackson was again in the lineup, doubling once and homering twice off former Cardinal and Dodger pitcher Dan Griner. Williams again pitched in the 4–0, two-hit victory.

"Shoeless Joe was a whole show in himself," the *Philadelphia Evening Public Ledger* said.[20] When Jackson hit his second dinger to clinch the series, "the Wilmington fans went money mad and showered him with greenbacks," the *New York Sun* reported. "For more than five minutes he was kept busy walking to the boxes and pulling in bills. After he had his fist full he walked over to a box directly behind home plate and handed them to his wife."[21] The *Inquirer* figured he'd scooped up sixty dollars, "not a bit backward about accepting the financial reward."[22]

Jackson returned to Wilmington, having played for three teams during his strange season. Old Sox teammates had stayed quiet after he'd jumped the team in May. Few thought badly of him, though, or shunned him during the summer. "Joe Jackson and Claude Williams made a brief call on the White Sox last night," the *Tribune* had said from Boston in July, "as they were in the harbor on a test trip with one of Uncle Sam's ships."[23] And Collins had seen him play in the recent playoff game in Philly.

"It is plain to us now that Jackson, Williams, Lynn and Felsch were wise guys when they left their major league affiliation to enter other occupations," an unnamed Sox player had told Robbins back on Labor Day. "Jackson was panned brown by some of the writers and was made a scapegoat, but we believe Joe did the right thing. There isn't a person who knows all the facts in his case but what backs him up and now it is plain to us that he and the other members of our club acted wisely in going when they did."[24]

The few original Sox left from the early season now scattered. They'd won a championship flag a year ago, when America had been active in the war but not yet fully committed on the battlefield. The team and the country were now vastly different.

Eddie Cicotte was coming off his worst season in the Majors, down from twenty-eight victories in 1917 to a dozen this year versus a league-leading nineteen losses. His ERA (2.77) wasn't bad, though, which indicated how little support he'd gotten from Sox batters. Eddie packed up and went home to Detroit and a job building patrol craft called Eagle boats at Ford's big River Rouge plant.

"Cicotte has a wife and two children to support," a wire service reported. "The veteran hurler was undecided just what to do, but after a chat with Billy Wreford, United States Employment Commissioner, entered the plant and will help build those sea devils to hunt down the U-boats."[25]

Eddie also pitched for an industrial team during what little was left of baseball weather in southeastern Michigan. September 22 he threw at Navin Field for American Car & Foundry, "when the team representing that plant played 14 innings to a 6 to 6 tie," according to the *Free Press*. Playing with him were Sox teammate Nemo Leibold and Tigers Bobby Veach, Oscar Stanage, and Archie Yelle, "all major leaguers and employed at useful work in Detroit at present."[26]

Other Sox were busy as well. Pitcher Joe Benz ended his season at eight-and-eight and began working for Illinois Steel in South Chicago. He lived up to his nickname Blitzen ("flash" in German) by decking a coworker he thought was spreading socialist propaganda. Shano Collins took a job with General Electric in his hometown of Pittsfield, Massachusetts. Dave Danforth went east too, to Baltimore Drydocks and Shipbuilding, where he played company ball with several other big leaguers. Reb Russell mined coal in southern Indiana and Mel Wolfgang found essential employment in upstate New York.

Chick Gandil "has been offered so many positions that he is on the fence" over which to accept, the *Daily News* reported.[27] He eventually went west and joined the Standard-Murphy industrial team in the Southern California War Service League, playing against Fred McMullin of the Pasadena Merchants. Frank Shellenback passed tests to enter pilot training with the army Air Service, but wasn't called after the armistice and instead pitched in the same circuit as Gandil and McMullin.

Pants Rowland turned down an offer to become a Knights of Columbus athletic director in France. He looked locally instead "for a place where he would be able to make good use of his athletic knowledge," the *Daily News* said. "This he found when the Thomas E. Wilson Company took him in as a sort of advisor to army and navy authorities on what to buy in the athletic paraphernalia line."[28]

Buck Weaver moved a hundred miles north to Beloit, Wisconsin, where his brother-in-law, Jim Scott, had pitched briefly for the Fairbanks-Morse industrial club in 1916. He wrote to Scott that he planned to work until drafted, but was never called. Fairbanks-Morse was the largest employer in the city of about 18,000 and had trouble keeping wartime workers. The general manager of the gas engine plant convinced Buck to study advanced mechanics and play ball on the company's semipro team, called the Fairies. Weaver later said he preferred the workaday world to professional baseball and wouldn't commit to returning to the Sox.

"I never knew much about big business before I got in with those fellows but now I am getting interested," he told Crusinberry. "I can see the possibilities for a young fellow in such a thing. It has never been a grind for me. I like it, and we like the small town to live in."[29]

Ray Schalk became the work-or-fight poster boy for those Sox who took wartime industrial jobs. The attention he received was no surprise, as he was a natural leader and go-getter.

"Cracker" Schalk had broken in with the club in 1912. "Who's the little cracker pants?" a player supposedly asked, prompting his nickname.[30] His debut as a Sox catcher a day before his twentieth birthday was the first major league game he'd ever seen. Now, for the first time in years, a battered and respected veteran, he found himself working somewhere other than a diamond during September.

Schalk hadn't completed high school but was a bright, ambitious, and personable man, more than capable of making his way outside baseball. His intelligence and abilities had been evident the previous fall when he'd returned to his downstate Illinois hometown, Litchfield, for a championship celebration and exhibition game. "I'll be busy in the bank a part of the time and will do some spinning over the roads in my car," he'd said.[31]

He landed a job this offseason at Great Western Smelting and Refining, less than a mile from Comiskey Park. The company produced brass, bronze, aluminum, silver, and other metals used in the construction of submarines, airplanes, and a great many other things. Cracker showed Crusinberry around the plant, pointing out a roaring and dangerous blast furnace.

"While it often has been exciting to watch Ray behind the bat at a ball game," the scribe wrote, "it was more interesting to see him tap a cupola furnace and charge a blast furnace than to see him peg 'em out at second." Schalk gave Jimmy a long interview:

> You see, I'm here to learn this business, so the boss makes me take a hand at every kind of work. The only way to learn all about it is to get into every department of it. Perhaps some day I'll be up in the front office in charge of some branch.
>
> It's hard work, all right, we all feel here we're doing something to help win the war. It might be more exciting to be a soldier at the front, but I had to take care of the folks, so will have to do my bit here.
>
> Baseball has been pretty good to me, but now I realize how little I knew about business, so I'm glad I can learn while still young. For eight years I did nothing to speak of except to play ball. I don't know whether I'll ever play any more professionally or not. . . . I get about ten minutes a day now for baseball. We have a half hour at noon and I eat my lunch sitting on the packing cases, then I get out in the yard and play catch with the boys until the whistle blows.
>
> It's a great life, all right, except in the morning. You see, the old alarm clock goes off at a quarter to 6, and I can't help but think of those other mornings when breakfast came about 10 o'clock. But I'll soon get used to it.[32]

Schalk worked so vigorously at the foundry, according to Harry Neily in the *American*, that "he grew a flock of callouses on his hands and learned a heap about the business."[33] He also managed to play a little weekend ball with a few other big leaguers. He faced Urban Faber on a local field in October when Red was on liberty from the navy. "In fact, a Sox or Cub rooter would have felt quite at home," Sy Sanborn wrote, "except that the players weren't lined up aright [*sic*], and it would have looked more natural to see Schalk handling Faber."[34] Later that month the catcher traded in his flannels and his work overalls for a business suit.

Ray "Cracker" Schalk, White Sox catcher, foundry worker. Chicago Tribune.

"Only last week the boss decided that Ray knew enough to represent the factory on the outside, and yesterday the young salesman inspected the entire plant of the Chicago Tribune to get a clear idea of just what newspapers did with the type metal which is part of his stock in trade," the paper said. "The little Sox star has been playing ball with a local semi-pro team on Sundays this fall and said he hoped to continue in baseball that way next season but might be too busy."35

A company executive told Robbins during the winter that Schalk had "exceeded our rosiest expectations. If he's a sample of what a ball player can do, they may send us some more just like him." The scribe also noted the catcher's other business activities. "Besides being in good with his firm in Chicago, Ray is the principal stockholder in the Litchfield Foundry and Machine company, is a stockholder in the Litchfield Creamery company, and is interested in the Litchfield Bank and Trust company." The scribe added, however, "He is under contract to catch for the White Sox in 1919."36

Schalk would catch again for Commy, without completely abandoning his interest in commerce and industry. He fondly recalled his time at the smelting company. "Sometimes, after hard work without a sale, I went to the office next day feeling rather blue and discouraged," he'd say. "I'd find two or three orders on my desk and half a dozen phone calls waiting for me. Nothing like that to cheer a fellow up."37

Cracker later acquired a successful Chicago area bowling alley, but was too much a baseball man to give up playing and eventually managing. His career would lead him into the Hall of Fame in 1955. "He kept eating, and sleeping, and cheering baseball until the end came," the *Tribune* said at Schalk's death fifteen years later.38

17

Jenks

The White Sox produced one war hero. Capt. Jim Scott, CPO Red Faber, and Pvt. Eddie Collins all served honorably, but never left the country. Joe Jenkins did. A year after aiding his club in winning the Major League championship, he helped the Allies defeat the Kaiser in France.

"Jenks" was the second Sox player after Death Valley Jim to don khaki, leaving soon after the 1917 World Series. Liked by teammates but rarely used in a game, he'd warmed up hurlers and generally kept things loose in the bullpen. "Joe Jenkins, White Sox third string catcher, has the softest snap of all the rookies," the *Daily News* had quipped. "He hasn't caught a game this year, yet he travels in limited trains, sleeps in lowers and stops at first class hotels. Joe isn't a slacker, either."[1]

A newspaper in Keokuk, Iowa, where he'd caught in the Minors, once called Jenkins "one of the most popular of the local players and a favorite with the umpires. Almost always smiling, seldom 'crabbing' and always ready for the call of the umpire, he was never put out of the game by an umpire and was a favorite with the fans."[2] Several years later, following the World Series, he was the life of the big party at Shanley's in Manhattan.

"Joe got up on the stage and made one of his witty speeches, much to the amazement and amusement of the after-theater crowd," said a paper in

Atlanta, where he'd also been a Minor Leaguer.[3] "Joe had kept quiet all year," the *Boston Globe* added, "but at 'Commy's' banquet he made it mighty clear that he, and not Rowland, was the fellow who had the relief pitchers right. The 'silver-tongued orator from the Platte' [William Jennings Bryan] never had anything on Jenkins, and if 'Buck' Weaver is going to do any more vaudeville this year, Joe is the boy he should get to put the stuff across."[4]

The catcher might normally have spent a lucrative winter speechifying in Chicago after winning the flag. But in wartime a barracks awaited him instead. "Joe Jenkins, captain of the Sox bull pen, has been drafted and will join his regiment," George Robbins reported after the series. He added that Jenks and Jim Scott "will be the boys at the front and fans and players will watch their movements with interest."[5] Jenkins had known from the start that sooner or later he'd take up arms for Uncle Sam.

"I'm thinking about this war," he'd said on a rattler north from Mineral Wells after drilling under Sergeant Smiley. "It's up to us young, unmarried fellows to get busy, and I'm going to be one of them within a few months."[6] He was lighthearted while awaiting his call, joking during his draft physical about his supposedly poor teeth, lungs, heart, and feet.

"But, doc, I want you to understand I don't for a minute want to be exempted," he'd said. "All I want Woodrow [Wilson] to do is to let me hang around till the Sox play the Giants. Then I want to go to the trenches. Look how I could cheer 'em up in the world's series. After we lick the Giants we'll go out and clean up the Turks—the real Turks."[7]

Jenks was registered for the draft at Hanford, California, where his father owned a ranch in the San Joaquin Valley. But he'd been born and reared in Shelbyville, Tennessee. After the World Series he visited relatives there and decided to enter the army with other men from the Volunteer State.

"Joe Jenkins, who was supposed to go with the next contingent from here, is now in the east, and the local board has arranged for him to report to an eastern cantonment," a Hanford newspaper said at the end of October 1917.[8] He and about seventy Tennesseans arrived November 15 at Camp Gordon, Georgia, a National Army cantonment near Atlanta. Jenkins and two other southerners from the minor leagues entered the third officers' training camp days into the new year.

"The strapping big fellow caught on to the military affairs from the outset as a private in a casual detachment of Company C, 167th Depot Brigade," an Atlanta scribe wrote. "Jenkins did not rise to the position of a sergeant, but he had the athletic instinct and the ability to think quickly. . . . The superiority of the athlete as an officer in the present cataclysm has been proved, and it would seem that all three stand a promising chance to win the black and gold hatcord."[9]

"He will start the grind Monday and will strive for a lieutenancy in the field artillery," the *Tribune* added of the catcher. "Jenkins made such a strong impression with his officers he was recommended. His name headed the list of enlisted men chosen from 40,000 troops."[10] But Jenkins wasn't the only big leaguer training at Camp Gordon. Brooklyn Dodgers pitcher Sherrod "Sherry" Smith from Mansfield, Georgia, was there too.

"Having been originally drafted from the minor leagues to the majors, and then drafted from the majors to the Army, the battery has been drafted into the series of intercantonment games for the championship of Uncle Sam's fighting forces at home and abroad," the *Brooklyn Eagle* said.[11] The big series never happened, but newspapers across the country ran photos of the two Sammies posing as pitcher and catcher in their khaki uniforms.

Joseph "Jenks" Jenkins, White Sox catcher, 2nd Lieutenant, USA. Spalding's Official Base Ball Guide 1919.

"Joe has written Chicago friends that he is coming along fine in the army," Harry Neily reported in the *Chicago Evening American* in late January.[12] When next heard from in early April, Jenkins and two other athletes in officer training bowed out of an army baseball game with the Southern Association's Atlanta Crackers, "pleading that they were not in condition on account of the extreme ardor of commission seeking."[13]

Jenkins's service record was destroyed in a massive archives fire decades later, along with millions of others. Details of his military history, therefore, are sketchy. He didn't complete officer training, the reason unknown, and sailed for the war April 25 as a private in the 327th Infantry. He stayed with the regiment in France no more than a few weeks before the army reassigned him to Company A, 132nd Infantry, Thirty-Third "Prairie" Division. Jenkins probably didn't oppose the unusual transfer and might even have finagled it. The 132nd was the old Second Illinois from Chicago.

"At the beginning every officer and man in the regiment was from Chicago and Illinois," the 132nd's commander, Col. Abel Davis, wrote in a unit history. "Among the replacements there came soldiers from other states, notably Tennessee. We have adopted them as our own and I am proud to say that they became a part of us."[14] Jenkins later penned a letter to Commy saying that "most of the men in my platoon are from the south side, and their favorite spot is the left field of the bleachers."[15]

After more training under British troops, the 132nd entered combat on Independence Day. Company A's commander was a captain who'd fought three years with a Canadian regiment and carried a shotgun in the field. Jenkins was now one of his sergeants. The regiment fought beside Australian Tommies to eliminate a German salient at Hamel along the Somme River north of Paris. The allied troops paid dearly for achieving their objectives. Some of the 132nd's wounded called their attack a costly mistake. "They brought back a story that somebody blundered July 4," a wire story said, "and as a result the 132d infantry was sent over the top for the first time against crack German troops, when the Illinois boys were only in that area to get their final training and not for assault work."[16]

"Before the fight was over the captain and lieutenants of his [Jenkins's] company were numbered among the casualties and as he was the senior sergeant he took command," the *Tribune* reported. "When that fight was over he was commissioned lieutenant for his valor and soldierly attainments."[17] The 132nd stayed with the Aussies until late August, then shifted southeast for attachment to the French Army.

"It was a proud moment when word reached the regiment that the front line trenches of the famous battlefields of Mort Homme [Dead Man] in front of Verdun were to be occupied by us," Colonel Davis wrote. The regiment occupied the position September 10. "Until Sept. 26 our men with the French to our right, and Americans to our left, held the Mort Homme hill and stood watch over the approach to the city of Verdun, where a million lives were given to stop the advance of the Huns."[18]

The sector remained quiet until September 26, when an enormous predawn artillery barrage opened the Meuse-Argonne offensive, the forty-seven-day push that forced an armistice upon Germany. Jenkins wore the second lieutenant's gold bar that had eluded him at Camp Gordon. Orders for the attack "designated the 132nd as the pivot for the whole movement," a history says, "for the regiment was resting against the west bank of the Meuse, and the object of the offensive was to drive the enemy off that bank and force him northward and eastward beyond the river."[19]

The regiment jumped off and achieved all its objectives in heavy fighting. The 132nd held the line on the west bank of the Meuse until October 4. After four days in reserve, the regiment went back into action, crossing the river at a place called Consenvoye. The casualty rate once more indicated the ferocity of the fighting.

"We have been scrapping for the past ten days on the Meuse, north of Verdun, and believe me the fighting has been hot and sharp," Jenks wrote Commy. "We have just been moved to a more quiet sector, the purpose for which is rest, and believe me, we can use it nicely. It is becoming more apparent that Germany is through, and in the last offensive I was in their spirit and morale was at a very low ebb. . . . I will bring something back in the line of a trophy for your office with me, as shipping it would be risky."[20]

The White Sox owner spoke October 22 about this or another of the lieutenant's letters. "Joe isn't a general yet," Commy told Harry Neily of the *Chicago Evening American*, "but he'll be something big if the war lasts long enough."[21]

Damon Runyon, now a war correspondent, also mentioned Jenks that day. It came near the end of his report about the combat death of Capt. Eddie

Grant, a former Giant infielder killed in the Argonne Forest. Runyon noted that Jenkins "was discovered yesterday scraping the mud off himself in a wayside billet. He had just come out of the line with the outfit. He has seen quite a lot of service."[22]

The 132nd again shifted position, arriving October 24 in the Troyon sector, 30 miles southwest of the German-held city of Metz. Johnny Evers, the former Chicago Cubs star second baseman, was in France too, as a uniformed athletic secretary for the Knights of Columbus. Although based in Paris, "The Crab" often visited the front to distribute chocolate and smokes and to chat about baseball and the news from home with the boys. He took a special interest in troops from Illinois and particularly Chicago.

Evers located Jenkins in frontline trenches that had been in enemy hands two days earlier. They'd last set eyes on one another a year earlier at Shanley's following Game Six of the World Series. They stood together now only 200 yards from German troops. Evers wrote about their meeting in his syndicated newspaper column back home:

> He was wearing his new bar on his shoulder, and his non-com stripe hadn't yet been cut off. He had been promoted under fire, for gallantry and nerve, when some others of the officers fell. . . . If you can't guess who it is, tell Comiskey that Lieut. Joe Jenkins sends his best regards and says that he is hitting them high up and far away.
>
> Jenkins naturally wasn't expecting me. He acted as if he saw a ghost then he jumped up, yelled, and we hugged each other and he demanded to know all about the White Sox and whether they won or not, and said he had been so darned busy he didn't have a chance to get any news at all.
>
> He didn't talk much of himself and I notice that the real fellows who are doing this big job never do. They want to tell what heroes the other fellows are, and Joe is prouder of his company than he is of anything else. He knows every man by name and they all know him. I think he is the most popular fellow with his soldiers that I ever saw—just as he was in baseball.

While we were talking a shell burst within a short distance of us and neither of us moved. He just waited until the jarring buzz died out of our ears and then went on talking baseball and asking the news from home. While we were talking orders came. What they were I don't know, but Joe Jenkins suddenly became Lieut. Jenkins, leader of a bunch of heroes.

"Good-by, Crab," he said, shaking hands; "I'll see you back in Chi when this is over."

We shook hands and then he swung around and said:

"All ready, fellows; let's go."

The men jumped up with a yell and Jenkins led the way out of the dugouts and the last I saw of them they were going forward, spreading out in a thinner line as they ascended the hill. I could hear the machine guns of the Germans sounding like buzz saws cutting through knots—and I felt better about ball players in their patriotism.[23]

Evers said in another account that Jenkins had shown him the sector out in the open until he asked how far away the Germans were. Shocked by his reply, the Crab said they should get under cover. "That's all right," Jenkins said, "those birds don't shoot very well and seldom hit anybody except by accident."[24] The tough little K. of C. man still took the lieutenant by the arm and led him away. Only after returning to New York shortly before Christmas did Evers admit what he'd left out of the printed tale.

"Hell was breaking all around," Evers said. "All of a sudden a big shell—it sounded to me like a whole ammunition dump—exploded about 150 yards to one side of us. Right in front of me a soldier, a young lad, ducked like a scared rabbit into a dugout. I followed just like that rabbit's brother. I was picking myself up from the bottom of the dugout when Jenkins stuck his head in the doorway and laughed, 'Ha! Ha! Ha! Johnny! What're you afraid of! Don't you know that shell is gone! You never see the one that hits you!'"[25] The violence of the shells raining down from both sides shocked Evers. "Take it from me," he said, "the front line trenches were never meant for health resorts."[26]

The Crab also reported that Jenkins was "receiving half his salary from the owner of the club he played with as long as he is over here."[27] Probably around the time the two chatted at the front Jenkins communicated again with Commy, assuring him that everything was all right. "I wrote you a few days ago," he said, "but since that time I have been in the front line for four days, having gone up to look over the situation with the major." Jenks continued:

Believe me, I am a brave man, but I did not bargain to eat any of these high explosives. One of the shells just missed me about ten feet. It hit on top of the trench and had it hit in the trench I would not be writing to you today.

To be honest with you, this is some league that I am in and it is a lot faster than the old American, for you know that when you boot one in this league you are through and can't come back.

Mr. Comiskey, I am doing fine and like it over here, everything being so different. Maybe the next time you write me you will have to address me as Maj. or Col. Jenkins.

Well, Mr. Comiskey, I will close now and will write you again as soon as I can get a few boches. Give every one my kindest regards.[28]

"Joe has done mighty well over there and the White Sox fans and all his friends can be very proud of him," Evers said later. "He takes so many chances that it's a wonder he hasn't been killed long ago."[29]

Jenks was alive November 11, and contrary to reports well and uninjured. The 132nd Infantry marched behind the withdrawing enemy army into Germany and eventually settled into billets in Luxembourg. At Christmastime, Jenkins, Christy Mathewson, Grover Cleveland Alexander, Sherry Smith, and a number of other big leaguers still overseas wired season's greetings to a Stateside newspaper.

"Doesn't look like the division I'm with will be home in the U. S. A. for Christmas and I'd give all of Europe to be in the old home town again," Jenkins said. "It can't be helped, though, so we'll have to make the best of it, as we are pretty sure it won't be very long before everything will be straightened out and we'll be on our way. Here's wishing Commy and all the boys on the other side the best ever." The lieutenant signed his wire, "Joe Jenkins, White Sox Catcher."[30]

The club also received word of George Lees, the young backstop they'd hoped would replace Jenks until he too had been called to the colors. Lees's father wrote to secretary Harry Grabiner in January, saying his son had emerged unscathed from heavy fighting near Verdun as a corporal with the 314th Infantry.

"On two occasions he was one of a few survivors of some of the bloodiest fighting in the closing chapters of the war," George Robbins wrote of the ex-steelworker, who'd once narrowly escaped being crushed in a mill accident. "George seems to have lived a charmed life. He missed the machine gun bullets and the bursting shells which were much more numerous than falling steel beams at Bethlehem, Pa."[31] Lees would return safely in the spring and play two seasons in the Minors before appearing in twenty games for the White Sox in 1921.

Lt. Joe Jenkins, meanwhile, reached home April 14, 1919, on the French liner SS *Rochambeau*. Among his companions in the 1,300 troops jamming the transport were Sergeant "Pete" Alexander of the Cubs (and 442nd Field Artillery) and outfielder Sgt. Mike Menosky of the Senators (and 338th Infantry). The three stood together in their khaki as the ship steamed from the Narrows toward a pier in the North (Hudson) River. A British officer misunderstood a Sammy's joke and asked the ballplayers if they were pawnbrokers. "No," the White Sox hero answered, "just pawns in Uncle Sam's game."[32]

18

Kenesaw

News of the armistice reached Chicago at five minutes before two a.m., Monday, November 11. The city had celebrated prematurely the previous Thursday, following a mistaken report. Now the flash was official: "Armistice signed."[1]

Bells tolled, sirens screamed, whistles shrieked. By 3 o'clock Chicago had gone mad. Parades began in the predawn darkness and wriggled all day through the city and suburbs. "Pandemonium was in the saddle wherever its citizens congregated," the *Daily News* said.[2] Charley Comiskey arose at the sound of the first factory whistle.

"I certainly never spent a more exciting moment in my life than I did this morning," Commy said. "First I am overjoyed at the coming of peace; second, at a prospect of the return of baseball. A few months ago things looked a bit dubious for playing ball next season, but this news has pleased me more than anything else in my career. The boys 'over there' certainly deserve credit for what they have brought about and I hope they may all be with us next summer."[3] He and manager Rowland hadn't yet planned for 1919. "There will be time enough for that later on," Commy said.[4]

The armistice had arrived faster than many expected, although none too soon for him and other baseball magnates. All were hard-pressed financially. "Almost every team had lost money because of the war; the Yankees and White Sox each claimed a net loss of more than $45,000 in 1918," Black Sox historian

Jacob Pomrenke writes, "and, in a rare gesture, White Sox owner Charles Comiskey chose to cut his own salary to $5,000, lower than even those of a handful of his own players."[5]

Commy was estranged now from Ban Johnson, but didn't join a late-November effort to oust him. Harry Frazee and Giants owner Harry Hempstead proposed drafting William Howard Taft as a one-man National Commission. They essentially hoped to make the former US president the Major Leagues' first commissioner. The push failed, the *St. Louis Post-Dispatch* noting, "The one-man commission is already in existence, with Byron B. Johnson playing the role of the commission."[6] Ban and Commy did clash again the following month, however, during the annual American League meeting in Chicago. The issue this time was the length of the 1919 season.

The pair had disagreed a year earlier on the same question. Now both men initially supported a normal 154-game schedule. Then Johnson bowed to National League pressure to play only 140 games and push back Opening Day to give military veterans time to return to their clubs. Frazee alone joined Commy in opposing their prexy, and a widely anticipated revolt by AL magnates never surfaced.

"Comiskey has refused to exert that power which he undoubtedly holds to force Johnson off his throne as virtual dictator of the league," the *Daily News* said.[7] Chicago players had clashed with gamblers at Fenway Park in 1917, but the Sox owner continued his current alliance with the "stormy petrel of the American league."[8] Commy defended Frazee against Johnson's desire to force him out over concerns about betting.

"Was any action ever taken against the Red Sox on the score of gambling under other ownerships?" the South Sider asked. "Why, then, should Johnson keep harping about gambling at Fenway park under Frazee?" Commy's following remark might have caused him regret later. "If Johnson has the good of baseball at heart," he said, "he will lay off the gambling end of it and not be so interested in buying out owners in the American league."[9]

The immediate task for the South Siders over the winter was to assemble a competitive roster. Players who'd jumped to paint-and-putty leagues became another contentious issue at the AL meeting. Many attendees anticipated a resolution barring these men in 1919. "After some discussion the measure was dropped and the matter of the shipyards ball player was left entirely to the owners," Jimmy Crusinberry reported.[10] The lack of any league directive left Commy to consult his own conscience about how best to handle those who'd so angered him. He could easily have unloaded everyone, especially Felsch and Jackson.

"Only seven clubs in the American and eight in the National League would be willing to sign this pair," editor Bob Maxwell quipped in Philadelphia. "As soon as they are placed on the auction block bidding will be brisk and Comiskey will have no trouble in disposing of them. Already the St. Louis Browns have claimed them because Phil Ball is a friend of Ban Johnson's and always supported the American League boss. St. Louis scribes believe Ban will put through the deal on that account."[11]

Maxwell dismissed concerns that fans would razz Jackson on his return, recalling Harlan playing at Reading, Pennsylvania, before a crowd of over 10,000. "The majority cared nothing about the ball game," Maxwell wrote. "They wanted to see Joe Jackson."[12]

Deciding what to do about the jumpers clearly would affect Commy's club for years—although exactly how many he certainly had no way of discerning. The magnate swallowed his anger and instead heeded his business instincts. He made no great pronouncement but let it be known the jumpers would be welcomed back in his ballpark.

"Here's a Christmas present Santa Claus has brought the baseball fans of the south side: Joe Jackson, greatest slugger in the game, is coming back," Robbins wrote December 24. "President Comiskey has relented and has acquiesced in plans to bring old Joe back to Chicago to wear a uniform of the White Sox." The scribe thought it was the right move. "Joe's career in the shipyards has been one of honor and unremitting toil," Robbins said. "To point a finger of scorn against him is to assail every man who worked in the shipyards, say friends of Jackson, who have come back to bat strong with President Comiskey."[13]

Another key decision during the winter involved Clarence Rowland. Few fans blamed the skipper for the awful past season. Commy wasn't known for the longevity of his managers, but Robbins reported that other AL magnates thought Pants was probably safe. "That President Comiskey has failed to mention his plans for 1919 does not affect Rowland's standing with the Old Roman or the probability of his early reappointment," he wrote.[14]

Collyer's Eye disagreed. "While Chicago publications have been reticent on the matter of a possible successor to Clarence Rowland as manager of the White Sox other cities on the American League circuit have been discussing a probable change with considerable interest not to say prolixity," the paper editorialized. "We are of the opinion that the White Sox may have a new leader the coming season."[15]

Commy waited until the last hours of the year to prove the *Eye* correct. He announced Rowland's firing shortly before boarding a Florida-bound train with his wife late December 31.

"Exit Clarence Rowland. Enter Bill 'Kid' Gleason," Crusinberry wrote New Year's Day. The new manager was a surprise, and little else was clear. "Just why Rowland was dismissed is a matter left unanswered by the boss of the Sox," Crusinberry added. "Outside of saying that he felt it a matter of his best judgment in his effort to give Chicago fans the best possible baseball results, the south side leader had nothing to say regarding the man let out."[16] Robbins couldn't explain the switch either.

"Kid Gleason's reappearance in Chicago will be welcomed as much as the departure of Clarence Rowland will be deplored," Robbins wrote. Appointing anyone other than the Kid as the new skipper, he added, "would have brought down on President Comiskey a volley of hot shrapnel shots from the scribes."[17]

The break between Commy and Kid has never been fully explained, nor has their reconciliation. "However, whatever caused the trouble seems to have been smoothed over, if Commy really had a hand in it, for Gleason is to get his chance—the chance to work for himself," wrote the Baltimore scribe who'd tracked Gleason down the previous summer.[18]

The Maryland writer noted that the Kid would become the fourth former Oriole managing in the majors, joining John McGraw of the Giants, Hughey Jennings of the Tigers, and Wilbert Robinson of the Dodgers. Pvt. Eddie Collins in Philadelphia was thrilled and abandoned any vague idea of retirement.

"When I say that the White Sox will go better than ever with Gleason at the helm, I mean to convey that harmony of the Paderewski sort will prevail in the ranks," the marine said. "This fellow Gleason—and the fans know it, too—is one of the greatest handlers of men for whom I ever had the pleasure of working.... Now that Gleason has been named, I look for most of the White Sox stars, about whom we have heard so many rumors of trade this winter, returning to Comiskey's club."[19]

Crusinberry wrote later that Gleason had convinced Commy to change his mind about the jumpers. The Kid had conceded, when asked, that he'd like to manage the White Sox. "But not unless you take back all those players who quit you," he'd added. "You know if I take the job, I want to win, and if I can get back the fellows of 1917, I think I can win. I don't want to go out there and try to do anything with a broken-down team."[20]

Gleason's first task was to bring Jackson, Williams, and Lynn back to Chicago. He visited the Wilmington shipyard January 4 in search of the three absent Sox. He found only Lefty, hanging on the side of a ship.

"Hey, there, how're you hitting?" Gleason shouted up. The hurler set aside his rivet gun and descended to shake the skipper's hand. Williams said as they chatted that Commy owed him $186 in back pay. The Kid said he'd take care of it. "I'll sign," Lefty replied, "just as soon as the money is sent to me."[21] Williams put Gleason in touch with Jackson, but nothing happened with the Harlan trio right away.

The first Sox jumper to reenter the fold actually was Felsch. He was still in Milwaukee, claiming to be unconcerned about his future but asking for a trade. "If I don't play in the big leagues," Hap said, "then I'll stick right here in Milwaukee and play in the Lake Shore league."[22] But February 10 he quietly slipped down to the Windy City to visit Commy at the South Side park.

"On entering the office he was ushered into the private room of the Sox owner and the pair got down to business," the *Daily News* said. "They were in conference for some time. When Felsch came out he wore a smile and was pleased to announce he had signed a contract for the season of 1919. . . . Today he forgot that he ever had any difficulties with Comiskey and they parted friends."[23]

Nemo Leibold's contract arrived the same day, and Ray Schalk turned up to sign his papers in person that afternoon. The star catcher was "making good in business," Crusinberry wrote, "but he didn't feel he could afford to quit the national game at the present time."[24] Pitchers Cicotte, Faber, and Benz had signed too. Other Major League clubs saw a similar influx of contracts from men eager for something resembling a normal season.

"If the playing profession has suffered to any appreciable extent," *New York Tribune* sportswriter W. J. "Bill" Macbeth wrote in mid-February, "it is looking upon the circumstance as unavoidable and bowing gracefully to a condition that was a direct result of the financial stringency of a world war. . . . Comiskey and Gleason have lined up almost enough for a White Sox nine."[25]

The next jumper to return was Byrd Lynn, who'd quit his shipyard job and gone home to his farm at Brookport, Illinois, near the Ohio River. The club received his contract in the mail February 19. "His signing indicates the others, Williams and Jackson, will follow suit," Crusinberry rightly predicted.[26]

Joe Jackson, like the second-string Sox catcher, had left the shipyard and was spending the winter at Savannah, Georgia. His contract showed up two days after Lynn's, with the same lack of fanfare. "I knew the big fellow [Jackson] would come around all right, and because he's going to be with us, the White Sox are almost sure to be in the fight for that old pennant," Gleason said.[27] Chick Gandil's contract came the next day. Williams's paperwork wasn't far behind.

Jackson's deal called for "about $5,500 a season and Mrs. Joe's traveling expenses," Robbins wrote in *The Sporting News*, "and here comes Lefty right into camp with his signed contract almost before the ink is dried on Joe's parchment. Mrs. Williams and Mrs. Jackson are chums and that may have had something to do with Lefty's actions." The only jumpers still holding out were Risberg and McMullin, who according to Robbins "have expressed a wish to remain on the Pacific Coast."[28]

But the Sox received Swede's signed contract March 17, five days before they were to leave for Mineral Wells. Buck Weaver came down from Beloit the same day, still threatening to play for Fairbanks-Morse.

"He just jumped on a train and came to town to see Comiskey," the *Daily News* said. "He found the big boss gone, but Kid Gleason was roosting in his office." The two men knew each other well. The Kid told Weaver how much the club valued him and explained what it could spend. Buck said, "if that was the best Commy could give and as the White Sox needed him he would accept. Whereupon Kid and Buck embraced and real tears of 1919 happiness laid the dust."[29] Sy Sanborn thought Gleason had prevailed by pointing out that the Sox played six or seven times a week, not twice like the Fairies. "If there is one thing Weaver would rather do than eat," Sanborn wrote, "it is play baseball."[30]

Commy also hoped to entice Capt. Jim Scott back to the diamond after his discharge. "I hear that Scott is in splendid condition and if he can deliver again in the big leagues I shall be more pleased than any one else," he said.[31] Scotty knew Beloit firsthand as well as from Weaver, and briefly considered working and playing ball again for the Fairies. He finally chose to pitch instead for the

San Francisco Seals, in the city where he'd been so popular during the war. Death Valley Jim would play nine more seasons in the PCL.

The final jumper, Fred McMullin, remained a holdout as spring training began. He even played for the Pasadena Merchants in a spring game versus the Cubs in California. Then the infielder wired Chicago the first day of April that his signed contract was in the mail and he would join the club at Texas. It wasn't an April Fool's joke. All six players who'd jumped the club in 1918 now were back under the tent—and after relatively little discord, further belying charges about Charley Comiskey's stinginess as an owner.

Commy was proud of those Sox players who'd helped America secure victory during the war. One by one the servicemen returned from their Stateside billets to exchange khaki or blues for flannels. Lt. Joe Jenkins later sailed home in time to become captain of the bullpen once more.

But Commy had fewer veterans than he would have liked. Of the thirty-seven men who'd appeared on Sox rosters during the two wartime seasons, only five had served in the armed forces. Of this quintet—Jenkins, Scott, Faber, Jourdan, and Eddie Collins—Jenks alone had left the United States or seen combat. According to White Sox publicists, however, the club had done far more. By one reckoning, its figurative service flag had nineteen stars for players who'd served.

Maj. Fritz von Kolnitz rated a star, although he hadn't played for the Sox since 1916 and never would play again in the big leagues. Sox prospects who'd donned khaki without ever getting into a regular season game counted too. Three—George Lees, George Payne, and Earl Keiser—had served in France, Corporal Keiser fighting with the Eighty-Ninth "Middle West" Division. Lees and Payne would make the club during later seasons.

The team's single gold star represented hurler "Connie" Constantineau, who had died of influenza while in the navy at Norfolk, Virginia. If they'd cared to stretch the point, the club might also have claimed a gold star for Pvt. Laverne "Larry" Chappell. The once-promising Sox outfielder (1913–15) likewise had perished during the pandemic, three days before the armistice, while in the army medical corps at San Francisco.

The other AL clubs reported similarly inflated figures. The number of service stars they claimed ranged from twelve for the Browns to twenty-four for the Tigers. National League figures roughly matched the American's. The Giants claimed a gold star for Captain Grant, killed in action, although "Harvard Eddie" had retired from baseball to practice law after the 1915 season. Both circuits exaggerated their wartime participation, hoping that fans would applaud their players' military service, believe the patriotic pronouncements, and overlook the jumpers. These hopes were largely realized.

Anger in Chicago toward Joe Jackson and fellow paint-and-putty players slowly dissipated. Commy and the Kid dismissed concerns about their slugger's return and denied plans for any trade. "Both seem convinced that Joe acted rightly in leaving the team early last summer to engage in essential work," Crusinberry wrote in February, "and both feel certain that Chicago's fans will be as strong as ever for Joe after he poles a few hits to the fences and drives in a few winning runs."[32]

The Sox opened the postwar season at St. Louis with the 1917 team largely reunited, although with the old cliques intact too. Commy's boys won six of seven games on the road, returned to the South Side, and ran their record to 10–2 during the first dozen contests.

Crusinberry's prediction about Jackson proved correct. Sy Sanborn noticed "a band representing the 'Joe Jackson Rooters' from the stockyards which aided in the entertainment" at the May 2 home opener, "and there were presentations for the athletes which included a gold watch for Jackson."[33] The rejuvenated Sox kept winning. "Whaling the massive rivet seems to have added more than passing impetus to Joe Jackson's swing," Grantland Rice wrote in the *New York Tribune*. "The Shoeless Wonder is assailing the ball with greater gusto than he has shown in seven or eight years."[34]

Shoeless Joe was luckier than others returning to the big leagues. Many military vets had subpar seasons in 1919, pitchers especially seeming to struggle, no matter whether they'd served overseas or within the United States. Red Faber came home from the Navy to post an 11–9 record after going 71–46 his first five seasons. Combat artilleryman Pete Alexander of the Cubs went 16–11, fine for most hurlers but disappointing for one who'd won thirty or more games each of the three seasons preceding his wartime service.

The reconstituted Sox, however, were nearly as good as they'd been during the hundred-victory season two years earlier. They won eighty-eight times while playing fourteen fewer games than in 1917. Eddie Cicotte, who hadn't served in the armed forces, returned to form and won a league-best twenty-nine contests while losing only seven. The sole Major League club to surpass the South Siders was National League champion Reds, which amassed ninety-six wins for the right to confront the Sox in the World Series.

The South Side club also shed its financial woes. Attendance at Comiskey Park soared from 195,000 in 1918 to 627,000 this season, and likewise from 3 million to 6.5 million across the Major Leagues.[35] The future looked bright. Then eight of Commy's players—the infamous Black Sox—disgraced their team and sport by conspiring with gamblers to fix the 1919 World Series. They intentionally lost the best-of-nine fall classic in eight games to Cincinnati. Joe Jenkins, in his last days as a big leaguer, sensed that something was amiss.

"We players, who were not involved in the payoff thought things were funny in that first game in Cincinnati," Jenks remembered decades afterward. "The last couple of days in the series everyone was talking. I roomed with Gandil. He was betting heavily on the series but I didn't think much of it as we used to get good odds and bet all the time. But I learned later he was betting against us," Jenkins added. "Yes, it was a terrible mess. . . . Charles Comiskey, the owner of our team, later sent us players who were not involved in the fix the difference in the losing and winning share."[36]

Of the half dozen players who'd jumped the club in 1918, only Lynn wasn't a conspirator. The other five—Jackson, Williams, Felsch, Risberg, and McMullin—all became Black Sox, along with Cicotte, Weaver, and Gandil. Most fans didn't know about the scandal until 1920, when a belated uproar shook the sport. It culminated that November when Major League owners overthrew the National Commission at last and unanimously elected Judge Kenesaw Mountain Landis as their first commissioner.

Kenesaw Mountain Landis, federal judge, baseball commissioner. Irving Knickerbocker, Bismarck (ND) Tribune.

Landis had first come to the magnates' attention in 1915 through his handling of the Federal League's antitrust suit versus the two established Major circuits. His unusual first name was a misspelling of the Civil War battle in which his father had been wounded. His reputation was that of a "fearless curmudgeon."[37] Humorist Will Rogers offered this explanation of his hiring: "The game needed a touch of class and distinction at the moment, and somebody said, 'Get that old guy who sits behind first base all the time. He's out here every day, anyhow.' So, they offered him a season's pass and he jumped at it."[38] Nobody was laughing over the Black Sox affair, though, and the commissioner banged down a decision that reverberates today.

"In 1921 Landis banned from baseball the seven [sic] Chicago White Sox players who had been charged with throwing the 1919 World Series ... despite the fact that they were acquitted in an Illinois state court trial in August of that year," the *American Bar Association Journal* recalled. "Although they later applied for reinstatement, Landis was adamant."[39] The *Tribune* agreed with the ruling.

"Judge Landis took his baseball position to give organized baseball a character bath," the paper editorialized. "With the Black Sox back in the game the bath would have looked worse than if it had been drawn from the Missouri river in flood time."[40]

The Great War in Europe affected everything—the world, the nation, the citizens of every state, city, and hamlet. Nothing ever was quite the same again, including Organized Baseball. Teams and entire leagues had shattered under wartime pressures. But at least the armed forces had recognized the game's value in helping instill the concept of teamwork in millions of uniformed Americans who contributed to the victory.

"It suddenly came to me that serving in the army has taught the men to obey orders and they all do it, without thinking of doing otherwise," Johnny

Evers wrote from France. "They obey as a matter of course. There will be four or five million young fellows after the war who have learned this lesson and they will make the best kind of ball player; the kind that works for the team, and managing a team of that kind of players will be the easiest work in the world."[41] Evers also observed that Sammies were "better sports and cleaner than they were before they got into the war."[42]

Spalding's Guide added that there was "no officer in the American army but what has appreciated what Base Ball did for his men. As a matter of fact, the game is a miniature warfare of bloodless combat between two sides, in which the physical and mental superiority and perfect athletic training of the best team conquers the other."[43]

The ex-servicemen playing for the 1919 White Sox—Collins, Faber, and Jenkins, plus newcomers Bill James, Tom McGuire, and combat veteran Win Noyes—all understood these truths. But their club also included a half dozen jumpers. A year earlier, these six had put personal needs ahead of their club's, some arguably for good reason. For them the meaning of team and teamwork was weakened if not erased altogether.

It's perhaps not surprising, then, that no returned veteran was tarred as a Black Sox, while five of the eight men out were jumpers. Why, though, had they chosen to throw the World Series? The war hadn't directly caused the scandal. A theory by sports historian Paul Gardner more than half a century later likely is still as sound an explanation as any:

> Baseball had for some time been living uneasily in the knowledge that bribes were being offered by gamblers, and that some players were accepting them. The players knew it was going on, and the owners knew it was going on. But more important, the players knew that the owners knew—and they knew that the owners were doing nothing about it for fear of a scandal that might damage organized baseball. Under such conditions it quite obviously did not pay to be honest.[44]

Ironically, had Commy ignored his better angels (or his bankers) and vented his fury on the jumpers, he might have avoided disaster. Even a fire sale of Jackson, Felsch, and the others would have given the Sox enough talent to form the nucleus of a new club—one that probably wouldn't have appeared in the 1919 World Series, thus avoiding the scandal that brought lifetime banishment to all eight Black Sox. Had such a revamped team somehow faced the Reds in the fall, Gandil, Cicotte, and Weaver alone couldn't have pulled off a betting conspiracy. It's equally unlikely they could have enticed enough new teammates into joining one, especially had Buck merely stayed silent instead of helping throw games.

No, the war hadn't caused the Black Sox scandal. But it had helped create the conditions that enabled it to happen. Wartime dominoes toppled in slow motion to change the sport. These events included jumps from the Majors to industrial teams; the ruined Comiskey-Johnson friendship; the weakening of the National Commission; the commission's subsequent demise; and the elevation of Judge Landis as commissioner. The cumulative effects are evident today. The eight Black Sox remained banned from Major League Baseball until 2025, and the relative guilt of Jackson and particularly Weaver still inspires debate.

The White Sox entered a long period of frustration and failure, comparable to the "curse of the Bambino" that beset the rival Red Sox. The South Siders didn't appear again in the World Series for four decades, until the "Go-Go Sox" bowed to the Los Angeles Dodgers in 1959, nearly three decades after Commy's death. They didn't win another championship until they swept the Houston Astros in 2005, fourteen years after the demolition of the old green ballpark that bore Charley Comiskey's name.

"Shoeless Joe came down to help them!" a fan yelped then in celebration. "You know, to clear the Black Sox!"[45] If so, the clean Sox—Cracker, Red, Pants, Death Valley Jim, others—accompanied Jackson to the Windy City. Warrior-catcher Lt. Joe Jenkins would have seen the cosmic joke in the name of Chicago's massive right-handed closer, Bobby Jenks. The other ghosts surely would have reminded the living Sox that they'd won only ninety-nine games in a longer season, one shy of the 1917 total. And a spectral old second baseman and captain might well have repeated what he'd once told a writer about serving in the marines.

"I learned from that bunch the meaning of spirit and determination," Eddie Collins had said. "What a lesson our White Sox could have learned from that corps."[46]

ACKNOWLEDGMENTS

Thanks to Christen Karniski for her early interest in this book, and to Jacob Pomrenke, Bill Lamb, Don Zminda, Rick Huhn, Jan Finkel, and Lindsay Bell for their help, encouragement, and suggestions. My gratitude as well to the Chicago History Museum, Chicago Public Library, University of Illinois Library, Old Worthington (Ohio) Libraries, and Lori Miller of Redbird Research in St. Louis.

NOTES

Chapter 1

1 "Major Leaguers May Enlist," *Chicago Daily News*, February 8, 1917.

2 "Ban Patriotic After Vacation at Dover Hall, *New York Tribune*, February 9, 1917.

3 "Military Training in Majors," *Chicago Examiner*, February 9, 1917.

4 John Alcock, "Dig Trenches, Target Drill for Players?," *Chicago Tribune*, February 9, 1917.

5 Murdock, "The Tragedy of Ban Johnson," 26.

6 "Club Owners Mobilize Men for War Drill," *Chicago Daily News*, February 16, 1917.

7 "If You Would Like to Be in the Ban Johnson Class Here Is a First Class Method to Do It," *Calgary Herald*, June 4, 1915.

8 "Baseball Gossip," *Lewistown (MT) Democrat*, June 3, 1915.

9 "He's Bossing More Millionaires Than Anyone Else in U.S.," *Syracuse (NY) Journal*, September 1, 1915. The town of Plattsburgh, New York, did not at the time use a concluding "h."

10 Bozeman Bulger, "Players Enthusiastic Over Plan to Give Them Military Drills in Camp," *New York World*, February 10, 1917.

11 John Alcock, "Military Drill for American League Assured," *Chicago Tribune*, February 25, 1917.

12 George S. Robbins, "Sergt. Smiley May Be Sox Army Tutor," *Chicago Daily News*, February 27, 1917.

13 Irving Vaughan, "Commy Seeks Drillmaster for the Sox," *Chicago Examiner*, February 23, 1917.

14 "White Sox Seek Drill Sergeant," *Chicago Tribune*, February 27, 1917.

15 Robbins, "Sergt. Smiley May Be Sox Army Tutor."

16 Malcolm MacLean, "Military Flavor Sure Thrills the Nerves of White Hose Athletes," *Chicago Evening Post*, March 8, 1917.

17 William Kennedy, "The Army All-Star Team," *Baseball Magazine*, June 1915.

18 "Baseball Nine Backed by U. S. to Promote Efficiency Among Soldiers," *Chicago Tribune*, April 18, 1915.

19 "Major League Club Secures Army Sergeant," *Honolulu Star-Bulletin*, March 17, 1917.

20 Irving Vaughan, "Too Many Cooks in A. L. Game," *Chicago Examiner*, February 28, 1917.

21 "Dilhoefer Liable to Get Regular Catching Job," *Chicago Day Book*, February 27, 1917.

22 George S. Robbins, "Lays Plans for So in the Training Camp," *Chicago Daily News*, February 26, 1917.

23 George S. Robbins, "Says Sox Luck Will Win League Pennant," *Chicago Daily News*, September 3, 1917.

24 George S. Robbins, "Buckner Rejoins the Sox," *Chicago Daily News*, February 14, 1917.

25 John Alcock, "Clubs Wait for Order to Engage Drill Masters," *Chicago Tribune*, February 28, 1917.

26 Walter S. Smiley, "Sergeant Smiley Tells of Drill Plans for Sox; Expects to Show Work Will Be Paying Investment," *Chicago Herald*, March 4, 1917.

27 Frederick G. Lieb, "Rain Halts Yanks' Work at Ball Park," *New York Sun*, March 3, 1917.

28 James Crusinberry, "Commy Books Sane Training Jaunt for Sox," *Chicago Tribune*, January 28, 1917.

29 William Evans, "Charles Comiskey, the Prince of Magnates," *Baseball Magazine*, December 1917.

30 Vaughan, "Commy Seeks Drillmaster."

31 George S. Robbins, "White Sox Training Cut to One Month," *Chicago Daily News*, January 4, 1917.

32 "U. S. Bares War Plot," *Chicago Tribune*, March 1, 1917.

33 "Plot Story True, Says Wilson, Senators Demand All Facts," *New York Evening World*, March 1, 1917.

34 "Uncover Plot Against Nation," *Washington Herald*, March 1, 1917.

35 David Rotroff, Sportively Speaking, *Chicago Daily News*, March 2, 1917.

Chapter 2

1 "White Sox Pull of [sic] Windy City Before Throng," *Davenport (IA) Democrat and Leader*, March 5, 1917.

2 "It Takes Two Diners to Fed Sox on Trip," *Chicago Daily News*, March 2, 1917.

3 John Alcock, "Away They Go! 3,000 Rooters Cheering Sox," *Chicago Tribune*, March 5, 1917

4 "Day's News Condensed," *Chicago Live Stock World*, March 5, 1917.

5 Alcock, "Away They Go!" Alcock was slightly mistaken; Walsh would pitch eighteen innings for the National League Boston Braves late in the 1917 season.

6 Robbins, "Buckner Rejoins the Sox."

7 George S. Robbins, "Gandil Goes on First for the White Sox," *Chicago Daily News*, March 1, 1917.

8 "Joy on Sox Special Speeding to Camp," *Chicago Daily News*, March 5, 1917.

9 Alcock, "Away They Go!"

10 G. W. Axelson, "White Sox and Followers Leave for Invasion of Texas Camp Tonight," *Chicago Herald*, March 4, 1917.

11 George S. Robbins, "Thousands Welcome Sox at Texas Camp," *Chicago Daily News*, March 6, 1917.

12 I. E. Sanborn, "Early Birds Find Snow at Camp of Sox," *Chicago Tribune*, March 6, 1917.

13 "White Sox Special Made Short Stop," *Wichita Beacon*, March 6, 1917.

14 "Sox Speed Southward," *Chicago Tribune*, March 6, 1917.

15 G. W. Axelson, "Sox Take Soldier Stuff Seriously; Put On First Drills, Tomorrow," *Chicago Herald*, March 6, 1917.

16 "Armed Participation in War Is Hinted by President Wilson," *Chicago Day Book*, March 5, 1917.

17 "Men in Arms Marching Along Historic Avenue Lesson for the World," *Washington Star*, March 5, 1917.

18 "Ball Players Here," *Enid (OK) Daily Eagle*, March 6, 1917.

19 Sanborn, "Early Birds Find Snow."

20 Robbins, "Thousands Welcome Sox."

21 Sanborn, "Early Birds Find Snow."

22 "Come to Mineral Wells Texas," display ad, *Chicago Daily News*, January 17, 1917.

23 I. E. Sanborn, "Eager Sox in Drill 3 Hours After Arrival," *Chicago Tribune*, March 7, 1917.

24 George S. Robbins, "Sox Start Training; Prepare for Drill," *Chicago Daily News*, March 7, 1917.

25 Chuck Swan, Talking It Over, *El Paso Herald*, March 9, 1917.

26 "Sox Go Into Camp," *Moline (IL) Daily Dispatch*, March 6, 1917.

27 Harry F. Pierce, "Chicago White Sox to Get Army Uniforms and Rifles," *St. Louis Star*, April 13, 1917.

28 Edward T. Collins, "Eddie Collins Tells Benefits of Military Drill," *Chicago Tribune*, April 15, 1917.

29 George S. Robbins, "'Tenshun! Company! Hep! Hep! Sox in Line," *Chicago Daily News*, March 8, 1917.

30 I. E. Sanborn, "'Tribune' Find Helps Rookies Beat Sox, 5 to 2," *Chicago Tribune*, March 9, 1917.

31 Robbins, "'Tenshun!"

32 "Comiskey Says Station Should Have Champ Ball Organization," *Great Lakes Recruit*, June 1917.

33 I. E. Sanborn, "Five White Sox Appointed Corporals," *Chicago Tribune*, March 11, 1917.

34 Ring W. Lardner, In the Wake of the News, *Chicago Tribune*, March 9, 1917.

35 "Preparedness at the White Sox Training Camp, *Chicago Daily News*, March 12, 1917.

36 Collins, "Eddie Collins Tells Benefits." *Baseball Magazine*, April 1916.

37 "Six Enlist Here," *Racine (WI) Journal-News*, April 20, 1916.

38 G. W. Axelson, "Sergeant Smiley Pins Chevrons on Five Members of the White Sox," *Chicago Herald*, March 11, 1917.

39 "Note About the White Sox," *Chicago Daily News*, April 4, 1917.

40 George S. Robbins, "White Sox Lose a Promising Player," *Chicago Daily News*, March 13, 1917.

41 "Edie Collins' Corps Used Slats for Drill; Hotel Maid Perplexed," *Akron (OH) Beacon Journal*, October 28, 1918.

42 "Recruiting Notes: 'White Sox' Drillmaster Retires," *United States Army Recruiting News*, July 1939.

43 George S. Robbins, "White Sox Doing Some Real Soldiering," *Chicago Daily News*, March 19, 1917.

44 John J. Ward, "'Death Valley' Jim Scott," *Baseball Magazine*, April 1916.

45 Mark Shields, "Jim Scott May Pitch Opening Game for White Sox," *Chicago Day Book*, March 15, 1917.

46 Mark Shields, "Jim Scott to Work Hard for Regular Berth with Sox," *Chicago Day Book*, March 6, 1917.

47 "Scott to Stick with Rowland; Boss Sees Star," *Chicago Tribune*, February 22, 1917.

48 W. S. Smiley, "White Sox Drill Sergeant Reports Great Progress by the Athletes," *Chicago Herald*, April 1, 1917.

49 Collins, "Eddie Collins Tells Benefits."

50 "Risberg Man to Take Berth of von Kolnitz," *Chicago Tribune*, March 14, 1917.

51 Robbins, "White Sox Lose a Promising Player."

52 "White Sox Can't Have Risberg Now," *Riverside (CA) Daily Press*, July 28, 1916.

53 "Risberg Man to Take Berth."

54 "Practice Grenade Throwing," *Racine (WI) Journal-News*, March 21, 1917.

55 George S. Robbins, "Sox Players Taught to Hurl Grenades," *Chicago Daily News*, March 20, 1917.

56 George S. Robbins, "O'Neill Drills Sox Players," *Chicago Daily News*, March 22, 1917.

57 "Panther Drill Under Dolly Gray," *Fort Worth Star-Telegram*, May 6, 1917. This wasn't William "Dolly" Gray, former Major League pitcher and outfielder who'd played with the 1909–1911 Washington Senators.

58 Brown, *The Chicago White Sox*, 83.

59 "'Pep' Is Missing, Says Gleason," *Chicago Herald*, April 7, 1917.

60 Harry Neily, "Gleason Gives Hose Edge on All Counts," *Chicago Evening American*, September 28, 1917.

61 "Preparedness!," *Chicago Tribune*, March 17, 1917.

62 I. E. Sanborn, "Sox Rout Foes in First Real Battle," *Chicago Tribune*, March 18, 1917.

63 "Trip," "Looking Them Over from the Pressbox," *Houston Post*, March 26, 1917.

64 "Trip," "Looking Them Over from the Pressbox," *Houston Post*, March 30, 1917

65 George S. Robbins, "Sox Play the Buffs with Faber on Slab," *Chicago Daily News*, March 24, 1917.

66 George S. Robbins, "Joe Jenkins—Some Recruit," *Chicago Daily News*, March 23, 1917.

67 John Alcock, "Up to Sox Pitchers to Win '17 Pennant, Comiskey Declares," *Chicago Tribune*, March 29, 1917.

68 Irving Vaughan, "Sox Halted in Wichita by Wind Storm," *Chicago Examiner*, April 4, 1917.

69 "House for War," *Chicago Tribune*, April 6, 1917.

70 "U. S. at War, Wilson Fiat," *Chicago Daily News*, April 6, 1917.

71 George S. Robbins, "Military Idea Game's Savior since Declaration of War," *Sporting News*, April 12, 1917.

72 "Sox Youngsters Blank Wichita," *Chicago Tribune*, April 7, 1917.

73 Robbins, "Military Idea Game's Savior."

74 "Mark Shields, "Elaborate Preparations for First Cub Game," *Chicago Day Book*, April 4, 1917.

75 George S. Robbins, "Sox Regulars Beat Ottumwa None 15-0," *Chicago Daily News*, April 6, 1917.

76 W. S. Smiley, "White Sox Drill Sergeant Speaks for Military Training," *Sporting News*, April 12, 1917. Various publications used "S." as his middle initial, but Smiley had no middle name. The army might have written this article for him.

Chapter 3

1   B. B. Johnson and John K. Tener, "Base Ball Assured," *Washington Star*, April 8, 1917.

2   Charles W. Murphy, "Murphy Says War Will Hurt," *Chicago Examiner*, April 15, 1917.

3   I. E. Sanborn, "White Sox Attack Routs Conquerors of Cubs, 7 to 4," *Chicago Tribune*, April 9, 1917.

4   "Exhibition Drill Times Should Begin Just Before Game Time," *St. Louis Star*, April 12, 1917.

5   I. E. Sanborn, "Enemy Gunners Routed by Sox at Finish, 7-2," *Chicago Tribune*, April 12, 1917.

6   "Gossip of the Sox Players," *Chicago Daily News*, April 12, 1917.

7   Sanborn, "Enemy Gunners Routed."

8   "Rain Prevents Second Tilt in Brown-Sox Mix," *Davenport (IA) Democrat and Leader*, April 13, 1917.

9   "It's Sy-cott Cicotte," *Chicago Evening American*, October 3, 1917.

10 "Cicotte Shuts the Browns Out Hitless," *St. Louis Globe-Democrat*, April 15, 1917.

11 Irving Vaughan, "Cicotte in No-Hit Victory over Browns; Sox Score 11 Runs," *Chicago Examiner*, April 15, 1917.

12   Sandoval, "Eddie Cicotte."

13   I. E. Sanborn, "27,00 See Sox Drop Opener to Browns, 6-2," *Chicago Tribune*, April 20, 1917.

14   "First in Fighting Men Is Place of Illinois," *Chicago Daily News*, April 19, 1917.

15   John Alcock, "War and Baseball to Share Same Bill at Sox Opener Today," *Chicago Tribune*, April 19, 1917.

16   Sanborn, "27,00 See Sox Drop Opener."

17   "White Sox Infantry Given Regimental Flag," *Chicago Examiner*, April 20, 1917.

18   "Sox Have the Stuff But Need Team Perfection," *Chicago Day Book*, April 20, 1917.

19   Sanborn, "27,00 See Sox Drop Opener."

20   "Ban Johnson Orders Drilling Continued," *Washington Times*, May 28, 1917.

21   "Humorous Occurrences in Sport Brought to Light," *Detroit Free Press*, August 6, 1917.

22   "White Sox on Way East," *Chicago Daily News*, May 31, 1917.

23   James Crusinberry, "Sox Compress Year's Thrills in 6-3 Victory," *Chicago Tribune*, June 6, 1917.

24   James Crusinberry, "Cicotte Allows Macks 3 Swats, Beats 'em, 4 – 0," *Chicago Tribune*, June 3, 1917.

25   F. C. Lane, "'Pants' Rowland, the Bush League Manager Who Made Good," *Baseball Magazine*, December 1917.

26   Jim Scott as told to Joseph S. McInerney, "Here Again—Gone Again," *San Francisco Bulletin*, September 18, 1917.

27   Lane, "'Pants' Rowland."

28   George S. Robbins, "Gandil and the Sox Head Agree on Pay," *Chicago Daily News*, March 9, 1917.

29   I. E. Sanborn, "Rookies' Rally Beats Sox Vets by 2 to 1 Count," *Chicago Tribune*, March 13, 1917.

30   Lane, "'Pants' Rowland."

31   Jim Scott as told to Joseph S. McInerney, "'Death Valley' Jim Scott Dopes Series," *San Francisco Bulletin*, September 15, 1917.

32   Wilbert and Hageman. *The 1917 White Sox*, 159.

33   John Alcock, "Set Your Seat for '17 Series! White Sox Purchase Gandil," *Chicago Tribune*, March 2, 1917.

34 J. Ed. Grillo, "Nationals, Led by Bob Groom, Come Back Strong," *Washington Star*, June 22, 1912.

35 Huhn, *Eddie Collins*, 141.

36 "Fighting Chick Gandil Makes Good with the Senator [sic] Team," *El Paso Herald*, September 20, 1917.

37 George E. Phair, Breakfast Food, *Chicago Examiner*, August 25, 1917.

38 George S. Robbins, "Debate Gameness of Sox and Giants," *Chicago Daily News*, September 12, 1917.

39 George S. Robbins, "Sox Go on Vacations; Plans of the Champs," *Chicago Daily News*, October 18, 1917.

Chapter 4

1 "Quota for First Draft Army Picked; Drawing Ended At 2.18 This Morning," *New York Tribune*, July 21, 1917.

2 "Draft Numbers Showing How Men Are To Be Called," *New York Tribune*, July 21, 1917.

3 "Calls Girls to Shame Slackers," *Chicago Herald*, April 11, 1917.

4 "Lashes Slacker Brides," *Chicago Daily News*, April 12, 1917.

5 "The Creed of a Slacker," *Chicago Daily News*, April 12, 1917.

6 "Sox Reach New York to Open Hard Series with Yanks Today," *Chicago Tribune*, July 25, 1917.

7 "White Sox Register for the War Draft," *Chicago Daily News*, May 24, 1917.

8 Kennedy, "The Army All-Star Team."

9 "Weaver of Sox Drawn Early in Draft Lottery," *Chicago Tribune*, July 21, 1917.

10 Daniel Rice, "Larry Cheney Is Looming Up As a Stand-by for Superbas," *Brooklyn Eagle*, March 29, 1917.

11 "Sox and Collegians in Clash," *Chicago Daily News*, April 23, 1917.

12 John Alcock, "Commy Hands $2,939 to Red Cross Funds; That Makes $5,158," *Chicago Tribune*, June 1, 1917.

13 "Joffre Day at Sox Park 'France Day' Is Plan," *Chicago Daily News*, April 25, 1917.

14 "White Sox Drillmaster Given Lieutenant's Rank," *Chicago Tribune*, June 12, 1917.

15 Zminda, *Double Plays and Double Crosses*, 1.

16 James Crusinberry, "Riot at Sox Game Started by Gamblers of Boston," *Chicago Tribune*, June 18, 1917.

17 Edward F. Martin, "Fans Crowd on Fenway Diamond," Boston Globe, June 17, 1917.

18 "Two Sox Served with Arrest Warrants," *Chicago Tribune*, June 19, 1917.

19 Sam Weller, "Sox Invade M'Henry at Treat Home Boys to 9 to 1 Trimming," *Chicago Tribune*, August 15, 1916.

20 Algren, *The Last Carousel*, 272.

21 "Notes," *Chicago Tribune*, September 25, 1917.

22 Sportsman, Live Tips and Topics, *Boston Globe*, June 18, 1917.

23 Crusinberry, "Cicotte Allows Macks 3 Swats."

24 I. E. Sanborn, "Sox Give West First Pennant in Many Years," *Chicago Tribune*, December 30, 1917.

25 "Jim Scott Quits Sox to Join Officers' Camp," *Chicago Examiner*, September 10, 1917.

26 "White Sox Notes," *Chicago Tribune*, July 7, 1917. This regular feature inserted a graphic of a single sock in the place of the words White Sox, and did the same for the Chicago Cubs. Hereafter cited as "Notes."

27 Lane, "'Pants' Rowland, the Bush League Manager."

28 "Macks Beat White Sox Before Army Officers," *Philadelphia Inquirer*, July 9, 1917.

29 "Macks Show Big League Frills and Beat Sox at Ft. Sheridan," *Chicago Tribune*, July 9, 1917.

30 James Clarkson, "3,500 Soldiers at Ball Game; Sox and Athletics Cheered," *Chicago Examiner*, July 9, 1917.

31 "National Race Is Getting to Be Runaway, But American Is as Tight as a Miser's Purse Strings," *Philadelphia Inquirer*, July 9, 1917.

32 James Crusinberry, "Mackmen Life White Sox Back to First Place," *Chicago Tribune*, July 9, 1917.

33 "National Race Is Getting to Be Runaway."

Chapter 5

1 I. E. Sanborn, "Sox Players 'Het Up' at Rough Road Trip for Game in Detroit," *Chicago Tribune*, July 30, 1917.

2 "Sox Lose Money of 14,000 Detroiters, Rain Stopping Game," *Chicago Tribune*, August 6, 1917.

3 "Rain Routs Both Tigers and Chicago," *Detroit Free Press*, August 6, 1917.

4 "White Sox Trio Ask Exemption," *Philadelphia Evening Public Ledger*, August 7, 1917.

5 Lane, "'Pants' Rowland, the Bush League Manager."

6 Wm. A. Phelon, "Baseball History in the Making," *Baseball Magazine*, September 1917.

7 "White Sox Lose Jim Scott," *Chicago Eagle*, August 4, 1917.

8 "Prize Drill of Sox Set for Thursday," *Chicago Tribune*, August 19, 1917.

9 "Phone Company of Engineers Off for East," *Chicago Tribune*, August 23, 1917.

10 "Military Day Today as White Sox Drill for Prize of $500," *Chicago Tribune*, August 23, 1917.

11 George S. Robbins, "Sox and Senators Drill for $500 Prize," *Chicago Daily News*, August 23, 1917.

12 E. E. Sanborn, "Army Pageant Dwarfs Game, But Sox Win," *Chicago Tribune*, August 24, 1917.

13 Sanborn, "Army Pageant Dwarfs Game."

14 J. Bradley Smollen, "Browns Win $500 Drill," *Chicago Examiner*, August 28, 1917.

15 Denman Thompson, "Griffith's Team Put Through Competitive Drill at Chicago," *Washington Evening Star*, August 24, 1917.

16 "American League Chatter," *Chicago Daily News*, August 28, 1917. The author of this unsigned piece was likely beat writer George S. Robbins.

17 "Browns Best in Army Work, Judge Rules," *Chicago Tribune*, August 28, 1917.

18 "Military Day Drills to Be Annual Feature," *Chicago Tribune*, August 26, 1917. The annual event Comiskey imagined never happened, although the Sox would hold what they called a military day in 1921 for thousands of disabled veterans, national guardsmen, and sailors from Great Lakes.

19 "Military to Honor Griffith," *Chicago Examiner*, August 25, 1917.

20 I. E. Sanborn, "28,000 See Sox Upset Johnson, 4 to 1," *Chicago Tribune*, August 26, 1917.

21 "Rush Negro Rioters to Border," *Chicago Tribune*, August 25, 1917.

22 "Colored Soldiers in the South," *Chicago Tribune*, August 29, 1917.

23 Lambert G. Sullivan, "Give Bats and Balls to Uncle Sam's Men," *Chicago Daily News*, August 25, 1917.

24. Sanborn, "28,000 See Sox Upset Johnson."
25. "Griff All Dolled Up for Big Time in Chicago Today," *Washington Times*, August 25, 1917.
26. Denman Thompson, "League Pennant May Depend on Play of Griffith's Team," *Washington Star*, August 26, 1917. Griffith's comment referred to the Philippine Insurrection following the Spanish-American War.
27. Sanborn, "28,000 See Sox Upset Johnson."
28. Denman Thompson, "White Sox Beat Johnson, 4 to 1," *Washington Star*, August 26, 1917.
29. "Chicago Sorry to See Griffmen Leave for Good," *Washington Times*, August 26, 1917. This accounting doesn't include the May 26 tie.
30. "Browns Best in Army Work."
31. "Browns Awarded Prize for Being Best Drilled Team in American League," *St. Louis Globe-Democrat*, August 28, 1917.
32. Smollen, "Browns Win $500 Drill."
33. "Browns Best in Army Work."
34. "Champion Browns and their Drill Master," *Sporting News*, September 6, 1917.
35. "Late News Items," *Sporting News*, August 30, 1917.
36. T. L. Huston, "Cap Huston Issues Solemn Warning to All Baseball Folk," *Brooklyn Eagle*, March 24, 1918.
37. Sanborn, "Sox Give West First Pennant in Many Years."
38. Charles A. Comiskey, letter addressed "To Whom it May Concern," August 26, 1916 [*sic*], Walter Smiley file, U.S. National Archives, St. Louis, MO.

Chapter 6

1. I. E. Sanborn, "30,000 Crowd Thrilled as Sox Win Two," *Chicago Tribune*, September 3, 1917.
2. "Tiges [sic] Fall Before Sox In Two Games at Chicago Sunday," *Detroit Times*, September 3, 1917.
3. "Told About the Tigers," *Detroit Free Press*, September 3, 1917.
4. George S. Robbins, "Sox Make Hard Fight to Keep Lead in 2d," *Chicago Daily News*, September 3, 1917.

5   "Notes," *Chicago Tribune*, September 4, 1917.

6   I. E. Sanborn, "Sox Widen Gap to 6 1-2 Games, Murphy Stars," *Chicago Tribune*, September 4, 1917.

7   E. A. Batchelor, "White Sox Beat Tigers Twice More," *Detroit Free Press*, September 4, 1917.

8   "White Hose Profit By Wildness of Tige Hurlers and Cop 2 Games," *Detroit Times*, September 4, 1917.

9   "Black Sox Juror Says He Doesn't Know 'Ty' Cobb!," *Chicago Tribune*, July 8, 1920.

10 "Tigers Sold 1917 Series, Risberg Tells Landis," *Detroit Free Press*, January 2, 1927.

11 Steinberg, "Dave Danforth."

12 Steinberg, "Dell Pratt."

13 Wilbert and Hageman, *The 1917 White Sox*, 209.

14 Zminda, *Double Plays and Double Crosses*, 8.

15 "Brownies' Revolt Ends; Owner Says He Was Misquoted," *St. Louis Post-Dispatch*, September 6, 1917.

16 "Johnson Confers with Ball," *Chicago Daily News*, September 10, 1917.

17 Wilbert and Hageman. *The 1917 White Sox*, 74.

18 C. B. Rourke, "Baseball Suits for Guards from 'Commy,'" *Chicago Daily News*, September 22, 1917.

19 I. E. Sanborn, "Troops Cheer as Sox Continue Sweep," *Chicago Tribune*, September 9, 1917.

20 "White Sox Notes," *Chicago Examiner*, September 9, 1917.

21 I. E. Sanborn, "Tribe Revolts, Ump Forfeits Clash to Sox," *Chicago Tribune*, September 10, 1917.

22 "Indians Lose by Forfeit," *Cleveland Plain Dealer*, September 10, 1917.

23 "'Death Valley' Jim Enters R.O.T.C. To-Day," *San Francisco Examiner*, September 11, 1917.

24 "Notes," *Chicago Tribune*, September 10, 1917.

25 Robert W. Maxwell, unsigned column, "Sharpe Sacrifices Reputation to Train Cornell Men to Play Game as if They Were Winning," *Philadelphia Evening Ledger*, November 15, 1917.

26 "Jim Scott Enrolls at Coast Officers' Camp," *Chicago Tribune*, September 12, 1917.

27 Harry Neily, *Chicago Evening American*, reprinted in "U. S. Army Life Agrees with Jim Scott," *Los Angeles Herald*, January 24, 1918.

28 James Crusinberry, "20,000 Fan See Sox Win in Tenth, 4-3," *Chicago Tribune*, September 17, 1917.

29 George S. Robbins, "White Sox in East; Sure of the Flag," *Chicago Daily News*, September 17, 1917.

30 Robbins, "Debate Gameness of Sox and Giants."

31 "Notes," *Chicago Tribune*, September 20, 1917.

32 John Alcock, "Phone Brings Glad News to Commy After 11 Lean Years," *Chicago Tribune*, September 22, 1917.

33 "Commy Is Overjoyed; Sends Thanks to Team," *Chicago Examiner*, September 22, 1917.

34 "Congrats to Commy from 'Over There' Sent by Capt. Huston," *Chicago Tribune*, September 26, 1917.

35 "In the White Sox Periscope," *Chicago Daily News*, September 24, 1917.

Chapter 7

1 George S. Robbins, "Shine Ball a Myth, Declares Cicotte," *Chicago Daily News*, October 17, 1917.

2 Malcolm MacLean, "Slab Miracle What Cicotte Will Be Named," *Chicago Evening Post*, September 7, 1917.

3 "White Sox Call the 'Shine Ball' a Bugaboo to Make Giants Tremble," *New York Times*, September 26, 1917.

4 "Ed Cicotte, Pitching Vet, Has New Delivery That's Tricky Yet Legal," *Dayton Daily News*, June 10, 1917.

5 Damon Runyon, "Giants Beaten, 2-1, by Home Run," *New York American*, October 7, 1917.

6 Sandoval, "Eddie Cicotte."

7 Billy Evans, "Stop Spitter and All Illegal Deliveries Can Be Eliminated," *Dayton Daily News*, January 13, 1918.

8 Robbins, "Says Sox Luck."

NOTES

9 H. G. Salsinger, "Ed Cicotte Says Mystery of His Puzzling Pitch Supplied by Players," *Binghamton (NY) Sunday Press*, March 23, 1952.

10 I. E. Sanborn, "White Sox vs. Giants," *Chicago Tribune*, October 1, 1917.

11 Runyon, "Giants Beaten, 2-1."

12 "World Series Notes," *Chicago Tribune*, October 7, 1917.

13 "What Faber Said," *Chicago Tribune*, October 9, 1917.

14 I. E. Sanborn, "White Sox Whale Giants, 7-2," *Chicago Tribune*, October 8, 1917.

15 "Faber Explains His Blunder," *Chicago Daily News*, October 8, 1917.

16 Commy Quits Game After Big Fourth," *Chicago Tribune*, October 8, 1917.

17 "Shines Again as Big Series Hero," *Sporting News*, October 18, 1917. Sportswriters often jumbled the name of the Griffith Ball and Bat Fund.

18 Irwin S. Cobb, "Davy Robertson and Psychology Win for Giants," *Boston Globe*, October 11, 1917.

19 George D. Underwood, "Big Baseball Army Is Well Handled," *New York Sun*, October 11, 1917.

20 James Crusinberry, "Fickle Gotham Makes Giants Heroes Again," *Chicago Tribune*, October 11, 1917.

21 Charles Dryden, "New York Goes Wild as Giants Beat Sox," *Chicago Examiner*, October 11, 1917.

22 Charles Dryden, "Giants Tie Up Series; 2 Homers by Kauff," *Chicago Examiner*, October 12, 1917

23 "Sox Fans Haven't Had Run for Their Money for the Last 22 Innings," *Chicago Examiner*, October 12, 1917.

24 James Crusinberry, "Sox Fans Slink Out of Gotham Silent Mob," *Chicago Tribune*, October 12, 1917.

25 Hugh S. Fullerton, "Sox Will Win Game and Series 'Sometime Before Thanksgiving.'—Fullerton," *Chicago Examiner*, October 13, 1917.

26 Robbins, "M'Graw Forces Come for Crucial Battle," *Chicago Daily News*, October 12, 1917.

27 Irwin S. Cobb, "M'Graw's Pet Plans Blow to Flinders," *Philadelphia Inquirer*, October 14, 1917.

28 I. E. Sanborn, "Sox Beat Giants, 8 to 5," *Chicago Tribune*, October 14, 1917.

29 Damon Runyan, "White Sox Rally and Beat Giants, 8-5," *New York American*, October 14, 1917.

30. "Worlds Series Notes," *Chicago Tribune*, October 14, 1917.
31. James Crusinberry, "Sox 'Big Push' Brings Bedlam," *Chicago Tribune*, October 14, 1917.
32. Louis Lee Arms, "Giants Spill All The Beans in Final Test," *New York Tribune*, October 16, 1917.
33. "Maybe Sox and Scribes Are More Friendly Now," *Chicago Tribune*, October 14, 1917. The author was likely Jack Lait, who wrote the preceding article.
34. James Crusinberry, "Gotham at Train to Welcome Sox with Mailed Fist," *Chicago Tribune*, October 15, 1917.
35. "White Sox Take World Title in Torrid Finish," *New York Times*, October 16, 1917.
36. Arms, "Giants Spill All The Beans."
37. Damon Runyon, "White Sox Win World's Championship on Errors by Giants," *New York American*, October 16, 1917.
38. Billy Birch, "Poor Old Heinie Writes Himself in the Record as Prize Boob of Series," *Chicago Herald*, October 16, 1917.
39. Frederick G. Lieb, "Giants' Defeat Is Fourth in World's Series," *New York Sun*, October 16, 1917.
40. "White Sox Take World Title."
41. "Catcher Rariden Tells How Collins Beat Zim," *New York Evening Journal*, October 16, 1917.
42. Stan Baumgartner, "Collins Went From Campus to A's," *Sporting News*, August 16, 1950.
43. James J. Corbett, "Foot Race Wins for White Sox," *Chicago Examiner*, October 16, 1917.
44. "Landis Calls White Sox Job Good Day's Work," *Chicago Tribune*, October 16, 1917.
45. "Prosperous Season for Major Leagues," *New York Times*, December 30, 1917.
46. James Crusinberry, "Statements," *Chicago Tribune*, October 16, 1917.
47. "Teams Perform Before Soldiers at Mineola," *South Bend (IN) Tribune*, October 17, 1917.
48. James Crusinberry, "Soldiers See Sox Clean Up Giants, 6-3," *Chicago Tribune*, October 17, 1917.
49. "Sox Beat Giants Again Before 15,000 Soldiers Of Rainbow Division," *New York Evening World*, October 17, 1917. The newspaper's crowd estimate was higher than most others.

50 Crusinberry, "Soldiers See Sox Clean Up Giants."

51 Larry Woltz, "Wild Mob Meets New Champions," *Chicago Examiner*, October 18, 1917. Other newspapers estimated the crowd at closer to 5,000 people. The *Examiner's* 50,000 figure might be a typesetting error, inserting an extra zero.

52 Fred A. Marquardt, "Wild Fans Hail Sox as They Reach City," *Chicago Daily News*, October 17, 1917.

53 Howard Johnson and Percy Wenrich, "Where Do We Go From Here?," Leo Feist, Inc., 1917.

Chapter 8

1 "Jim Scott of Sox Here to Join Camp of Presidio Officers," *San Francisco Chronicle*, September 11, 1917.

2 "Jim Scott Admitted to Presidio Camp," *Bakersfield Californian*, September 12, 1917.

3 "Death Valley Jim Scott Admitted to Presidio Camp," *San Francisco Call*, September 11, 1917.

4 "Officers' Training Camp," *Buffalo (WY) Voice*, July 6, 1917.

5 Bert Lowry, "Midwinter Baseball Is Not Favored by Coast League Bosses," *San Francisco Call*, September 18, 1917.

6 Lowry, "Midwinter Baseball Is Not Favored."

7 Joseph S. McInerney, "Jim Scott Says Sox Board of Will Outhink [sic] M'Graw," *San Francisco Bulletin*, September 14, 1917.

8 "White Sox Daily Drills Helped Captain James Scott, Now Here, Earn Commission at Presidio," *Tacoma (WA) Daily Ledger*, December 14, 1917.

9 E. G. B. Fitzhamon, "Digging In Is Hard Job at Presidio," *San Francisco Examiner*, October 19, 1917.

10 "Shrapnel," *San Francisco Bulletin*, October 17, 1917.

11 "Baseball Gossip," *San Francisco Call*, September 17, 1917.

12 "Merced Bears Badly Beaten by Richmond," *San Francisco Chronicle*, September 24, 1917.

13 "Scott Can't Even Follow Ball Games," *San Francisco Chronicle*, October 8, 1917.

14 "Ten Thousand Fans See Big Leaguers Win from Coasters," *San Francisco Examiner*, November 12, 1917.

15 J. J. Alcock, "Weaver Intent on Footlights' Poolroom to Go," *Chicago Tribune*, October 10, 1915.

16 "'Too Many Cooks,' But 'Death Valley' Jim Finally Weds," *San Francisco Examiner*, November 18, 1917.

17 "Meet Captain Jim Scott!," *San Francisco Bulletin*, November 26, 1917.

18 "White Sox Daily Drills Helped Captain James Scott."

19 "Dr. Palmer Says All California Is Hooverizing," *Honolulu Star-Bulletin*, December 6, 1917.

20 "Jim Scott Now a Captain," *Chicago Daily News*, November 26, 1917.

21 James Crusinberry, "How Jim Scott Made Good," *Chicago Tribune*, February 17, 1918.

22 Robert W. Maxwell, unsigned column, "Barrow, Red Sox Manager, Working Overtime for C. Mack in Search for Ball Players," *Philadelphia Evening Public Ledger*, February 21, 1918.

23 "Commy Says Play Is Safe Next Year," *Rock Island (IL) Argus*, November 27, 1917.

24 "Receives Wife's Congratulations," *Canton (OH) Daily News*, December 10, 1917.

25 "Risberg Will Coach Soldiers' Ball Club," *San Francisco Chronicle*, December 5, 1917.

26 "'Swede' Handles Team at Presidio," *San Francisco Bulletin*, December 29, 1917.

27 "McCredie Wants to Go into Northwestern Baseball League," *Ogden (UT) Standard*, December 7, 1917.

28 "Here Is Man Who Will Make Germans 'Duck,'" *Tacoma (WA) Sunday News-Ledger*, December 9, 1917.

29 Larry Woltz, "Jim Scott Heard From," *Chicago Examiner*, January 16, 1918.

30 Henderson, *The Ninety-first*, 395.

31 "Capt. James Scott Likes the White Sox Chances to Repeat," *Chicago Examiner*, January 31, 1918.

32 Grantland Rice, "Somewhere in America," *Atlanta Journal*, January 15, 1918.

33 George S. Robbins, "White Sox Work for Cleanup To-day," *Chicago Daily News*, May 30, 1918.

34 "Capt. Jim Scott Works with Sox," *Chicago Tribune*, May 31, 1918.

35 George S. Robbins, "Scott's Work in Army Pleases Comiskey," *Chicago Daily News*, July 5, 1918.

36 George S. Robbins, "Baker Rule a Blow to Nation's Morale," *Sporting News*, July 25, 1918.

NOTES

37 Bill Yeager, "Jim Scott Has Fine Lineup on His Team," *San Francisco Examiner*, August 17, 1918.

38 "Camp Lewis Ball Club Hands Naval Camp 9-0 Beating," *Vallejo (CA) Evening Chronicle*, August 27, 1918.

39 Eddie Murphy, "Plenty of Baseball Games to Be Played and No Chance to Say Game Is Dead Here," *Oakland Tribune*, August 22, 1918.

40 "Camp Lewis Team Wins Baseball Tournament," *San Jose Mercury Herald*, August 23, 1918.

41 "Camp Lewis Ball Team Winners," *Vancouver (BC) Sun*, September 4, 1918.

Chapter 9

1 George S. Robbins, "World Series Coin Split by White Sox," *Chicago Daily News*, October 18, 1917.

2 "Here They Are—Buck and Mack," *Chicago Defender*, November 10, 1917.

3 James Crusinberry, "White Sox Make Trail of Mirth of Return Trip," *Chicago Tribune*, October 18, 1917.

4 I. E. Sanborn, "Sox Players Put Coin into Bonds," *Chicago Tribune*, October 19, 1917.

5 Reid J. Murdock, "Kid Gleason's Promises to Sox Wreck South Side Team," *Chicago Collyer's Eye*, July 13, 1918.

6 Nelson Algren, "Charles Comiskey," undated typed manuscript, Charles Comiskey file, National Baseball Hall of Fame, Cooperstown, New York.

7 George S. Robbins, "Sox Fans Wonder Whether Commy or Weaver Will Yield," *Sporting News*, March 13, 1919.

8 J. B. Sheridan, "Charles A. Comiskey, "The Noblest Roman" in Baseball," *El Paso Times*, October 21, 1917.

9 Lamb, *Black Sox in the Courtroom*, 7.

10 Hoie, "1919 Baseball Salaries and the Mythically Underpaid Chicago White Sox," 17, 31.

11 Harry Neily, "Commy Thinks He Has Real Ball Team," *Chicago Evening American*, March 4, 1918.

12 "Prosperous Season for Major Leagues."

13 Sanborn, "Sox Give West First Pennant."

14. "Slight Chance for Shorter Schedule," *Norwich (CT) Bulletin*, November 22, 1917.
15. I. E. Sanborn, "Ball Magnates Eye New Army Rules in Drawing 1918 Plans," *Chicago Tribune*, November 26, 1917.
16. "Commy Says Play Is Safe."
17. Leo Fischer, "Sox Leave on Spring Trip Mar. 16," *Chicago Daily News*, December 29, 1917.
18. Robbins, "Sox Fans Wonder."
19. "White Sox Duds Packed," *Chicago Daily News*, March 8, 1918.
20. George S. Robbins, "White Sox Trainer Ready for Getaway," *Chicago Daily News*, March 8, 1918.
21. Harry Neily, "Buckner Again Will Train Sox," *Chicago Evening American*, March 9, 1918.
22. George S. Robbins, "Sox Change Trainers Before Start South," *Chicago Daily News*, March 15, 1918.
23. I. E. Sanborn, "Sox Off Today on First Lap of 1918 Race," *Chicago Tribune*, March 16, 1918.
24. "Rowland Fires Bill Buckner as White Sox Trainer," *Chicago Defender*, March 23, 1918.
25. Robbins, "Sox Change Trainers."
26. George S. Robbins, "Buckner May Get His Old Post Back," *Chicago Daily News*, January 6, 1919.
27. Huhn, *Eddie Collins*, 306.
28. I. E. Sanborn, "Danforth Has Caused Quite a Bit of Trouble," *Washington Post*, September 19, 1923.
29. "Fans Glad to See Buckner as White Sox Trainer," *Chicago Defender*, February 11, 1922.

Chapter 10

1. Dan Daniel, High Lights and Shadows in All Spheres of Sport, *New York Sun*, March 26, 1918.
2. Charles A. Comiskey, "Comiskey Park for Government If Wanted," *Brooklyn Standard Union*, January 19, 1918.

3   "No Military Training For Baseball Players," *New York Tribune*, March 13, 1918.

4   John Alcock, "Rowland Leads Sox to Texas Camp," *Chicago Tribune*, March 17, 1918.

5   I. E. Sanborn, "Joe Benz Ready for First Game," *Chicago Tribune*, March 17, 1918.

6   "Snapping of Towel Puts Red Kuhn Out of Army and Ball," *Indianapolis News*, March 19, 1918.

7   George S. Robbins, "White Sox Players in Train Wreck," *Chicago Daily News*, March 18, 1918.

8   I. E. Sanborn, "Sox in Wreck; Lose Practice," *Chicago Tribune*, March 19, 1918.

9   George S. Robbins, "Eddie Cicotte Hurt in Auto Collision," *Chicago Daily News*, March 20, 1918.

10 I. E. Sanborn, "Ban on Autos and Golf for Sox and Golf," *Chicago Tribune*, March 21, 1918.

11 George S. Robbins, "Gen Wood Sees Sox Play His Camp Team," *Chicago Daily News*, April 12, 1918.

12 "Reb Russell, Felsch, Coach Gleason, Hass Not with White Sox," *Chicago Tribune*, March 18, 1918.

13 I. E. Sanborn, "Ray, Young Pitcher, First of White Sox to Get His Release," *Chicago Tribune*, March 27, 1918.

14 "Raid Alleged Poolroom in Shadow of Church," *Philadelphia Inquirer*, March 8, 1918.

15 "Gleason Not a Holdout; Expects to Report Soon," *Chicago Examiner*, April 8, 1918.

16 Comiskey Believes Baseball Necessity," *Chicago Daily News*, April 16, 1918.

17 "Baseball Notes," *Reading (PA) News-Times*, May 10, 1918.

18 James Crusinberry, "'Kid' Gleason Appointed Manager of the White Sox," *Chicago Tribune*, January 1, 1919.

19 "'Commy' Tells His Side of the Felsch Story," *Chicago Tribune*, January 1, 1919.

20 C. Starr Matthews, "Gleason Now Manager," *Baltimore Sun*, January 1, 1919. Gleason had begun his career in Baltimore more than thirty years earlier.

21 George S. Robbins, "Gleason Leads Sox; Rowland Is Deposed," *Chicago Daily News*, January 2, 1918.

22 Reid Murdock, "Sox Fans See Little Hope for Flag in Absence of Kid Gleason," *Chicago Collyer's Eye*, May 4, 1918.

23 I. E. Sanborn, "Sox Win from U.S. Marines in Texas, 11-2," *Chicago Tribune*, April 2, 1918.

24 Charles Dryden, "White Sox Wallop Hosts—Beat Marine Nine, 11 to 3," *Chicago Examiner*, April 2, 1918.

25 I. E. Sanborn, "Boys 'On Toes' for Sox Game at Camp Logan," *Chicago Tribune*, April 3, 1918.

26 I. E. Sanborn, "Sox Get More than Ball in 13-7 Clash," *Chicago Tribune*, April 4, 1918.

27 "White Sox Notes," *Chicago Tribune*, April 5, 1918.

28 Garrett H. Graham, "Ellington Efficiency," in *Ellington 1918*, 11.

29 George S. Robbins, "Sox Are Hit Hard by Draft," *Chicago Daily News*, July 21, 1917.

30 "Gossip of the Sox Players," *Chicago Daily News*, April 5, 1918.

31 I. E. Sanborn, "10,000 Funston Boys Watch Sox Bombard Camp's Team, 13 to 1," *Chicago Tribune*, April 13, 1918.

32 I. E. Sanborn, "Sox Win Last Game on Training Tour; Return Home Today," *Chicago Tribune*, April 15, 1918.

33 "White Sox Sign Collegian," *New York Sun*, November 21, 1917.

34 "Gossip from the Sox Trip," *Chicago Daily News*, April 3, 1918.

35 "This Keiser O. K.," *Chicago Tribune*, December 28, 1918.

Chapter 11

1 Dan Daniel, High Lights and Shadows in All Spheres of Sport, *New York Sun*, February 7, 1918.

2 Robert W. Maxwell, "Magnates Likely to Revoke Waiver Rule," *Philadelphia Inquirer*, February 13, 1918.

3 "Chicken Feed," *Chicago Tribune*, February 11, 1918. The Dodgers were often called the Robins while Wilbert Robinson, "Uncle Robbie," managed the club.

4 "May Compromise on the Spit Ball," *New York Herald*, February 11, 1918.

5 I. E. Sanborn, "Major League Prices Cover Fans' War Tax," *Chicago Tribune*, March 3, 1918.

6 "Patriots All!," *Chicago Tribune*, June 3, 1918.

7 "Girls Usher at Major League Parks; Find Time to Watch their Favorites," *Rock Island (IL) Argus*, July 18, 1918.

8 "American League Bingles," *Chicago Daily News*, April 17, 1918.

9 George S. Robbins, "Rowland's Stars Cannot Hold Browns," *Chicago Daily News*, April 16, 1918.

10 I. E. Sanborn, "25,000 Fans See White Sox Drop Opener, 6 to 1," *Chicago Tribune*, April 17, 1918.

11 Charles Dryden, "18,000 See Champions Tumble Under 17 Hits," *Chicago Examiner*, April 17, 1918.

12 Robbins, "Rowland's Stars Cannot Hold Browns."

13 "American League Bingles."

14 George Robbins, "Rowland Looks 'Em Over," *Great Lakes Recruit*, March 1918.

15 Hugh Edmund Keough as "HEK," "In the Wake of the News," *Chicago Tribune*, September 13, 1910.

16 "Chouinard Playing at Crystal Theater," *Green Bay Gazette*, February 14, 1912.

17 "Notes of the Sox," *Chicago Examiner*, April 17, 1918.

18 Seymour, *Baseball: The People's Game*, 338. Since publication Dorothy Seymour has been widely credited as coauthor with Harold.

19 Jimmie Corcoran, "Noted Athletes in the Navy," *Great Lakes Recruit*, September 1917.

20 Buzzell, *The Great Lakes Naval Training Station: A History*, 155.

21 "Major League Players Nucleus of Navy Teams," *New York Tribune*, March 12, 1918.

22 "Call to Outdoors Issued for Ball Men," *Great Lakes Bulletin*, April 3, 1918.

23 "Baseball Brevities," *Chicago Tribune*, March 24, 1918.

24 "Athletic Field and Ball Park at Great Lakes," *Chicago Tribune*, April 1, 1918.

25 "Too Cold for Sox Game," *Chicago Daily News*, April 20, 1918.

26 "White Sox Ball Game Is Off," *Chicago Daily News*, April 19, 1918.

27 "American League Drives," *Chicago Daily News*, July 31, 1918.

28 I. E. Sanborn, "Champ Sox Hit Road in Rusty Form After Rainy Day Idleness," *Chicago Tribune*, April 24, 1918.

29 "Joe Jackson Put in Class One Today," *Greenwood (SC) Evening Index*, May 1, 1918.

30 "Joe Jackson Placed in Class One and Must Serve in Army," *Greenville Daily News*, May 1, 1918.

31 "Joe Jackson Ready to Go for Boches," *Greenwood Evening Index*, May 2, 1918.

Chapter 12

1. George S. Robbins, "Jackson Asked to Wilmington Yard?," *Chicago Daily News*, May 22, 1918.
2. George S. Robbins, "Von Kolnitz Scores Critics of Jackson," *Chicago Daily News*, February 1, 1919.
3. Keith, *Rich Man's War, Poor Man's Fight*, 69-70.
4. George S. Robbins, "Public with Ban in Lining Up Dodgers," *Sporting News*, May 23, 1918.
5. Bob Pigue, The Sporting Spotlight, *Memphis News Scimitar*, December 9, 1918.
6. "Jackson's Status," *Chicago Tribune*, May 3, 1918.
7. "Hap Felsch Is Sox Absentee," *Chicago Daily News*, May 9, 1918.
8. I. E. Sanborn, "Shipyard Jobs Offered to Players, Sanborn Finds," *Chicago Tribune*, May 20, 1918.
9. "Jackson Ordered to Be Examined," *Greenville Daily News*, May 11, 1918.
10. "Joe Jackson 100 P. C. Sound, Says Doctor," *Philadelphia Inquirer*, May 12, 1918.
11. "Sox Beat Macks After Uphill Fight of 11 Rounds, 5 to 3," *Chicago Tribune*, May 11, 1918.
12. I. E. Sanborn, "Joe Jackson Leaves for War Service and Sox Lose 6 to 4," *Chicago Tribune*, May 14, 1918.
13. I. E. Sanborn, "Jackson Notifies He's Due for Early Call in Draft," *Chicago Tribune*, May 13, 1918.
14. Robert W. Maxwell, "Walker, J. Collins Smash Home Runs," *Philadelphia Evening Public Ledger*, May 13, 1918.
15. Robbins, "Public with Ban."
16. "Joe Jackson Must Resign in Two Weeks," *Washington Times*, May 13, 1918.
17. Howard Mann, "Jackson, Under Draft, Quits Sox for Shipyards," *Chicago Evening Post*, May 14, 1918.
18. Fleitz, *Shoeless*, 73.
19. "Retreats to a Ship Yard," *Sporting News*, May 16, 1918.
20. James S. Carolan, "Joe Jackson Quits Sox to Help Build Ships," *Philadelphia Evening Public Ledger*, May 14, 1918.

21 "Sox Manager Sends Joe Jackson Away with Best Wishes," *Chicago Tribune*, May 14, 1918.

22 Robbins, "Jackson Asked to Wilmington Yard?"

23 Hornbaker, *Fall from Grace*, 124.

24 "Jackson Starts Ship Yard Job," *Chicago Tribune*, May 15, 1918.

25 "Joe Jackson Peeved, Says He's Out of Big League Ball," *Wilmington (DE) Evening Journal*, May 24, 1918.

26 Robbins, "Public with Ban."

27 David Rotroff, Sportively Speaking, *Chicago Daily News*, May 27, 1918.

28 "Absence of Regulars Shoots Big Holes in White Sox Lineup," *Chicago Collyer's Eye*, May 18, 1918.

29 "Notes," *Chicago Tribune*, May 16, 1918.

30 Seymour, *Baseball: The People's Game*, 234.

31 John Alcock, "Johnson Raps Ball Players Seeking to Evade Draft," *Chicago Tribune*, May 17, 1918.

32 Louis A. Dougher, "Yankees Proud of Those Who Joined Colors, Don't Mention Rest," *Washington Times*, July 2, 1918.

33 "Southpaw" substituting for Paul Purman, Going Back Over the Sport Trail, *Madison Wisconsin State Journal*, May 20, 1918.

34 Bob Dunbar, Sporting Comment, *Boston Herald*, May 14, 1918.

35 "The Case of Joe Jackson," *Chicago Tribune*, editorial, June 6, 1918.

36 Letter signed L. M. P., "Voice of the People," *Chicago Tribune*, June 13, 1918.

37 "Jackson Wants to Keep Harland Job," *Wilmington Evening Journal*, May 21, 1918.

38 J. H. Keene, Keen Stuff, *Harrisburg (PA) Patriot*, June 12, 1918.

39 "Jackson Wants to Keep Harland Job."

40 "Friends of Jackson Pleading His Case," *Lincoln (NE) Star*, June 16, 1918.

41 "Joe Jackson Called to Report Here for Immediate Service," *Greenville Daily News*, May 19, 1918.

42 Robert W. Maxwell, "Uncle Sam Refused to Favor Athletic Heroes; 'Shipbuilders' Must Go," *Philadelphia Evening Public Ledger*, May 21, 1918.

43 "The South Carolina Federation of Women's Clubs," *Greenville (SC) Daily News*, May 25, 1918.

44 Robbins, "Jackson Asked to Wilmington Yard?"

45 "Draft Board Overruled," *New York Times*, May 22, 1918.

46 "'Red' Faber in Draft; Passes Physical Test," *Chicago Examiner*, April 25, 1918.

47 "Williams and Lynn are to Build Ships," *Chicago Daily News*, June 11, 1918.

48 "Comiskey Wipes 2 Shipbuilders Off Sox Roster," *Chicago Tribune*, June 12, 1918.

49 "Notes," *Chicago Tribune*, June 12, 1918.

50 "Notes," *Chicago Tribune*, June 15, 1918.

51 George S. Robbins, "Invoke Fans' Loyalty as Sox Strike Squall," *Chicago Daily News*, June 15, 1918.

52 James Crusinberry, "Ty and Tigers Drive White Sox to the Second Division," *Chicago Tribune*, June 25, 1918.

Chapter 13

1 "'Work or Fight,' Choice Given Men within Draft Age," *Washington Evening Star*, May 23, 1918.

2 Oscar C. Reichow, "Baseball Men Find Hope in Revised Fiat," *Chicago Daily News*, May 23, 1918.

3 "Ball Players in Confusion over Federal War Work Edict," *Chicago Tribune*, May 24, 1918.

4 "What Officials Say About New Crowder Order," *New York Tribune*, May 24, 1918.

5 "American League Bingles," *Chicago Daily News*, June 5, 1918.

6 "Chief Yeoman Faber; Will Join Navy," *Cascade (IA) Pioneer*, June 13, 1918.

7 I. E. Sanborn, "Sanborn Tells Why Sox Won't Run Up Flag," *Chicago Tribune*, May 19, 1918.

8 I. E. Sanborn, "Two Sox Stripped of Uniforms; Pennant Raised, Victory 4-1," *Chicago Tribune*, June 12, 1918.

9 "Sox Turn Last Stand into Rally that Nets 7 to 4 Triumph," *Chicago Tribune*, June 15, 1918.

10 "Notes," *Chicago Tribune*, July 29, 1918.

11 I. E. Sanborn, "Good Ship Sox Sunk Despite Yeoman Faber," *Chicago Tribune*, June 16, 1918.

12 "Faber, Sox 'Ace,' Now Is a Jackie," *Chicago Tribune*, June 18, 1918.

13 George S. Robbins, "Desertions Rouse Old Roman's Anger," *Sporting News*, June 20, 1918.

14 "Sol Grabiner Was Faber's Recruiting Aid," *Great Lakes Bulletin*, June 12, 1918.

15 Jimmy Corcoran, "Daily Sport Log," *Great Lakes Bulletin*, June 20, 1918. Corcoran's byline was "Jimmy" in the station newspaper but "Jimmie" in the station magazine.

16 Jimmy Corcoran, "Daily Sport Log," *Great Lakes Bulletin*, June 14, 1918.

17 Jimmy Corcoran, "Daily Sport Log," *Great Lakes Bulletin*, June 22, 1918.

18 George S. Robbins, "Clevelanders Route Shellenbach [sic]," *Chicago Daily News*, June 22, 1918.

19 "American League Drives," *Chicago Daily News*, June 28, 1918.

20 Reid J. Murdock, "White Sox Riddled by Discord Now 4 to 1 Shots to Win Flag," *Chicago Collyer's Eye*, June 22, 1918.

21 Jimmie Corcoran, "With the Athletes," *Great Lakes Recruit*, June 1918.

22 "Faber Hands New Athletic Field Big Boost," *Great Lakes Bulletin*, July 3, 1918.

23 Paul L. Jones, "Station Club to Issue Defy to Champs," *Great Lakes Bulletin*, July 9, 1918.

24 Paul L. Jones, "Our Sailors Maul Pfeffer as Faber Blanks Pier Tars," *Great Lakes Bulletin*, July 26, 1918.

25 "Jackies Attack on Jeff Pfeffer Beats Pier Nine," *Chicago Tribune*, July 26, 1918.

26 Robbins, "Baseball Is Booming."

27 "Great Lakes Scuttles Nine of Fleet, 6 to 2," *Chicago Tribune*, August 4, 1918.

28 Fred A. Marquardt, "Great Lakes Nine Fights to Keep Lead," *Chicago Daily News*, August 5, 1918.

29 Jimmie Delaney, "The Station Nine Is Victor Over Fleet," *Great Lakes Bulletin*, August 6, 1918.

30 "Again Winning Fame," *Cascade Pioneer*, August 8, 1918.

31 John Alcock, "Red Faber Hurls Great Lakes Crew to Championship," *Chicago Tribune*, August 6, 1918.

32 I. E. Sanborn, "Cubs Thrilled by Navy Life as They Beat Jackies, 5 to 0," *Chicago Tribune*, August 28, 1918.

33 Oscar C. Reichow, "Inside Story of Cubs-Great Lakes Game," *Great Lakes Recruit*, October 1918.

34 "Local Boy Pitches Great Game, But Ex-Leaguer Has The Breaks," *Davenport* (IA) *Democrat and Leader*, September 16, 1918.

35 George S. Robbins, "'Navy World Series' Baseball Prospect," *Chicago Daily News*, October 2, 1918.

36 "Hopped Out of Navy Quickly," *Boston Post*, December 14, 1918.

37 "Chief 'Red' Faber to Don Civies Soon," *Great Lakes Bulletin*, December 31, 1918.

38 John B. Foster, "Base Ball and the Service: Great Lakes (Ill.) Naval Training Station," in Foster, *Spalding's Official Base Ball Guide 1919*, 181.

Chapter 14

1 "Notes," *Chicago Tribune*, June 17, 1918.

2 I. E. Sanborn, "Fans Mingle Joy and Regret as Sox Beat Nick Altrock, 3-0," *Chicago Tribune*, June 17, 1918.

3 Denman Thompson, "Base Ball Fans in Chicago Showing Lack of Interest," *Washington Evening Star*, Monday, June 17, 1918. Retrosheet shows attendance for those three days as 3,600, 7,400, 11,800. https://www.retrosheet.org.

4 Nitz, "Happy Felsch."

5 Bill Bailey, "'Work or Fight' Status Worry to Players," *Chicago Evening American*, July 3, 1918.

6 Malcolm MacLean, "Hap Surprises Baseball World by Jumping Job," *Chicago Evening Post*, July 2, 1918.

7 George S. Robbins, "Will Comiskey Quit? He's Lost 8 Players," *Chicago Daily News*, July 3, 1918.

8 George S. Robbins, "Sox Drop Opener to Browns by 2-0 Score," *Chicago Daily News*, July 1, 1918.

9 "Happy Felsch Quits White Sox for Job at $125 per Month," *Chicago Tribune*, July 2, 1918.

10 "Hap Refuses to Worry Over His White Sox Job," *Milwaukee Evening Sentinel*, January 9, 1919.

11 "'Commy' Tells His Side of the Felsch Story."

12 "Hap Felsch Signs with Kosciuskos," *Sheboygan (WI) Press*, July 3, 1918.

13 Sporting Arbiter, *Milwaukee Sunday Sentinel*, May 26, 1918.

14 Murdock, "Kid Gleason's Promises." Felsch hit .252 in 1918, a steep drop from .308 the previous season.

15 Bailey, "'Work or Fight' Status."
16 "Poles to Play Beloit Fairies," *Milwaukee Evening Sentinel*, July 18, 1918.
17 Bailey, "'Work or Fight' Status."
18 George S. Robbins, "Bricklayer Latest Sox Recruit," *Chicago Daily News*, June 13, 1918.
19 "Notes," *Chicago Tribune*, July 17, 1918.
20 James Crusinberry, "Jack Quinn May Yet Play with Sox; Case Up for New Hearing," *Chicago Tribune*, February 1, 1919.
21 "Comish Awards Quinn to Yanks," *Chicago Tribune*, August 25, 1918.
22 "Comiskey Tells His Story of Black Sox and Feud with Ban," *Cleveland Plain Dealer*, January 13, 1929.
23 Spatz and Steinberg. *Comeback Pitchers*, 95.
24 Brown, *The Chicago White Sox*, 78.
25 "Sox Turned Down in Quinn Appeal," *Chicago Tribune*, February 5, 1919.
26 Ban Johnson, "Making the American League," *Saturday Evening Post*, March 22, 1930.
27 "Albany Parks Lose to Felsch and Stars, 13-1," *Milwaukee Sentinel*, October 14, 1918.
28 "Vaughn Outpitches Benz," *Chicago Daily News*, October 14, 1918.
29 "Happy Felsch Not Worried Over Job with White Sox," *Chicago Tribune*, December 21, 1918.

Chapter 15

1 James Crusinberry, "Sox Neither Work Nor Fight; Lose Two Games, 2-0 and 4-3," *Chicago Tribune*, July 2, 1918.
2 "Notes," *Chicago Tribune*, July 2, 1918.
3 "Secretary Baker Calls Baseball a "Nonessential," *Chicago Daily News*, July 19, 1918.
4 "Work or Fight Rule Does Not Worry Sox," *Chicago Tribune*, July 20, 1918.
5 "Notes," *Chicago Tribune*, July 20, 1918.
6 "American League Gossip," *Chicago Daily News*, July 22, 1918.
7 "Sox Will Continue Season," *Chicago Daily News*, July 23, 1918.

8 "Ruling Favors Game Is View of Fans," *Chicago Daily News*, July 26, 1918.

9 George S. Robbins, "Magnates at War on World Series Dates," *Chicago Daily News*, July 30, 1918.

10 Robbins, "Magnates at War."

11 John Alcock, "Close Season Aug. 20, Then World Series, Johnson's Plan," *Chicago Tribune*, July 30, 1918.

12 "Notes," *Chicago Tribune*, July 31, 1918.

13 "Owners Overrule Johnson Closing Plan," *Chicago Tribune*, August 4, 1918.

14 "Owners Overrule Johnson."

15 Ed Bang, "Movement on Foot to Oust Johnson as Head of Junior League, Says Bang," *Cleveland News*, reprinted in *Chicago Collyer's Eye*, August 10, 1918.

16 Louis Lee Arms, Facts and Fancies, *New York Tribune*, August 6, 1918.

17 "Tener Steps Down as League Leader," *New York Times*, August 6, 1918.

18 John Alcock, "Frazee Blamed for Turning Fire on Ban Johnson," *Chicago Tribune*, August 11, 1918.

19 Hugh S. Fullerton, "Cleveland Confident of Grabbing Lead in Boston," *New York Evening World*, August 15, 1918.

20 George S. Robbins, "Rowland Is to Lead Sox in New Season," *Chicago Daily News*, December 10, 1918.

21 "Owners Overrule Johnson Closing Plan."

22 George S. Robbins, "Magnates Cool Hells in Halls of 'War,'" *Chicago Daily News*, July 26, 1918.

23 "Notes," *Chicago Tribune*, July 28, 1918.

24 "Notes," *Chicago Tribune*, July 29, 1918.

25 George S. Robbins, "Rowland Is to Lead Sox in New Season," *Chicago Daily News*, December 10, 1918.

26 Ring W. Lardner, In the Wake of the News, *Chicago Tribune*, August 3, 1918.

27 James Crusinberry, "Sox Take First in Hitfest, 10-3; Lose Other, 4-1," *Chicago Tribune*, August 4, 1918.

28 "Burlesque Baseball by White Sox Hands Indians Game, 11-2," *Chicago Tribune*, August 13, 1918.

29 Mittermeyer, "Eddie Collins."

30 "In the Wake of the War," *San Francisco Examiner*, November 30, 1917.

31 "Eddie Collins Is Still on Waiting List for Army Draft," *Harrisburg (PA) Telegraph*, December 6, 1917.

32 "Collins to War?," *Chicago Tribune*, December 14, 1917.

33 "M'Mullin and Risberg Leave Sox to Enlist," *Chicago Tribune*, August 8, 1918.

34 "E. Collins Quits," *Chicago Tribune*, August 11, 1918.

35 Matt Gallagher, Strictly Baseball, *Los Angeles Herald*, August 29, 1918.

36 Eddie Murphy, "Hanlons Are Outclassed by Alameda Club," *Oakland Tribune*, September 10, 1918.

37 Louis A. Dougher, Looking 'Em Over, *Washington Times*, November 9, 1918.

38 James Crusinberry, "White Sox Leave for Final Drive on East Front," *Chicago Tribune*, August 9, 1918.

39 George S. Robbins, "Eddie Collins Joins the Marines," *Chicago Daily News*, August 10, 1918.

40 "E. Collins Quits."

41 "Games at Boston End E. Collins' Play with Sox," *Chicago Tribune*, August 14, 1918.

42 George S. Robbins, "Sox Will Scatter After Games Sept. 2," *Chicago Daily News*, August 30, 1918.

43 "Eddie Collins Lover of the Marines," *Albany (NY) Journal*, December 18, 1918.

44 "Eddie Collins in Farewell Game Helps Beat Boston, 6-2," *Chicago Tribune*, August 16, 1918.

45 "Eddie Collins and Connie Mack Laud 'Silk' O'Loughlin," *Philadelphia Evening Public Ledger*, December 21, 1918.

46 Spick Hall, "Eddie Collins Now in U.S. Marine Corps," *Philadelphia Evening Public Ledger*, August 19, 1918.

47 "Collins Enlists in U.S. Marines," *Philadelphia Inquirer*, August 20, 1918.

48 "Sox and Yankees Battle It Out for Fourth Place," *Chicago Tribune*, August 19, 1918.

49 Eddie Collins as told to Jim Leonard, "From Sullivan to Collins," *Sporting News*, October 25, 1950.

50 Robert W. Maxwell, "Eddie Collins Plans to Stick with Marines Until He Hears the Officer Say 'Fire-d,'" *Philadelphia Evening Public Ledger*, December 10, 1918.

51 "Eddie Collins, White Sox Infielder, Still a Marine," *Syracuse (NY) Post-Standard*, December 18, 1918.

52 "Perry and Perkins Sign with Athletics," *Philadelphia Inquirer*, February 7, 1919.

Chapter 16

1. George S. Robbins, "Sox Get Contract Notices," *Chicago Daily News*, August 23, 1918.
2. George S. Robbins, "White Sox in Toledo for a Short Visit," *Chicago Daily News*, August 27, 1918.
3. "Sox Given Shock; Must Play Today at Massillon, O.," *Chicago Tribune*, August 28, 1918.
4. Mitchell Woodbury, "Ninth Inning Rally Gives Rail-Lights Win Over Sox," *Toledo News-Bee*, August 30, 1918.
5. Matt Foley, "Sox Beaten in Last Tilt Here," *Chicago Herald and Examiner*, September 2, 1918.
6. "No Joy Attends Sox Closing Day," *Chicago Tribune*, September 2, 1918.
7. "Sox Do a Fadeout by Dropping Pair to Detroit Tigers," *Chicago Tribune*, September 3, 1918.
8. "Cobb and Pinelli Entertain the Fans," *Chicago Daily News*, September 3, 1918. "Flier" was frequently spelled "flyer" during the early years of aviation.
9. "Travesty Games Mark Baseball's End in Detroit," *Detroit Free Press*, September 3, 1918.
10. George S. Robbins, "Sox Dethroned; A. L. Shaken," *Chicago Daily News*, December 31, 1918.
11. Clarence H. Rowland, "'Cubs May Expect a Hard Fight': Rowland," *Chicago Daily News*, September 5, 1918.
12. Figures compiled from Baseball-reference.com, July 19, 2024.
13. Louis Lee Arms, "Facts and Fancies," *New York Tribune*, August 23, 1918.
14. "World Series to South Side," *Chicago Daily News*, August 28, 1918.
15. James Crusinberry, "Red Sox Grab First World's Series Battle From Cubs, 1-0," *Chicago Tribune*, September 6, 1918.
16. Total 1917 World Series attendance was 186,654, falling to 128,483 the following year. Figures compiled July 18, 2024, from Baseball-Reference.com.
17. "Cub Boss Sends Thanks to Sox," *Chicago Tribune*, September 15, 1918.
18. Edgar Forrest Wolfe as Jim Nasium, "Harlan Team Is Ship Yard Champ," *Philadelphia Inquirer*, August 29, 1918.

19 "Wonder If Painter Worried Any," *Washington Times*, August 30, 1918. Reprinted elsewhere, the article likely originated in the *Times*, where columnist Louis A. Dougher had coined the phrase "Joe the Painter."

20 "Harlan Wins Coxe Trophy," *Philadelphia Evening Public Ledger*, September 16, 1918.

21 "Jackson's Homers Defeat Standards," *New York Sun*, September 15, 1918.

22 "Harlan Team of Wilmington Wins Championship of Ship Yard Leagues," *Philadelphia Inquirer*, September 15, 1918.

23 "Notes," *Chicago Tribune*, July 14, 1918.

24 George S. Robbins, "'Aw, Get in the Army' Was Coast Fans' Cry," *Chicago Daily News*, August 2, 1918.

25 "Cicotte Now Working as an Eagle Builder," *Philadelphia Evening Public Ledger*, October 5, 1918.

26 "Makes Appearance Here As Member of Semi-Professional Ball Club," *Detroit Free Press*, September 23, 1918.

27 George S. Robbins, "Sox Will Scatter After Games Sept. 2," *Chicago Daily News*, August 30, 1918.

28 "His New Job," *Chicago Daily News*, September 21, 1918.

29 James Crusinberry, "Work So 'Soft' 'Buck' Might Not Play," *Chicago Tribune*, January 4, 1918.

30 David Condon, "Ray Schalk, Hall of Fame Catcher, Dies," *Chicago Tribune*, May 20, 1970.

31 George S. Robbins, "Sox Go on Vacation; Plans of the Champs," *Chicago Daily News*, October 18, 1917.

32 James Crusinberry, "Ray Schalk Dons Real Overalls in Metal Plant," *Chicago Tribune*, September 15, 1918.

33 Harry Neily, "Schalk Outs His Old Pep into Business," *Chicago Evening American*, October 28, 1918.

34 I. E. Sanborn, "Fans Jam Semi-Pro Park to See Garden City Beat Logans," *Chicago Tribune*, October 7, 1918.

35 "Firm Advances Schalk in Job," *Chicago Tribune*, October 27, 1918.

36 George Robbins, "Ray Schalk Makes Good in Business," *Chicago Daily News*, February 12, 1919.

37 Malcolm MacLean, "Schalk Hopes to Quit Game for Real Business," *Atlanta Constitution*, May 18, 1919.

38 Condon, "Ray Schalk."

Chapter 17

1. George S. Robbins, "Gossip of the Sox Players," *Chicago Daily News*, June 1, 1917.
2. "St. Louis Drafts Joe Jenkins," *Keokuk (IA) Daily Gate City*, September 16, 1913.
3. Malcolm MacLean, "Jenkins, Ex-Cracker, Happy-Go-Lucky Chap, Promoted Under Fire," *Atlanta Constitution*, December 8, 1918.
4. Walter Barnes, as "Sportsman," Live Tips and Topics, *Boston Globe*, September 24, 1917.
5. Robbins, "Sox Go on Vacations."
6. MacLean, "Jenkins, Ex-Cracker."
7. George S. Robbins, "Joe Jenkins Tested by War Examiner," *Chicago Daily News*, August 27, 1917. The Ottoman Empire was allied with Germany and the Central Powers during World War I.
8. "Name Twenty-three Kings Boys Who Are to Leave Next Sunday Morning," *Hanford (CA) Morning Journal*, October 31, 1917.
9. Reuben A. Lewis, "Joe Jenkins and Bowden Win Places, *Atlanta Sunday American*, January 6, 1918. The writer was mistaken. Cavalry officers wore black and gold hat cords, whereas Jenkins trained for the infantry, which wore blue.
10. "Jenkins of Sox Wins Place in Officers' Camp," *Chicago Tribune*, January 6, 1918.
11. "Crack Big League Battery Working for Uncle Sam," *Brooklyn Eagle*, January 11, 1918.
12. Neily, "U. S. Army Life Agrees."
13. "Military Is Routed by Civilians," *Atlanta Georgian*, April 7, 1918.
14. Abel Davis, "Battle History of the 132nd Infantry," *Chicago Tribune*, June 1, 1919. The article largely duplicates Davis's book, *The Story of the 132d Infantry A. E. F.*, Luxembourg, n. p., 1919.
15. "Jenkins Brings Sox Hun Trophy," *Chicago Tribune*, January 12, 1919.
16. "Illinois Yanks Assert Mistake Cost Heavily," *Freeport (IL) Journal-Standard*, December 27, 1918.
17. George C. Briggs, "Alex, Back from France, Talks Ball for Cub Fans," *Chicago Daily News*, April 15, 1919.
18. Davis, "Battle History of the 132nd Infantry."
19. A. V. Becker, "The 132nd Infantry," in *Illinois in the World War* 1, 322.
20. "Jenkins Brings Sox Hun Trophy."

21 Harry Neily, *Chicago Evening American*, reprinted in "White Sox Now Have 16 Men in Service," *Los Angeles Evening Herald*, October 22, 1918.

22 Damon Runyon, "Eddie Grant Died Leading His Battalion," *New York American*, October 23, 1918.

23 Johnny Evers, "Sees Joe Jenkins Lead Men to Attack," *Chicago Daily News*, November 25, 1918.

24 "Doughboys' Work Finished; Eager to Get Home for Opening of Pennant Races," *Ithaca (NY) Daily News*, December 24, 1918.

25 "Same Old Johnny Evers Home from France," *Albany Evening Journal*, December 17, 1918.

26 Jack Veiock, "Johnny Evers Not Strong for Trenches," *Los Angeles Herald*, December 26, 1918.

27 Evers, "Sees Joe Jenkins Lead."

28 George S. Robbins, "Death Ten Feet Off, Writes Joe Jenkins," *Chicago Daily News*, December 20, 1918. The date of the letter isn't stated.

29 "Johnny Evers Loses No Time in Denying," *The Sporting News*, December 26, 1918.

30 "Send Greetings Through Post," *Boston Post*, December 25, 1918.

31 George S. Robbins, "Big League Owners May Honor Heroes," *Chicago Daily News*, January 16, 1919.

32 Briggs, "Alex, Back from France."

Chapter 18

1 "Chicago Gets Out of Bed; Bedlam Reigns in Loop," *Chicago Tribune*, November 11, 1918.

2 "Terms Leave Foe Powerless," *Chicago Daily News*, November 11, 1918.

3 Fred A. Marquardt, "Peace Brings Talk of Baseball Again," *Chicago Daily News*, November 11, 1918.

4 I. E. Sanborn, "Major Moguls Forget Pastime for Armistice," *Chicago Tribune*, November 12, 1918.

5 Jacob Pomrenke, "Prologue: Offseason, 1918-19," in Pomrenke et al., *Scandal on the South Side*, 5.

6 John E. Wray, Wray's Column, *St. Louis Post-Dispatch*, December 2, 1918.

7   "Comiskey Keeps Plans to Himself," *Chicago Daily News*, December 30, 1918.

8   George S. Robbins, "Will Confer Jan 16 on Baseball Topics," *Chicago Daily News*, December 13, 1918.

9   George S. Robbins, "Comiskey Pans Ban and Upholds Frazee," *Chicago Daily News*, December 18, 1918.

10 James Crusinberry, "Sox Chances Depend upon Attitude of Ship Leaguers," *Chicago Tribune*, December 19, 1918.

11 Robert W. Maxwell, "Jackson and Felsch, Barred by Comiskey, Sought by Yankees," *Philadelphia Evening Public Ledger*, December 14, 1918.

12 Maxwell, "Jackson and Felsch."

13 George S. Robbins, "Comiskey Lifts the Ban on Joe Jackson," *Chicago Daily News*, December 24, 1918.

14 Robbins, "Rowland Is to Lead Sox."

15 Editorial item, *Chicago Collyer's Eye*, December 21, 1918.

16 Crusinberry, "'Kid' Gleason Appointed Manager."

17 Robbins, "Gleason Leads Sox."

18 Matthews, "Gleason Now Manager."

19 "'A Real New Year's Present,' Exclaims White Sox Captain," *Philadelphia Public Ledger*, January 2, 1919.

20 James Crusinberry, "For the Fan," *Eagle Magazine*, May 1919.

21 "Big Day for the Ints [sic]," *Baltimore Evening Sun*, January 6, 1919.

22 "Hap Refuses to Worry Over His White Sox Job," *Milwaukee Evening Sentinel*, January 9, 1919.

23 "Felsch Is to Play with Sox This Year," *Chicago Daily News*, February 10, 1919.

24 James Crusinberry, "Hap Felsch Appears to Sign Contract; Schalk Also in Line," *Chicago Tribune*, February 11, 1919.

25 W. J. Macbeth, "Ball Tossers Seem Eager To Sign Up for Season," *New York Tribune*, February 16, 1919.

26 James Crusinberry, "White Sox Champions of 1917 Rallying Under Kid Gleason," *Chicago Tribune*, February 20, 1919.

27 James Crusinberry, "Joe Jackson Signs; Ship Leaguers' Case Now Up to the Fans," *Chicago Tribune*, February 22, 1919.

28 Robbins, "Sox Fans Wonder."

29 "Weaver Signs with Sox," *Chicago Daily News*, March 17, 1919.
30 I. E. Sanborn, "Two Sox Players and One Cub Enter Fold for Spring Trip," *Chicago Tribune*, March 18, 1919.
31 I. E. Sanborn, "Comiskey Eager to Give Scott Chance on Team," *Chicago Tribune*, March 15, 1919.
32 Crusinberry, "White Sox Champions of 1917 Rallying."
33 I. E. Sanborn, "Browns Crab White Sox Inaugural by Winning, 11 to 4," *Chicago Tribune*, May 3, 1919.
34 Grantland Rice, The Sportlight, *New York Tribune*, May 4, 1919.
35 Nitz, "Happy Felsch," and other sources.
36 Tom Meehan, "Hanford's Jenkins, Black Sox Innocent, Talks of One Big Smirch on Baseball," *Fresno Bee*, May 13, 1962.
37 Allen, "Lawyers, Law, and Baseball," 1530.
38 Bill Corum's Column, *Washington Times*, October 5, 1937.
39 Allen, "Lawyers, Law, and Baseball," 1532. Fred McMullin, also indicted, wasn't present during the trial because California had refused to extradite him.
40 "Black Sox Acquitted, but Out," editorial, *Chicago Tribune*, August 4, 1921.
41 Johnny Evers, Evers in France, *Troy (NY) Times*, October 21, 1918.
42 Johnny Evers, "Says Soldiers Are Not Rough at Sport," *Chicago Daily News*, November 20, 1918.
43 "Base Ball in France," in Foster, *Spalding's Official Base Ball Guide 1919*, 203.
44 Gardner, *Nice Guys Finish Last*, 190-191.
45 John Kass, "Fans Ditch as Joy Reaches a Fever Pitch," *Chicago Tribune*, October 28, 2005.
46 Collins, "From Sullivan to Collins."

BIBLIOGRAPHY

Algren, Nelson. *The Last Carousel*. Seven Stories, 1975.
Allen, Richard B. "Lawyers, Law, and Baseball." *American Bar Association Journal* 64 (October 1978): 1530–5.
Brown, Warren. *The Chicago White Sox*. G. P. Punam, 1952.
Buzzell, Francis. *The Great Lakes Naval Training Station: A History*. Small, Maynard & Company, 1919.
Ellington 1918. [United States Army Air Service?], 1918.
Fleitz, David L. *Shoeless: The Life and Times of Joe Jackson*. McFarland & Company, 2001.
Foster, John B., ed. *Spalding's Official Base Ball Guide 1919*. American Sports Publishing, 1919.
Gardner, Paul. *Nice Guys Finish Last: Sport and American Life*. Universe Books, 1975.
Genslinger, Charles Henry. *Final Report of Clark C. Griffith Ball and Bat Fund*. Clark C. Griffith Ball and Bat Fund, 1919.
Hall, Tom G. "Wilson and the Food Crisis: Agricultural Price Control During World War I." *Agricultural History* 47, no. 1 (January 1973): 25–46.
Henderson, Alice Palmer. *The Ninety-first: The First at Camp Lewis*. Tacoma: John C. Barr, 1918
Hoie, Bob. "1919 Baseball Salaries and the Mythically Underpaid Chicago White Sox." *BaseBall* 6, no. 1 (Spring 2012): 17–34.
Hornbaker, Tom. *Fall from Grace: The Truth and Tragedy of "Shoeless Joe Jackson"*. Sports Publishing, 2016.
Huhn, Rick. *Eddie Collins: A Baseball Biography*. McFarland & Company, 2008.
Keith, Jeanette. *Rich Man's War, Poor Man's Fight: Race, Class, and Power in the Rural South during the First World War*. University of North Carolina Press, 2004.
Lamb, William F. *Black Sox in the Courtroom: The Grand Jury, Criminal Trial and Civil Litigation*. McFarland & Company, 2013.
Mittermeyer, Paul. "Eddie Collins." SABR BioProject, sabr.org/bioproject.
Murdock, Eugene C. *Ban Johnson: Czar of Baseball*. Greenwood Press, 1982.
Murdock, Eugene C. "The Tragedy of Ban Johnson." *Journal of Sport History* 1, no. 1 (Spring 1974): 26–39.
Nitz, Jim. "Happy Felsch." SABR BioProject, sabr.org/bioproject.
Pomrenke, Jacob, Rick Huhn, Bill Nowlin, and Len Levin, eds. *Scandal on the South Side: The 1919 Chicago White Sox*. Society for American Baseball Research, 2015.
Richter, Francis C., ed. *The Reach Official American League Base Ball Guide for 1919*. A. J. Reach Company, 1919.
Sandoval, Jim. "Eddie Cicotte." SABR BioProject, sabr.org/bioproject.
Seymour, Harold. *Baseball: The People's Game*. Oxford University Press, 1990.

Spatz, Lyle, and Steve Steinberg. *Comeback Pitchers: The Remarkable Careers of Howard Ehmke and Jack Quinn*. University of Nebraska Press, 2021.
States Publication Society. *Illinois in the World War: An Illustrated Record Prepared with the Coöperation and Under the Direction of the Leaders in the State's Military and Civilian Organizations*, vol. 1. States Publication Society, 1920.
Steinberg, Steve. "Dave Danforth." SABR BioProject, sabr.org/bioproject.
Steinberg, Steve. "Dell Pratt." SABR BioProject, sabr.org/bioproject.
Sweeney, W. Allison. *History of the American Negro in the Great World War*. G. C. Sapp, 1919.
Wilbert, Warren N., and William C. Hageman. *The 1917 White Sox: Their World Championship Season*. McFarland & Company, 2004.
Zminda, Don. *Double Plays and Double Crosses: The Black Sox and Baseball in 1920*. Rowman & Littlefield, 2021.

INDEX

Note: page numbers in *Italics* refer to figures

African Americans
  baseball   11
  military   11, 60, 61, 92, 117
  trainers   103
Agathon club   175
Alcock, John
  1917 season   29, 47, 74
  1918 season   165
  military drilling and   12
  spring training   4, 16, 17, 112
alcohol   18, 156
Alexander, Grover Cleveland   195, 196, 206
Algren, Nelson   50, 104
Altrock, Nicholas   153
American Car & Foundry   181
American League
  1917 standings   51–3, 56
  1918 season   148, 163–6, 177
  1919 season   198, 199
  drill competition   20–1, 58, 63
  drillmasters   111
  Felsch's return to   157
  Gandil's record   41
  Griffith fund collections   107
  infighting   167
  leadership   3
  loss of players   137
  military drilling   8–10, 12, 21, 64
  records   77, 205
Argonne Forest   193
Arms, Louis Lee   84, 85, 166, 177
athletes
  industrial salaries   137

  in military   95, 99, 100 (*see also* baseball players)
Atlantic City, NJ   116
Atlantic Coast shipyards   179
Atlantic Fleet team   149–50
Axelson, G. W   19, 23

Bailey, Bill   155, 157
Baker, Newton   163–5
Ball, Phil   70–1, 199
Baltimore Drydocks Shipbuilding   181
Baltimore Oriole managers   201
Bang, Ed   166
Barry, Jack   126, 149
Barry, Thomas   36, 37, 58
baseball, transferable skills   93
baseball bats   21, 58. See *also* baseball equipment
baseball equipment
  to Canadians   5
  donations   48, 118
  to France   81–2 (*see also* baseball bats; baseballs; Clark C. Griffith Bat and Ball Fund)
baseball games)
  attendance   33, 47, 68, 82, 84, 105, 111, 165, 177, 178, 206
  cancelation   127
  exhibition for soldiers   87
  exhibition in Hawaii   92
  exhibition in Mexico   8
  ticket prices   121–3
Baseball Hall of Fame   185
baseball players
  enlistment   51, 81

gambling and   206, 209
participation in war   3–4, 57, 119–20, 208–9
play while enlisted   145
salaries   105, 107
shortage   106
strike   178 (*see also* athletes)
baseballs   27. *See also* baseball equipment
baseball season, shortening   106, 107, 164–5, 177
Batchelor, E. A.   129
B. B. N. G.   22, 26, 30, 51, 58, 92
Benton, John   82, 84–6
Benz, Joe
   1917 season   39
   1918 season   163
   bonds   104
   draft   45
   employment   181
   German heritage   22
   return to Sox   202
   singing   38
Bernoudy, Albert   146
Bethlehem Steel Baseball League   134, 138, 178
Bethlehem Steel company   140
Black Sox
   circumstances   209–10
   economic grievances   104, 105
   legacy   210
   participants   206–7
   ruling   208
   Tigers *vs.* Sox   69–70 (*see also* gambling)
Boston Braves   8, 51
Boston Globe   49, 51
Boston Red Sox
   1917 season   39, 53, 75
   1918 season   165, 171–3
   Detroit *vs.*   70
   fracas   49–51
   pennant   73, 74
   players   35
   World Series   13, 177, 178

Brooklyn Dodgers   8, 111, 149
Brown, Warren   28, 160
Buckner, Maggie   60
Buckner, William   *108*
   background   11
   Cicotte pitches   78
   dog   48
   family   60, 117
   firing   107–10
   spring training   18
   Walsh and   16
   World Series check   103
Buffalo Soldiers   61. *See also* African Americans, military
businessmen   6, 13, 26, 34, 183–5

Camp Fremont   100
Camp Funston   118
Camp Gordon   189
Camp Grant   147, 150
Camp Lewis   96, 97, 99–100
Camp Logan   61, 117
Camp Mills   81, 84
Camp Perry   99, 163
Camp Randall   47
Canada   5, 101, 107, 163
Carlson, Hal   150
catchers   119, 158
Chappell, Laverne   204
Chemical Warfare Service   176
Chicago Cubs
   exhibition games   151
   ownership   8
   players   26
   spring training   13
   usherettes   123
   work-or-fight   143
   World Series   80, 177
Chicago Daily News
   1917 home opener   36
   1918 season   107, 142, 164
   American League governance   198
   armistice   197
   army aviators   176

Buckner and   11, 109
Chouinard's experience   124
Clark Griffith Day   61
draft   44–5
drilling   9, 22, 23, 59, 64, 95
exhibition games   9
Faber enlistment   144
feeding of team   15
Felsch and   131, 161
France Day   47
game cancelation   127
Gandil and   42
Gleason's absence   115
Harlan employees   141
Jackson's career   136
Jenkins' personality   187
Lees' appearance   119
player losses   157
returning Sox   202, 203
Risberg and   27
Scott and   34, 99
Smiley and   18
Sox employment   181, 182
Tigers *vs.* Sox   68
Von Kolnitz and   26
war declaration   14
war tax   123
work-or-fight   143
World Series   88, 103
Chicago Day Book   11, 19, 25, 31, 37
Chicago Defender   49, 103, 108–10
Chicago Evening American   28, 105, 155, 184, 190, 192
Chicago Evening Post   10, 77, 134, 155
Chicago Examiner
   1918 season   123
   baseball gear   60
   Chouinard and   126
   Cicotte and   35, 71
   drills   4, 9, 59, 63
   enlistments   52
   Faber's draft   140–1
   Gandil and   42
   Gleason's absence   115

marine pitcher   117
Scott and   95, 98
Smiley and   10
World Series   82, 86, 87
Chicago Herald
   draft   44
   drilling   23, 25
   fundraising   60
   Gleason and   28
   patriotism   58
   players' attitudes   19
   Smiley's articles in   12
   World Series   85
Chicago Herald and Examiner   176
Chicago, IL, soldiers from   191, 193
Chicago Tribune   185
   1917 home opener   36
   1918 season   166, 168, 175, 176
   American League standings   52
   A's *vs.* Sox   38
   attendance   165, 167–8
   baseball-military link   10
   Black Sox   208
   calling game   56
   Chouinard and   125
   Cicotte's victories   74
   Collins' play   173, 174
   Comiskey Park staff   122
   Comisky's travel   13
   draft   45, 46, 158
   drilling   9, 12, 18, 28, 30, 57, 58, 63
   enlistments   169, 170, 172
   Faber's pitching   145, 149, 150
   Felsch and   156, 161
   fundraising   80
   Gleason disappearance   114
   Jackson's draft status   131
   Jackson's employment   135, 137, 138
   Jenkins in army   189, 191
   manual of arms   22
   naval baseball team   127
   naval enlistees   146
   plant inspection   185
   player desertions   141–2

Quinn acquisition   160
riots   49–50, 61
Schalk's love of baseball   185
Scott and   72, 99
shine ball   153
Smiley's commission   48
spring training   4, 16, 18, 118
Tigers *vs.* Sox   68, 69
train accident   20
war declaration   14
White Sox visit   180
Williams and   34
work-or-fight   163, 164
World Series   83
Chicago White Sox
  1917 pennant   74
  1918 season   106, 107, 110, 112, 148, 153, 157, 163, 168, 175–7
  1919 roster   185, 199, 202, 204
  1919 season   205–6
  1921 roster   196
  dog   48–9
  downfall   210
  drillmaster   9–11
  image   103
  infield   39–41
  management 1925-6   109
  racist accusations   108–9
  service record   204–5
  uniforms   34
  world tour   24
chief petty officers (CPOs)   126
Chouinard, Felix   *124*, 125, 141, 148
Cicotte, Edgar   *79*
  1917 season   39, 53, 59–60, 67, 68, 71, 73, 74
  1918 season   123, 124, 180–1
  1919 season   206
  accomplishments   77–8
  army team *vs.*   117
  A's *vs.*   53
  Boston *vs.*   49, 51
  Buckner and   103
  car accident   113
  as conspirator   207
  draft   45
  at Ellington Field   118
  pitching quality   35, 80
  return to Sox   202
  spring training   16
  World Series   82, 83
Cincinnati Reds   26, 206
City League (Chicago)   125
Clark C. Griffith Bat and Ball Fund   48, 60–2, 81–2, 107
Clark Griffith Day   60–3
Cleveland, OH   99, 165
Cleveland Indians   16, 49, 64, 71–2, 171–2
Cobb, Irwin   81, 83
Cobb, Ty   73, 176
Collins, Edward   *172*
  1917 home opener   37
  1918 season   123, 131
  background   168
  Buckner and   109
  drilling   21–3, 25, 30
  Felsch's departure   156
  Gandil and   41–2
  illness   113
  military service   168–9, 171–3, 187, 204, 211
  return to baseball   174, 201
  as spectator   179, 180
  spring training   16
  trade   26
  work-or-fight   163
  World Series   85–87
  wristwatch   145
Collins, John   45, 72, 181
Collyer's Eye   104, 105, 136, 148, 156–7, 200
Comiskey, Charles   *7*
  1916 team   39
  1917 season   29, 74
  1918 season   165–7, 176, 177
  1919 roster   205
  armistice   197

INDEX

Buckner firing 107–9
cancelations 127
drilling 6, 12, 21, 22
enlistments 72, 73, 141, 146, 170, 172
Felsch's departure 155, 156
Gleason and 115–16
Jenkins' correspondence 192, 195
Johnson and 7, 159, 160, 167, 198
military support 8–9, 57, 60
player acquisitions 26
players' accident 113
postwar staff 199–204
rifles 28
salaries 92, 104–5, 107, 115–16, 172, 195, 198, 201, 203
Scott and 25, 93, 96
shortened schedule 106
Smiley and 65
travel 13, 15–17
Von Kolnitz and 27
war contributions 46–8, 60, 71, 111, 143, 177
work-or-fight 164
World Series 84, 87, 206
Comiskey, Louis 17, 74
Comiskey Park
attendance 61, 80, 122, 145, 149, 153–4, 163, 167–8, 176–8, 206
cancelations 127
demolition 210
dog 49
flags 144, 147
manual of arms 22
patriotism 36–7, 58, 61, 68, 71
staff 122–3, 178
war tax 121–2
World Series 80
comptometer 122
Constantineau, Leo 120, 204
Cook, Harriet Belle. *See* Scott, Harriet Belle Cook
Corbett, James 86
Corcoran, Jimmy 147, 148
Crane, Sam 86

Crowder, Enoch 137, 143, 164, 173
Crusinberry, James
1918 season 142, 163, 168, 178
A's vs. Sox 38, 53
Browns vs. Sox 73
calling game 49
diamonds 104
Gleason's absence 115
Jackson's return 205
Quinn and 159
Schalk's employment 183
Scott and 96
shipyard players 199, 201
Sox manager and 200
team travel 13
Weaver's employment 182
World Series 82–4, 87
Cunningham, George 67–8

Danforth, Dave
1917 season 37, 39, 68, 72
1918 season 123, 163, 176
Browns vs. 34, 35
Buckner and 109–10
employment 181
physical 56
spring training 20
World Series 82
Daniels, Dan 121
Davis, Abel 191
Dean, John 59
Delaware River Shipping League 179
Des Moines Boosters 34
Detroit, MI 181
Detroit Tigers 12, 55–6, 67–9, 176, 205
Dewey, George 36
diamonds 104
Dorey, Halstead 8, 12
Dougher, Louis 138, 171
Douglas, Phillip 151
draft
1918 season 106, 153
age 45
Collins' enlistment and 169

drill and   64
evasions   137, 173
exemptions   44–5, 56, 57, 129, 130, 134, 140, 157
Jackson's classification   127–30, 135–6, 138–40
Jacobs' status   158
physicals   56, 132, 140, 188
recruiting and   112
registration   43–6
Dreyfuss, Barney   165
drillmasters
1917 season   33
1918 season   111
need for   8, 9
reassignment   64, 65 (*see also* military drilling)
Driscoll, John   127
Dryden, Charles   8, 82, 117, 123
Durning, Dick   149, 150

Eagle boats   181
Ebbets, Charles   111, 121–2
Edmund, Hugh   125
Ellington Field   118
England   4, 24
Evans, William   13, 78
Evers, John   80, 81, 87, 193–5, 208–9

Faber, Urban   *146*
1917 season   39, 55, 60, 63, 68, 72, 74
1918 season   123, 124
1919 season   206
Browns *vs.*   35
illness and injury   147, 150
machine guns   116
military service   140–1, 144–6, 167, 187, 204
naval baseball   147–52
recreational baseball   184
return to Sox   202
Sox loss of   157
World Series   79–86
Fairbanks-Morse   151, 182, 203

Fairies   182, 203
Federal League   10, 125, 208
Felsch, Charles   131
Felsch, Oscar   *154*
1917 season   39
1918 season   154–5, 157
brother   131, 156
as conspirator   207
departure   155–7, 167
draft   45
German heritage   22
grenade practice   27
physical   56
post-Sox activities   159–61
return to pro ball   199, 202
shine ball   77
World Series   80, 85
Fenway Park   49, 50, 198
flag presentations   37, 147–8
food   15–16, 18
Ford River Rouge plant   181
Fort Barry   94
Fort Crockett   116–17
Fort Sheridan   52–3, 65, 80, 147
Fort Worth Panthers   27–8
Fournier, Jack   20
France
baseball gear to   81–2
Knights of Columbus   181
soldiers in   81, 98, 190–3, 204
World Series score in   80
France Day   47
Frazee, Harry   49, 121, 122, 166, 198
Fullerton, Hugh   82, 166–7

Gainer, Del   149
gambling   49, 115, 198, 206, 209. *See also* Black Sox
Gandil, Arnold   *40*
1917 season   39, 40
car accident   113
draft   46
at Ellington Field   118
employment   181

gambling   70, 206
humming   38
physical   56
return to Sox   203
spring training   16, 29
temperament   16, 41–2
World Series   85
Gardner, Paul   209
General Electric   181
George V, King of Great Britain   24, 37
German heritage   22
Germany
    armistice   192
    Mexico and   14
    sports in   4
    submarine warfare   6
    U.S. army in   195
    U.S. war declaration   30
Gibson, Smith   12, 48, 63
Gleason, William   *114*
    1919 roster   202–3, 205
    absence   114–16, 131, 148, 156
    description   28
    draft   45
    drilling   27
    Gandil and   16
    as manager   200–1
    spring training   16, 19
Goofs. *See* Yannigans
Gowdy, Hank   51, 81
Grabiner, Harry
    draft   44, 45
    Lees' combat and   196
    military supplies   36
    spring training   17, 18
    ticket prices   123
    World Series   88, 103, 177
Grabiner, Sol   146, 151
Graney, Jack   72
Grant, Edward   192–3, 205
Gray, Wilbur   27–8
Great Lakes Naval Training Station
    active duty players   145
    Chouinard at   125–6

Comiskey at   146
    pregame march   44
    Rowland at   124–5
    sports facility   127, 148, 149, 151
    team   141, 148, 150, 152
    train from   124
Great Western Smelting and
    Refining   183
Greenville, SC   127–8, 130–2, 135, 139
Griffith, Clark   *62*
    1918 season   165–167
    shine ball   36, 153
    war contributions   47–8, 60, 62–3, 80
    work-or-fight   164
Griner, Dan   179

Haas, Bruno   120
Hageman, William   41, 70, 71
Halas, George   127
Hamel   191
hand grenades   27, 93
Hardgrove, William   157
Harlan & Hollingsworth shipyard
    Jackson at   133–5, 178, 179
    Sox at   135, 139–41
Harper, George   176
Hasbrook, Bob   103
Hempstead, Harry   198
Henry, Fred   120
Herrmann, August   159
hidden-ball trick   176
Hoie, Bob   105
Holke, Walter   86
home guard   64
Hornbaker, Tim   135
Houston, TX   29, 61
Houston Astros   210
Houston Buffaloes   29, 118
Huhn, Rick   41, 109
Huston, Tillinghast L'Hommedieu
    1917 pennant   74
    in army   44
    drilling idea   3, 6, 8, 31

drillmaster for 12
purpose of drill 64

Illinois
  Black Sox trial 208
  soldiers from 191, 193
Illinois-Indiana-Iowa League 21, 158
Illinois National Guard 57–8, 60–1, 71, 117
Illinois Steel 181
industrial baseball
  California 170, 171
  competition 148
  player quality 137–8
  shipbuilding 134
  Sox players 157, 181
influenza 151, 161, 173, 204, 205
International League 159
Iowa 30, 34, 151

Jackson, Joseph *133*
  1917 season 39
  accident and illness 113
  background 26
  Browns *vs.* 34
  as conspirator 207, 210
  draft 45, 127–33, 135–6, 138–40
  drilling 22, 27
  illiteracy 45, 134, 139, 140
  industrial success 178–80
  nicknames 138
  return to Sox 199–203, 205–6
  Sox loss of 157, 167
  spring training 16, 20
  World Series 85
Jackson, Katie 130, 132–4, 203
Jacobs, Otto 158
James, Bill 209
Jenkins, Joseph *190*
  1917 season 29, 73
  Black Sox 206
  combat 191–6
  draft 119, 188–9
  in Houston 29
  personality 187–8, 193
  physical 56
  return to Sox 204
  service record 190, 204
  World Series 83
Jennings, Hughey 201
Joffre, Joseph 47
Johnson, Byron Bancroft *5*
  1917 season 33
  1918 season 165, 166
  Ball friendship 199
  calling game 56
  Comiskey and 7, 159, 160, 167, 198
  drilling 3, 8, 9, 12, 21, 31, 37–8, 58, 59, 64, 112
  enlistments 169
  Jackson's departure 137
  ouster 198
  shine ball 36, 78
  shortened schedule 106
  slander and 70–1
  work-or-fight 144, 164
Johnson, Walter 60, 63, 77, 81
Jones, Fielder 34, 37, 63, 70, 123
Jones, John Paul 150

Kansas 18, 30, 118
Kauff, Benny 82
Kaufman, John 125, 126, 148
Keiser, Earl 120, 204
Keith, Jeanette 130
Kenney, Franklin
  1917 home opener 36
  draft 44
  drillmaster 9, 10, 12
  grenade practice 27
Kit and Comfort Club 60
Knights of Columbus 181, 193
knuckleball 35
Kosciusko club 155, 159
Kuhn, Charles 112, 127

Lake, Harry 119
Lake Shore League 155, 157

Lamb, William   105
Landis, Kenesaw Mountain   69–70, 74, 86, *207*, 208
Lane, F. C.   39, 40
Lardner, Ring, Sr.   22, 168
Lavan, John   70–1
Lees, George   119, 157, 196, 204
Leibold, Harry   34, 39, 164, 181, 202
Leksell, Charles   30
Leonard, Hubert   74
Leonard, Joe   125, 127
Leon Springs, TX   51
Letterman General Hospital   100
Leverenz, Walter   100
Lewis, George   80, 100, 151
Liberty Loan drive   104, 123, 143
Lieb, Fred   85
Litchfield, IL   183, 185
Los Angeles Dodgers   210
Loudermilk, Grover   123
Luderus, Fred   159
Lusitania   6
Luxembourg   195
Lynn, Byrd
  1917 season   29
  backup   119
  Black Sox   207
  return to Sox   201, 202
  Sox loss of   141, 157, 167

Macbeth, W. J.   202
machine guns   116. *See also* rifles
Mack, Connie   38–9, 74
Mackall, Ed   103
MacLean, Malcolm   10, 77, 155
Macon, GA   12
Major Leagues
  1919 rosters   202
  banning   208, 210
  draft   44, 169
  finances   105, 111, 197
  governance   93, 198, 207–8
  industrial players   134, 135, 138
  military players   100, 118, 126–7, 150, 170
  PCL players *vs.*   94
  postwar success   206
  shutdown   31
  war support   47–8
Maranville, Walter   81, 149, 150
Mare Island   100, 150, 151
marriages
  players'   94–5, 136
  war and   44, 46, 56, 127–30, 141, 169
Mathewson, Christy   195
Maxwell, Robert
  Collins' duties   174
  Jackson and   133, 139
  Scott and   72, 96
  shipyard players   199
McBride, George   80
McCain, Henry   9, 58
McClellan, Hervey   120
McGraw, John   82, 201
McGuire, Tom   209
McMullin, Fred
  as conspirator   207
  departure   169–71
  industrial ball   181
  return to Sox   203, 204
  riot   49–51
  talent   41
Menosky, Mike   196
Merced Bears   93
Meuse-Argonne offensive   192
Mexico   14
Military Day   58–60
military drilling
  attitudes toward   11, 13, 23–5, 30, 51
  benefits   13, 25, 30–2, 64–5
  competition   20–1, 57–9, 63–4
  Ft. Worth Panthers   27–8
  at games   28, 34, 35, 37, 47, 58–9
  idea of   3–4, 6
  marines   116
  Scott and   92 (*see also* drillmasters)
Milwaukee Gas Light Company   155, 157

Mineral Wells, TX   13, 20
Minor Leagues
   Chouinard in   125
   drilling   28
   finances   106
   Gandil in   16
   Jenkins in   187, 188
   Lees in   196
   players   96, 117, 127, 134, 135, 170, 189
   shutdowns   159
   war support   47–8
Mitchell, Fred   151
Mittermeyer, Paul   168
Mort Homme   191, 192
Murdock, Eugene   4
Murphy, Charles   33

Nasium, Jim. *See* Wolfe, Edgar Forrest
National Commission
   exhibition games   84
   overthrow   207
   Quinn and   159, 160
   reconfiguration   198
   rules   93
National League
   1917 season   33
   1918 season   164, 165, 177
   1919 schedule   198
   drilling   8, 111
   finances   105
   service records   205
Naval Auxiliary Reserve Officers' Training School   149
Navin Field   181
Neily, Harry
   army baseball   190
   Buckner and   107
   Gleason and   28
   Jenkins' service   192
   salaries   105
   Schalk's employment   184
New York Giants
   exhibition games   87

   pitchers   79
   service record   205
   trainer   103
   World Series   82, 83, 85–6
New York Ship club   179
New York Sun, World Series   85
New York Yankees
   active duty players   145
   drilling   3, 12, 48, 63
   finances   197
   Quinn with   159, 160
Nitz, Jim   154
Noyes, Win   209

Oakland, CA   100
officers   91, 95
Officers Training Camp   96
Ohio   175–6
Ohio National Guard   51
O'Loughlin, Francis   56, 173
O'Neill, Joe   30, 103, 164, 175
Owens, Clarence   72

Pacific Coast League
   closure   159
   infielders   40
   McMullin and   170
   Risberg and   26
   Scott and   92–94, 204
Parris Island, SC   174
Pasadena Merchants   170, 181, 204
patriotism
   drilling   33, 65
   at games   36–8, 58, 60, 61, 64, 71
   industrial jobs   137
   Major League teams   205
Payne, Fred   134
Payne, George   120, 204
PCL. *See* Pacific Coast League
Pennant (dog)   48
pennies   121–2
Pershing, John   8
Pfeffer, Jeff   149
Philadelphia, PA

gambling   115
Gandil and Collins in   41
physicals   56, 132, 136
Smiley in   38
Philadelphia Athletics
   1917 season   38–9, 52–3, 73–4
   1918 season   168
   Collins with   41
   draft   44
   Giants *vs.*   82
   Sundays   55
Philadelphia Inquirer   52, 115, 121, 179, 180
Philadelphia Navy Yard   174
Philadelphia Phillies   179
Pigue, Bob   131
Pinelli, Ralph   176
pitchers   120, 123–4, 158–9, 206
pitches   35, 36, 77–8
pitching   25, 39, 68, 93
Plank, Eddie   35, 37
Plattsburg Movement   6, 23
Polo Grounds   81, 84, 179
Pomrenke, Jacob   198
Pratt, Derrill   70–1

Quinn, John Pincus   158–60

Rariden, William   86
Red Cross
   Comiskey contributions   46, 47, 143, 177
   drill prize   64
   tax donations   121, 122
Registration Day   43–4
Rice, Daniel   46–7
Rice, Grantland   98, 205
Rickey, Branch   29
rifles   21, 23, 28, 94. *See also* Springfield rifles
Risberg, Charles   69
   1917 season   29, 40
   acquisition   26–7
   air service   118

army baseball   96, 170
Black Sox   69–70, 207
departure   169–71
draft   46
exhibition games   92
return to Sox   203
Robbins, George
   1917 pennant   73
   1918 season   124, 142, 167, 168, 175
   Buckner and   11, 108, 109
   Collins' enlistment   171, 172
   Comiskey's wealth   104
   Faber's pitching   151
   feeding of team   15
   flag raising   147
   Gandil and   42
   Gleason's departure   116
   industrial teams   134–5
   Jackson's career   136, 140
   Jackson's draft status   129–31, 133
   Jackson's salary   203
   Jenkins and   29, 188
   Lees' luck   196
   military baseball   149
   military drills   22, 23, 27, 30
   naval enlistees   146
   postwar Sox staff   199–200
   Schalk's work ethic   185
   Scott's appearance   99
   shine ball   78
   Tigers *vs.* Sox   68
   train accident   112–13
   World Series money   103
Roberson, Charles   120
Robertson, Dave   85
Robinson, Wilbert   201
Rochambeau   196
Rock Island Arsenal   151
Rock Island train   15
Roosevelt, Theodore   6
Rotroff, David   14, 136
Rowland, Clarence
   1917 roster   57
   A's *vs.*   52

Black Sox 69–70
Browns vs. 34
Buckner firing 109
Chouinard and 124–5
Detroit vs. 55
draft 44, 45
drilling 11, 21, 23, 31
employment 171, 181–2
Felsch's departure 155
firing 200
Gandil's temperament 41
Gleason and 114–16
grenade practice 27
Jackson's departure 135, 136
pitchers 39
rifles 28
Scott and 25
singing 38
spring training 16, 118
train accident 112
Von Kolnitz and 26
wartime roster 119, 120, 124, 157–9, 167, 172, 176, 177
work-or-fight 164
World Series 82, 87, 88
Ruether, Walter 100
Runyon, Damon
shine ball 78
as war correspondent 192–3
World Series 80, 83, 85, 86
Russell, Ewell
1917 season 37, 39, 72
1918 season 123
employment 181
World Series 83
Ruth, Herman 49, 51, 77

SABR. *See* Society for American Baseball Research
Sallee, Harry 80, 83
Sanborn, Irving
1917 season 36, 37, 67
1918 season 123, 127, 132
army team 117

baseball finances 106
bonds 104
Browns vs. Sox 34, 35
Buckner firing 108, 109
Clark Griffith Day 60, 63
drilling 18, 28, 58, 65
Gleason's absence 114
Great Lakes park 151
gun explanation 117
Indians' kicking 72
Jackson's popularity 205
Kuhn accident 112
patriotic scene 71
pennants 144
recreational games 184
Risberg and 40
shine ball 153
spring training 20, 22, 23, 28, 29, 118–19
Sundays 55
Tigers vs. Sox 68
train accident 113
war tax 122
Weaver's return 203
World Series 79, 81
Sandoval, Jim 36, 78
San Francisco, CA 72, 100
San Francisco Presidio
Scott at 56, 74–5, 91–5, 99
Risberg at 118, 170
San Francisco Seals 93, 204
San Pedro submarine base 170
Schalk, Ray *184*
1917 season 72
1918 season 157, 158
backup for 119
Buckner and 103
car accident 113
draft 46
drilling 23
employment 182–5
return to Sox 202
riot 49
spring training 16, 29

Schauer, Alexander   53
Schupp, Ferdinand   82
Schwab, Charles   140
Scott, Harriet Belle Cook   94-7, 99
Scott, Jim   97
   1917 season   37-9, 74-5
   background   24
   Browns vs.   34
   commission   95, 96
   drilling   23
   enlistment   51-2, 72-3, 119, 141
   as entertainer   125
   industrial team   182
   marriage   94-5
   military service   101, 187, 188, 204
   physical   56
   postwar baseball   203-4
   report to Presidio   91
   Risberg and   40
   singing   38
   as spectator   163
   spring training   16, 20, 28
   suspension   24-5, 57, 95
service baseball   148-50, 170
Seventh Regiment armory   80
Seymour, Harold and Dorothy   126, 137
Shanley's Restaurant   87, 187, 193
Shawkey, Bob   145
Sheldon, Raymond   58, 59, 64
Shellenback, Frank   158, 181
Sheridan, J. B.   105
Shibe Park, draft   44
Shields, Mark   25, 31
shine ball   35-6, 77-8, 82, 153
Shipbuilders' League   171
shipyards
   necessity   140
   players at   119, 132-6, 141, 157, 171, 180, 181, 199
   salaries   137
   travel past   164 (*see also* United States Shipping Board Emergency Fleet Corporation)
Shore, Ernie   49

singing   38
Smiley, Walter   *17, 31*
   1917 season   33-9
   background   9-11
   benefits of drilling   32
   commission   48, 65
   drill competition   57, 59, 63
   as drillmaster   12
   exhibition game drilling   47
   influence   27, 28, 30
   rapport   24
   spring training   18-23, 25
   World Series   80
Smith, Sherrod   189, 195
Society for American Baseball Research   36, 78, 105, 154, 168
South Carolina   26, 127-8, 136, 139
Southern California War Service League   170, 181
Southern Pacific Company   170
Spalding's Official Baseball Guide   152, 209
Spatz, Lyle   160
Sporting News
   army baseball   99
   drilling   30, 32, 64
   Gowdy at World Series   81
   Jackson's draft status   131, 133, 134
   returning Sox   203
   salaries   107
sportswriters   8, 122
Spreckels, Hank   147
Springfield rifles   21, 28, 36, 58. *See also* rifles
spring training
   1918 season   107, 112
   drilling   3-4, 9, 13, 21-3, 25
   postwar   204
Stanage, Oscar   181
Standard Shipbuilding   179
Standard-Murphy industrial team   181
Steel League. *See* Bethlehem Steel Baseball League
Steinberg, Steve   70, 160

St. Louis Browns
   1917 season   36, 37, 70, 73
   1918 season   123, 157
   1919 season   205
   drilling   12, 34, 35, 63, 64
   games   34–5
   Jenkins and   29
   players   199
   service record   205
   training   13
St. Louis Cardinals   118
St. Paul Saints   33
Sundays   24, 51, 52, 55

Taft, William Howard   198
Tearney, A. R.   21
Tener, John   33
Tennessee   188–9, 191
Terry, Zebulon   26, 40
Texas
   Felsch injury   131
   military regiments   11
   spring training in   12–17, 19, 20, 116
Texas League   27–29, 118, 131
Thomas E. Wilson Company   182
Thompson, Denman   59, 63, 153
Three-I League. *See* Illinois-Indiana-Iowa League
Tinker, Joe   10
Toledo Railways & Light Company   175–6
trains   15–20, 112–13
Troyon sector   193

umpires   171, 187
uniforms
   baseball   34, 80, 107, 117
   military   58–9, 126, 147, 148
Union Iron Works   170, 171
United States
   neutrality   6
   role in war   19
   war declaration   14, 30

United States Shipping Board Emergency Fleet Corporation   133, 138, 140
U.S. Army
   1918 season opener   123
   athletic gear   182
   Ban Johnson in   4
   baseball in   10, 24, 45, 92, 96, 98–100, 117
   "disappearing" gun and mortar   116–7
   drill competition   63
   enlistments   27, 51, 169, 170
   illiteracy   139
   lessons   208–9
   nicknames   48
   officers   95
   players in   72–3, 106, 112, 119, 120
   recruiting office   36
   sergeants for drilling   8, 12
   western department   57
   World Series   80
U.S. Army Fifth Company, San Francisco Presidio   92, 94
U.S. Army Twenty-Fourth Infantry   61
U.S. Army Twenty-Fifth Infantry   92
U.S. Army Thirty-Third "Prairie" Division   117, 191
U.S. Army Forty-Second "Rainbow" Division   81
U.S. Army Eighty-Ninth "Middle West" Division   118, 204
U.S. Army Ninety-First "Wild West" Division   98
U.S. Army 122nd Field Artillery   71
U.S. Army 132nd Infantry   191–3, 195
U.S. Army 314th Infantry   196
U.S. Army 327th Infantry   190
U.S. Army 370th Infantry   60–1
U.S. Army Air Service   118, 120, 181
U.S. Army Company C 167th Depot Brigade   189
U.S. Army Company F, Camp Lewis   96
U.S. Marines
   1918 season opener   123

baseball teams   117
enlistments   171, 173, 174
Jackson's contact   138
lessons   211
maneuvers   39
nicknames   48
pregame march   44
Sox visit   116
U.S. Navy
  1918 season opener   124
  athletic gear   182
  baseball in   100, 126–7, 151
  Chouinard in   126
  enlistments   120, 141, 170, 173
  Faber in   144–6
  nicknames   48
  pregame march   44
  yeomen   126, 144

Veach, Bobby   181
Venice Tigers   92
Verdun   191, 192, 196
Vernon Tigers   26, 159, 160
Von Kolnitz, Alfred   26, 129, 204

Walsh, Ed   16, 24, 74, 104
war tax   121–3
Washington Senators
  1917 season   63
  1918 season   153
  attendance   111
  Clark Griffith Day   60–1
  drill competition   58, 59
  Faber vs.   145
  Gandil with   16, 41
  ownership   48
Washington Star   19
Wattelet, Leonard A.   98
Weaver, George   50
  baseball finances   107
  as conspirator   207, 210
  draft   46
  employment   163, 182
  as entertainer   125

exhibition games   52
father's death   113
grenade practice   27
machine guns   116
marriage   94–5
physical   56
return to Sox   203
riot   49–51
singing   38
talent   40
Tigers vs.   68
World Series   80–1
Weeghman, Charles   8, 46, 177, 178
Weeghman Park   10, 44, 177
Western League   30, 34, 120
Wichita Witches   30
Wilbert, Warren   41, 70, 71
Wilhelm II, Kaiser   6, 14
Williams, Claude
  1917 season   39, 67
  Boston vs.   49
  Browns vs.   34, 73
  as conspirator   207
  departure   141, 157, 167
  return to Sox   201, 203
  White Sox visit   180
  World Series   83
Wilmington, DE   119, 133
Wilson, Woodrow   6, 19, 140
Wisconsin
  employment   182
  exhibition games   47, 147
  military recruits   23
  Scott in   25
  semipro league   155
Wisener, Winfred   34, 63
Witt, Lawton   149, 150
Wolfe, Edgar Forrest   179
Wolfgang, Meldon   39, 181
women   123
Wood, Leonard   6, 8
Woodland Bards   71, 81, 117, 178

work-or-fight   143, 155, 163, 164, 177
World Series   210
World Series (1916)   13
World Series (1917)   79–86
  botched plays   80–1, 85–6, 141
  celebrations   87, 88
  checks   103–4
  Jenkins in   187, 188
  pitching   77, 79
  scoreboards   94
World Series (1918)
  date   167
  format   177, 178
  possibility   164–6
World Series (1919)   206–8

World War I
  armistice   151, 192, 197
  duration   3
  effects   208, 210
  neutrality   6
World War II   65, 100
Wreford, Billy   181
Wyoming   57, 72

Yannigans   28, 30, 35
Yelle, Archie   181
Young Men's Christian Association   95, 173

Zimmerman, Henry   85, 86
Zimmermann telegram   14
Zminda, Don   49, 70